HOPE US, LORD!
PROPHETIC INVITATIONS, Part 1

HOPE US, LORD!
PROPHETIC INVITATIONS, Part 1

By Alvin C. Bernstine

"For whatever things were written before were written for our learning, that we through the patience and comfort of the Scriptures might have hope."
(Romans 15:4, NKJV)

© 2018. Alvin C. Bernstine.

No part of this book may be reproduced or transmitted in any form, by any means, electronic or mechanical, including photocopying, recording, or by any information storage or retrieval system without the express permission in writing from the author.

ISBN: 978-0-9767020-5-4

DEDICATION

In Memory of Her: Maxine Miles Hismith,
my amazing Mother

INTRODUCTION

As I pondered this meditative journey, inevitably I was compelled to ask myself, "What will shape these terse and admittedly subjective musings?" I understood that I needed some literary and social boundaries within which to contain my imaginative impulses, while maintaining my provocative edge. I concluded that the use of Scripture, biblical reflections, social events, socio-political realities, community mood, history, literature, cultural arts, literary expressions, life experiences, and personal reflections ought to be adequate resources to allow for creative, but provocative boundaries. More importantly, I wanted the framing of this spiritual adventure to be couched within prayerful and persistent appeals to God in response to whatever resources I consulted and prophetic probing I mined.

I have surmised that prayer and the prophetic are inextricably bound to one another. My assumptions are powerfully supported by an amazing homiletician with prophetic sensitivities, Lenora Tubbs Tisdale, Professor of Homiletics, Yale Divinity School. Dr. Tubbs Tisdale cites that "There are at least three types of prayers that need to be reclaimed and reconnected with the church's prophetic mission: (1) prayer in which we seek discernment for the particular witness God would have us make; (2) prayer in which we are honest with God about our fears, our differences, and our struggles; and (3) prayer in which we regain the ability to lament and to mourn before God the brokenness of our world."[1] I hope this adventure connects in some way to all three of those prayerful experiences.

It seems obvious that one spiritual activity that appeals to God (prayer), and another activity that is compelled by God (the prophetic), could meditatively co-exist. Moreover, the subsequent tension between prayerful appeal and prophetic compelling beckons us to creative participation. Paramount to this adventure, I extend an invitation to creatively consider a prayerful and persistent appeal to God derived from the enigmatic, yet prophetic yearning of an African American cultural idiom: "You hoped us…" This strange and compelling statement enriches this quest to regain our prophetic footing.

From where did this cultural idiom come? I do not know its origins. I can only share with you where I found it. What does it mean? I offer an interpretation based upon considerable instances where I encountered it. I was blessed to spend a significant part of my life and formative ministry years in the Southern parts of America. Having been born and raised in California, I remain amazed at the rich legacy of the African American experience that is so vividly expressed in the South. There is not only the Southern dialect but there are cultural expressions unique to the South. One such expression, I frequently encountered after preaching. Someone would come up, smile, shake my hand and say, "You hoped me."

---

[1] Tisdale, Tubbs Lenora, Prophetic Preaching: A Pastoral Approach, (Westminster John Knox Press, Louisville, KY, 2010), p. 33.

INTRODUCTION

At first I thought this, at best, an odd expression. At worst, it represented a poor expression of grammar. However, as I pondered the expression in light of the Southern legacy of racial oppression and systemic violence, I concluded that African Americans are not bound to English grammatical purity. While the language of the conqueror/oppressor may be dominant, it is not always definitive. Oppressed people are known to use the language of their oppressors in subversive patterns and constructions. Much of the New Testament is framed in such language, and the African American community of my hometown, Oakland, California, proudly engages in "Ebonics." Our once enslaved ancestry, Southern blacks, likewise used language to give expression to their reality. Thus, the phrase "you hoped me," provided a linguistic mutation of the noun "hope" into a verb.

Hope for African Americans can never be limited to a person, place, or thing. Hope must be action, a lived-out experience in the face of the horrid realities of systemic oppression and perpetual violence. "You hoped me" represents a hopeful acknowledgement of help needed and provided for people whose life experiences have been darkly distorted with the potential for deathly despair.

"And now abide faith, hope, love; but the greatest of these is love (1 Corinthians 13:13)." This incredible text has fueled the ethical mandate of Christendom throughout the years with its focus on the "greatest of these." The love focus of this text has shown up often to embellish the loving aspirations of those who adventure into the journey of holy matrimony. However, it is best used when served as the primary text that anchors the love mandate of the Christian witness. I seek not, neither do I desire to diminish the love focus of this invaluable text. My sole aim and desire is to consider and reflect upon another of the vital "these three." I want to reflect upon the implications of hope. In a sense, to hope is to create the possibility for love. There is no love without hope, and no hope without love.

Hope is the indispensable dynamic for all who dare to live beyond what is. Hope moves us out of the dungeons of our deepest fears and encapsulates our noblest dreams. Aristotle noted that "Hope is a waking dream." All great religions are constructed on the foundation of hope, and without hope, religion deteriorates into fascist ideologies that fuel terror and rule by violence, intimidation and fear, or succumb to an impotent, self-indulged pietism. The noted psychologist, Erik Erikson, stated, "Hope is the enduring belief in the attainability of fervent wishes."[2]

The power of hope transcends religions and even racial distinctions. All people need what hope provides. Confucius viewed hope as indispensable to personal growth when he said, "Hope can be very useful for your self motivation." Emily Dickinson, an Anglo American, stated wisely:

---

2 Erikson, Erik H., Childhood and Society, (W.W. Norton & Co, 1950), p. 118.

INTRODUCTION

> "Hope is the thing with feathers
> That perches in the soul
> And sings the tune without the words
> And never stops at all."

The Tibetan prophet, the Dalai Lama, notes that "No matter what sort of difficulties, how painful experience is, if we lose our hope, that's our real disaster." The inimitable Langston Hughes powerfully stated:

> "Hold fast to dreams,
> For if dreams die
> Life is a broken-winged bird,
> That cannot fly."

The Apostle Paul staked considerable value on hope. "Therefore, since we have such hope, we use great boldness of speech (2 Corinthians 3:12)." In fact, he considered a life without hope as being completely unbearable (1 Corinthians 15:19). Jesus has been aptly identified as the hope of glory (Colossians 1:27).

My dear friend, Diana, in a recent paper, noted that "Hope can be said to "urge us forward" even though we do not know where the path will lead, who or what we will encounter, or how we might be changed or transformed during the process. The Apostle Paul "intensified the challenge" in his letter to the Romans by saying, "Hope that is seen is not hope. For who hopes for what is seen?"[3]

Although I firmly believe and agree that the "greatest of these is love," I do not think we fare well by minimizing, overlooking, or diminishing the power and importance of the other two aspects of "these three," in particular, hope. Thus, this writing will engage in what I consider hopeful imagination. I want to meditatively infuse hope as an indispensible faith dynamic, essential to prophetic engagement. I am aware that "hopeful imagination" is clearly a play on Walter Brueggemann's invaluable publication, Prophetic Imagination. I use it as a confessional opening to what I am doing. I consider Brueggemann a life-tutor in Old Testament study, and am not ashamed to play off anything he has written or said. In fact, Brueggemann noted that "Hope is clearly understood as a dreamlike alternative imagination which accepts God's intent as more powerful than the present, seemingly intransigent circumstance."[4] This writing represents me probing and provoking the "dreamlike alternative imagination" and considers my personal struggle to

---

3 Becton, Diana, The Search for the Abundant Life, a class assignment prepared at Pacific School of Religion, Berkley, CA, 2014.

4 Brueggemann, Walter, A Commentary on Jeremiah: Exile and Homecoming, (Eerdmans, Grand Rapids, MI, 1989), p. 289.

remain hopeful in "seemingly intransigent circumstances." Thus, I committed myself to a year-long reflection on the prophetic, with the hope of nurturing my own prophetic hopefulness.[5]

I am convinced that maintaining prophetic hope is a difficult and challenging undertaking in the American church, particularly the African American church. Too much of what is expected of the local pastor, and sometimes desired of the pastor, conflicts with the prophetic mantle. In an effort to maintain relevancy and appeal, my own journey has been wrought with fits and turns that ultimately compromised the prophetic. I believe the prophetic ministry of the church has been tragically co-opted by the marketing model of capitalism, and renders most pastors into the impotent role of a Christianized CEO. As CEOs, the demands of the market not only drain us of prophetic strength, market-driven demands blind us to our prophetic responsibilities, especially when the church is the primary object of our prophetic protestations.

I found poignantly helpful the words of the prophet of Czechoslovakia who stated:

Hope is definitely not the same thing as optimism. It is not the conviction that something will turn out well, but the certainty that something makes sense, regardless of how it turns out. In short, I think that the deepest and most important form of hope, the only one that can keep us above water and urge us to good works, and the only true source of the breathtaking dimension of the human spirit and its efforts, is something we get, as it were, from "elsewhere." It is also this hope, above all, which gives us the strength to live and continually to try new things, even in conditions that seem as hopeless as ours do, here and now.[6]

Truly this meditative experience is driven by the belief in something we get from "elsewhere." I join with Bishop Desmond Tutu, who aptly stated, "Hope is being able to see that there is light despite all of the darkness." Our world has normalized darkness, and prophetic light fueled by hope is urgently required. Thus, for each meditation, I have endeavored to do the following:

First, I consider a biblical text. I consider one that I believe has prophetic significance (and I believe all of the Bible has prophetic significance). Secondly, after having considered/read the text, I offer a general observation of it. Thirdly, I provide a brief and cursory examination of the text. My examinations are poignant and not academically

---

5 While most of the reflective process was expressed during a year (2015), its completion extended over the course of three years. In 2015, I inexplicably hit a wall and struggled over the course of two years to complete three months of reflection. It was truly painfully befuddling. I felt as if I had exhausted my bank of knowledge and life experiences. I now believe I would have been better assisted if I had shared my struggles with friends and my faith family. I'm convinced now that writing is not a solo adventure. We need people, even if the work is individually undertaken.

6 Havel, Vaclav, Disturbing the Peace: A Conversation with Karel Hvizdala, (Knopf, New York, NY, 1980), p. 181-82.

profuse. Fourthly, I offer some form of prophetic implication and/or observation that the text might have for ministry. Finally, I close with a brief prayerful prostration – a hopeful appeal to God. These words reflect my own effort toward seeking God's help to heighten my prophetic sensibilities and responsibilities. In the words of Jan Richardson, these are admittedly Rough Translations, that cry out that we:

> Hope nonetheless.
> Hope despite.
> Hope regardless.
> Hope still.
> Hope where we had ceased to hope.
> Hope amid what threatens hope.
> Hope with those who feed our hope.
> Hope beyond what we had hoped.
> Hope that draws us past our limits.
> Hope that defies expectations.
> Hope that questions what we have known.
> Hope that makes a way where there is none.
> Hope that takes us past our fear.
> Hope that calls us into life.
> Hope that holds us beyond death.
> Hope that blesses those to come.[7]

While I started this journey in 2014 (refer to footnote), I hit a writer's block toward the end of the year and stopped writing with less than three months to go. For nearly two years I plodded along, inexplicably uninspired. It felt as if I had exhausted my knowledge bank and depleted my imaginative capacities. It was a bit scary! Ironically, this worked in my favor. The time I lost, I literally won, because it allowed me to test my prophetic assumptions in the aftermath of the national, as well as the international anxiety prompted by the election of America's 45th President. Donald J. Trump offers the prophetic community a symbolic gateway to prophetic angst. The few days that I had to go back hopefully have had a real-time effect and are not disruptive to chronological flow. Perhaps unbeknownst to all of us, Mr. Trump unmasked the idols to which this country truly

---

[7] Richardson, Jan, Circle of Grace: A Book of Blessings for the Seasons, (Wanton Gospeller Press, Orlando, FL, 2015), p. 108.

bows: whiteness and maleness – and his election and white male-dominated administration should stir up prophetic resistance.

In a recent newspaper article, Archibishop Warda was noted to have said, "Hope is not a concept to be understood. It's a way of life. If we want to live in a peaceful community...we have to work. We want to change the future, it starts now."

In any event, I pray that these writings will help cultivate the mantra used by the African American prophet, Jesse Louis Jackson, who encourages us to "keep hope alive."

Exodus 1:8-14

"A Stalking Horse"

Prophetic Invitations. That is the literary grid in which I meditatively adventure this year. As a Christian, a preacher, community leader and an avid student of the Bible, I begin this meditative adventure where prophecy in the Bible traditionally and legitimately begins – with Moses. Moses represents the paradigm from which biblical prophets are modeled and mentored. However, Moses comes from somewhere. He is a product of a people who were living their lives within specific oppressive social, political, economical, and even psychological arrangements. Thus, a common characteristic of the primary biblical prophets is that they all, in some way or another, bounce their prophetic urgencies off the prophetic mantle of Moses. I invite us to do as they did.

Today's text stirred up a basic exegetical mandate I learned early in my academic journey, as I ventured to understand the preaching ministry. I was told that a text without a context is a pretext. While I might not have understood all of the implications of that observation when I first heard it, I understand them better now. A text without a context sets up the preacher, or teacher, to engage in pretentious proclamations. What he or she espouses is to speak words with no basis in biblical reality. In other words, he or she is pretending. One synonym for a pretext is a "stalking horse." A lot of preaching and teaching has become like a stalking horse: fancy prancing with no functional intent.

The prophetic ministry of Moses was birthed in a context where the powers expressed fear of losing their powers by becoming more oppressive. As I write these lines on the first day of the year, I am gazing out the window at the city of Las Vegas. Whatever else Las Vegas might be known for, it serves as one of the primary symbols of American pretentiousness. The glitter and glitz of this city is made possible because fear-based personalities are providing pretentious escape from the oppressive realities of American life. Jackpot economics is a slick scheme to perpetuate more oppression, with its seductive cathedrals of glitz and greed.

I challenge you to look out of the window of your context and identify how the powers have expressed fear of losing their powers by becoming more oppressive. Prophetic meditations are the byproduct of contextual analysis and compassionate sensitivity. Can you identify the stalking horse tendency within your life, community, or ministry? How are these stalking horses symbolized and manifested?

PRAYER:
Gracious God, may our efforts to share the faith be ever mindful of the biblical context in which our witness is shaped. Hope us, Lord. Deliver us from any and every effort to bypass the honest and responsible study of the Word and our world. In Jesus's Name. AMEN.

Exodus 1:15-21

"No Obligation"

Moses not only comes from a context, or emerges from somewhere, he is a product of a people who had a particular experience. Moses's people had been the primary subjects of a long night of oppression. Oppression had become so deathly pervasive, it invaded the birthing process of Moses's people. The evil scheme to put to death all of the young males constituted the denial of hope and the precariousness of life for an oppressed people.

I recall a conversation I had with the late Reverend Robert Stephens. I was concerned about the lack of truth-telling in this text by the midwives. The midwives clearly do not speak truthfully about the continued birth of the male children, who represented the hope and life of God's people. My dear friend informed me that the oppressed are under no obligation to engage in "maximum veracity with the oppressors." In other words, oppressed people do not owe those who oppress them the full truth about anything that intensifies their oppression and threatens to extinguish their hope and life.

The dynamics of oppression contain a lot of assumptions, one of which is that those who are oppressed should be willing subjects to their oppression, and they should have no problem accommodating oppression. What would happen in the life of oppressed people if we united, like Puah and Shiprah, and refused to no longer accommodate our own oppression? Two women, the oppressed of the oppressed, viewed themselves as not being obligated to provide maximum veracity to those who oppressed them. Unfortunately, many women and many African Americans continue to accommodate their own oppression. We remain complicit with the powers that deny us power and access to justice and equality.

Today will truly provide you and me opportunities to decide who we are truly obligated to. I invite you to examine the times in your life where you provided oppressive constructs with maximum veracity. What was your obligation then and what is your obligation now? I contend that the incredible midwives of our text ultimately were not employed by those who they worked for. Their obligation to God overruled their obligations to an oppressive employment system, and they "chose to obey God."

PRAYER:
O God, I am not always clear on what I should say to those who oppress me. Hope us, I pray, to be ever mindful of our obligation to You. May the words we speak reflect that who we may work for is not always our Ultimate Employer. AMEN.

Exodus 2:1-10

"She Saw, She Drew"

Prophetic activity takes place when something beautiful is being threatened by something obviously evil and someone decides to take courageous and creative action. Life, no matter how conceived, is beautiful. Hope in the midst of despair is beautiful. The life and hope of an oppressed people is a beautiful reality and must be nurtured and maintained, even at great risk.

It is noteworthy that Moses's life was protected from birth not by men, who are the assumed protective agents of life, but by women, the historical objects of oppression. Women were the protective agents of prophetic activity because they were able to see something in a child. Note that everything hinges upon what the women "saw." Moses's mother saw that her son was beautiful. Moses's sister saw where Moses was hidden, and saw Pharaoh's daughter find him. Pharaoh's daughter saw the child in the basket. She also saw that Moses was a child of the oppressed. When Moses's sister saw what Pharaoh's daughter saw, she saw an opportunity to reconnect Moses with his mother with the protective blessing of Pharaoh's daughter. Moses's name means "drew out of water," which was what Pharaoh's daughter did. Perhaps God saw a human agent of liberation being drawn out of a river of oppression.

In every city of America, life is being threatened by something obviously evil. Nothing is more obviously evil than dangerous weapons in the hands of immature men. It's strange how people without the means to adequately sustain and maintain life can find easy access to dangerous weapons. Unfortunately, in communities of massive ignorance and poverty, dangerous weapons are too easily available.

Our young men, who are most at risk by the easy access of dangerous weapons, will only be saved and nurtured when someone sees them as beautiful and becomes courageous and creative enough to draw them out. As an African American father, I must admit that I don't always feel adequate to protect my sons and the sons of my community from so much obvious and oppressive evil. Perhaps we need a generation of Puahs, Shiprahs, and Miriams, and the resourcefulness of some compassionate Pharaoh's daughters to see, protect, nurture, and provide for the hope and life of our communities.

Prophetic personalities emerge out of the combined efforts of people who can see and those who have the resources and capacity to draw them out. We must not allow our oppression to limit the creative impetus of those who see and are courageous enough to do something imaginative and different.

What do you see in the faces of young men of color? Is there any beauty there worthy of you taking a risk to save? If not, why not?

PRAYER:
O God, I don't always see what I need to see, and do not always have access to the resources to nurture and provide for life and hope. Hope us, I pray, to not be intimidated by the sisters who do see, and can see how to sustain and provide for life beyond oppressive realities. AMEN.

Exodus 2:11-15

"Premature Engagement"

Every life-changing movement lives or dies by timing. Doing the right thing, even for God, demands that it is done at the right time. Conversely, to do the right thing at the wrong time is usually a waste of time. Nothing hurts a movement more than to be off schedule. Prophetic engagement demands doing the right thing at the right time.

Biblically speaking, there is no childhood Moses. Moses moves swiftly from being a babe in an basket to a grown man. As a grown man, he seemed to possess enough social awareness to detect that something was terribly wrong with the way society was organized. His response to obvious evil and injustice was to assert himself with a particular expression of injustice. It is noteworthy that Moses's engagement into addressing obvious evil and injustice was untimely, misapplied, and virtually unwelcomed. There was no social climate or community appetite for prophetic engagement. He directed his prophetic rage upon the wrong person. Moses was to speak directly to power, not a pawn of power. Moreover, his involvement was not well received by those most affected by oppression.

As I write these lines, Marvin McMickles's book, Where are All the Prophets? haunts me. It haunts me with the obvious. There is obvious evil in our communities, country, and world, and there is an obvious absence of prophetic engagement. This does not mean that no one is doing anything to address obvious evil. It merely suggests that what is being done has obviously not gained the social traction to engage a community-wide movement. Perhaps we are experiencing a pre-Midian blackout, where prophetic engagement is untimely, misapplied, and unwelcomed. I pray for prophetic timeliness for a world that is surely in need of a prophet.

What are your thoughts on being a prophetic presence in the world? Who do you perceive to be a prophet? Why? Where are the prophetic movements in our world and what are they doing?

PRAYER:
O God, may our time be synchronized with Your time. Hope us, I pray, to not move without divine synchronization so that our time will not result in a waste of time. We look to You to engage us in the "fulfillment of time." AMEN.

Exodus 2:16-25

"Drawing Water"

Prophetic engagement is a process. It is a process that leads us into strange venues of preparation. There are times when what we do seems to have nothing to do with what we feel destined to do. The process of engagement often calls us to develop other areas of our humanity in order for us to be more human in what we do. Without a humanizing process, a prophetic taskmaster can be as oppressive as a profit-driven taskmaster.

Moses's journey into Midian is a strange twist. The story landed him in a context where he encountered some interesting experiences. To begin, he witnessed women drawing water. His name means "drawn from water." He was drawn from water, and some women drew him from water. Secondly, he courageously asserted himself with regard to another act of obvious evil and injustice. The women who came to draw water were being subjected to the assumed privileges of male entitlement. We are not given the detail of this encounter, but something obviously unjust was being perpetrated. Thirdly, Moses was identified with those who oppressed him. Although he was clearly viewed as a Hebrew in Egypt, in Midian he was viewed as an Egyptian.

In a small and not widely read book, entitled Moses and Monotheism, Sigmund Freud, the father of modern day psychotherapy, identifies Moses as an Egyptian. Perhaps the Midian process was a time for Moses to become clear about his identity. Finally, he married and became a father. His first child was named in reference to his life experience. Gershom means "stranger." Prophetic engagement can cause a person to feel like a stranger.

As I consider the work of prophetic engagement, I reflect upon the times I felt like a stranger. I have often found myself alone within settings with no prophetic companions. I've had painful moments with no clergy brothers or sisters to share the prophetic burden. Perhaps the absence of serious prophetic engagement is because preachers are not inclined to be strangers. We assume pseudo residency rather than embrace our alien status. The process of prophetic engagement is a time where we have to bring to birth the stranger within us. We have to content ourselves with being "drawn from water."

How have you experienced the prophetic experience? Are you comfortable being a stranger? What has sustained you when the world you live in treats you like a stranger?

PRAYER:
Lord, as much as you are mindful of the cries of oppressed people, You must be mindful of the prophet in exile. Hope us, I pray, to be sensitive to the prophets who feel like strangers. May our burden of work be relieved by the assurance that You hear, remember, and have acknowledged the stranger. AMEN.

Exodus 3:1-8

"Prophetic Intrusions"

Prophetic ministry is an intrusion upon a normal life. Anyone who would engage in prophetic activity must consider its disruptive nature. It may be that when the systems of society are discomforting for anyone, no one should be comfortable with a well-ordered, or so-called normal life. No one should adjust to a world upheld by systemic injustices. In 1956, Martin Luther King, Jr. addressed the N.A.A.C.P. and said that, "(Perhaps) the salvation of the world lies in the hands of the maladjusted."

The image within our text is a man going about a daily routine. Life had become normal for Moses. He was a man with a wife, a child, a job, and a supportive community. He had adjusted to a particular lifestyle. He had been provided with patriarchal privileges to maintain a socially acceptable standard of life. While engaged in the work of maintaining his patriarchal privileges, he noticed something unusual. A bush was ablaze and was not being consumed.

Moses's response represents the pivotal response to prophetic ministry. Moses turned aside. He turned aside from his normal life. He turned aside from participating in the well-ordered industry of his patriarchal benefactor. He turned aside from his vocational responsibilities. In turning aside, he encountered what is representative of prophetic urgency, which was a fire burning that did not go out. The inextinguishable flame of prophetic urgency demanded a reverent response to the prophetic call that consequently disrupts the normal. The willingness to turn aside positioned Moses to hear afresh what he had sought to avoid: God's call to engage in the awesome task of prophetic ministry. Turning aside allowed him to affirmatively respond, "Here I am."

How immersed are you in the normal proceedings of life? Have you so immersed yourself in maintaining what is socially acceptable that you can comfortably ignore prophetic intrusions? The seduction of American consumerism, materialism, and hedonistic living can consume the best of us. Prophetic engagement has suffered because too few want to turn aside. I pray this year will provide moments when the urgency of God can disrupt the lives of a few prophets. God can use some people who are compelled to turn aside. God can use a few more people to join the "creatively maladjusted."

PRAYER:
O God, forgive us for bypassing turn-aside moments. Hope us, I pray, to be open to fresh moments when the inextinguishable fire of prophetic ministry will be recognized and embraced. Grant us experiences where we can renew our call to prophetic responsibility. AMEN.

Exodus 3:9-15

"Who Sent You?"

Questions of legitimacy quite naturally dog prophetic engagement. There is always the question, or questions, about what and who legitimates prophetic engagement. Prophets never get a free ride, or a pass into the work of prophetic ministry. In 2008, during the presidential campaign of Barak Obama, the Reverend Jeremiah Wright was unfairly thrust into the fray and cruelly demonized for being who he had been throughout his entire ministry. The issue was not so much what he said, but the fact that he was not legitimized by the so-called powers that be. I believe the more painful experience was the inexplicable sense of rejection by his own people.

The ministry of Moses begins with the honest questions of legitimacy. There was no question about the reality of oppression. There was no question about the fact that oppression was creating cry-filled trauma for a people. Furthermore, there was even no question about the fact that God was compassionately concerned about the plight of the oppressed people. The questions centered on prophetic legitimacy. The first is the question of personal audacity. Who am I to make such a bodacious claim against imperial powers? The second, and I believe the most challenging one, is who legitimates the prophet to the oppressed people? Prophetic ministry always faces the challenge of legitimacy, and, I believe, rightfully so.

As I look upon the African American clergy scene, I see a mad scramble for validation. Preachers are claiming academic validation without ever attending a class. Many are purchasing degree-claiming documents without ever having written a paper. I see greedy grasping for titles that make false claims of ecclesiastical authority, elevating people to positions with no valid communal support. In the midst of all the mad scrambling for validation, authentic prophetic legitimacy is being avoided. No one is daring a Mosaic quest of asking who am I to make bodacious claims against imperial powers? Or, who do I claim legitimates my claim to speak for an oppressed people? Every prophetic voice should honestly grapple with the questions of legitimacy.

What legitimates what you do? How have your claims to ministry or service been validated? How have such claims been received by the community?

PRAYER:
Lord, I am not always emboldened by the call to speak on Your behalf. I confess a fear of the wrath of the imperial powers, as well as the painful rejection of my own people. Hope us, I pray, to become comfortable with the discomfort of prophetic legitimacy. AMEN.

Exodus 3:16-22; 6:14-27

"Building Prophetic Community"

Prophetic engagement is always community focused. There is no solo-centric aspect of authentic prophetic engagement. We may experience aloneness, but the ministry of the prophetic is about community. Unfortunately, the American mantra of rugged individualism has infected the total drama of American Christianity. We are a nation of hero worshippers. We equate greatness with doing it alone. However, the egregious community concerns of the prophetic can only be realized by building a prophetic community.

The call of Moses to prophetic engagement is incomplete without the acknowledgement of the need to involve the oppressed community. The concern of God for Moses to speak to the children of Israel included involving the established leadership of the community. The elders represented people who could best connect the prophetic tradition with the prophetic urgency of Moses's call. For Moses, prophetic engagement was not done in a vacuum, or within a silo of individualism. Moreover, the confrontation with Pharaoh would be best served with community representation. The inclusion of community leaders provided a support system that could undergird the prophetic initiative.

I have struggled to find support in what I sensed God was up to with the traditional foci of established church leadership. In fact, it has been rare to find a cadre of leaders who viewed ministry beyond their individual roles as local pastors, or denominational leadership. Religious ritual and institutional maintenance dominates the thinking of most established church leaders. Years ago, Dr. Jeremiah Wright sought to involve the religious community in Chicago in an anti-apartheid campaign. He sent out 2,000 letters asking that each church place an anti-apartheid sign in front of their churches, in support of the South African anti-apartheid movement. He received three replies, and of the three, two were white congregations.

Who in your community supports your prophetic inclinations? Is there a community that nurtures the prophetic? If not, what will it take to get you involved in creating space for prophetic engagement?

PRAYER:
God, I acknowledge Your concern for community. You understand better than me that what You want accomplished involves community. Hope us, I pray, to cultivate a spirit of community building as a part of prophetic engagement. May we be open to others who are also concerned about the obvious expressions of evil besieging our communities. AMEN.

Exodus 4:1-17

"Struggling with Inadequacies"

Prophetic engagement brings us face-to-face with our own inadequacies. Anyone who would honestly obey God's call to prophetic ministry confronts his or her own inadequacies. The Bible is filled with reluctant, and even rebellious prophets. Most of us do not see ourselves as competent for the enormous tasks of social transformation. In fact, I would be suspicious of anyone who assumes prophetic ministry with exuberant confidence. Such an exuberant approach would indicate at least two things: a self-centered delusion or a psychological disorder. The enormous task of convincing God's people to begin living life in a different way involves a trust in God beyond personal competence.

A perspective on Moses's call to lead God's people might need to consider the people as Moses's greatest challenge. Moses seems to view the perspective of the people as crucial to prophetic legitimacy. Moses's concern for how the people would receive him occupied the bulk of his reservations. From his perspective, the people would be reluctant to receive him because he lacked personal confidence and capacity. He did not foresee a welcoming community, nor did he see himself as being competent for the task. God's response was to transform Moses's view of what was in his hand, and to provide for him a capable spokesperson. What Moses had in his hand would be more than enough when used in the cause of God, and God was known to give speech to the mute. Finding someone else to do for God what God wanted Moses to do was not an option.

I have never gotten used to people's compliments of my abilities. I know me. I know what my struggles are when it comes to doing what God wants done. Like Moses, I struggle with people's perspectives. Why should these people believe what I'm saying about their reality? In reality, who are we that people should believe us? What is it about me that people should follow me? I have no delusions about my presence before people. Likewise, I know the true level of my competence and capacity. The fact of God is the one thing that emboldens prophetic ministry. Prophetic ministry should always find its source in the competence and capacity of God.

What are your views of yourself? Do you easily fit your ministry? What role does God play in your ministry?

PRAYER:
O God, I acknowledge my incompetence and inadequacies for this assignment. The kickback of the people challenges me, and my capacities seem so small. Hope me, I pray, to see within me a possibility, so that I will access myself better to Your service and glory. AMEN.

Exodus 3:18-22

"God-centered Initiatives"

Prophetic engagement requires an obedient response to a strange-acting God. Whenever God is clearly at the middle of something, it rarely makes sense. In fact, God-centered initiatives always seem strange. God-centered requests escape the parameters of human logic, reasoning, and understanding. Try as we will, and we have, we can never reduce the beckoning of God to our reductionist thinking. A long-standing rumor in my community is that "God moves in mysterious ways, His wonders to perform."

The directives of God to Moses are strange. God directed Moses to rally the elders of Israel to a confrontation with Pharaoh. Moses was then directed to tell Pharaoh what he, a fugitive criminal and an enslaved people, were going to do. Interestingly, he does it in the form of a request. The request for freedom was the freedom to worship. God then informed Moses what Israel was going to do to their oppressors. They were going to plunder by asking their oppressors to give them silver and gold. What has worship to do with plunder? This is a strange initiative.

Worship is basically our lifting up praise and adoration to God. Plunder, however, is the violent seizure of property belonging to another. When worship is considered as subversive (Brueggemann), a connection is made with plunder. To worship the Lord was literally an affront to the imperialistic powers of Pharaoh. Likewise, the plunder of the Egyptians represented a reclaiming of deprived resources and privileges as a result of the imperialistic power.

Currently, worship has been domesticated in America. Worship in America often sanctions and promotes the ideological claims of being an American, at the expense of being loyal to Jesus. The loose and easy way in which politicians spew out "God bless America" makes it not difficult to see where Christian worship has become a tool of imperialistic powers. God-centered initiatives, however, call us to consider how worship prepares us to reclaim what the "enemy" has taken.

Who is truly at the center of your worship? When was the last time the worshippers of your community plundered the enemy in worship?

PRAYER:
O God, prepare us in our worship to respond to Your strange initiatives. We confess that much of what You want us to do does not fit what we claim to know about You. Hope us, I pray, and grant us a faith perspective to respond to Your strange initiatives. AMEN. AMEN.

Exodus 4:18-27

"From Killing to Kissing"

The work of prophetic engagement can be likened to a love-hate relationship. On the one hand, there are moments when the work of addressing obvious evil for the good of an oppressed people seems a likely journey to death. Just being on the way of doing what God wants done feels like the Lord has positioned us to be killed. The journey for equal rights for African Americans is littered with the bodies of the martyred. The LGBTQ community engages in daily laments about violent responses to their quest for civil rights. It's painfully true, and glaringly unavoidable: people get killed doing prophetic ministry.

On the other hand, the work of prophetic ministry has moments when we experience a depth of kinship that is likened to no other. We encounter a depth in our relationship with fellow sufferers that is likened to a kiss. Whenever another brother or sister can experience true kinship in redemptive suffering, it's like being on the mountain of God.

Moses's journey to Egypt is strangely interrupted. The text says, "And it came to pass on the way, at the encampment, that the Lord met him and sought to kill him." This is a strange text and commentary on the narrative. Stranger yet is the fact that the assault of God is interrupted by an assault from Moses's wife, Zipporah. Zipporah whipped out a knife and circumcised her son "and cast it at Moses's feet." Her words declare a depth of kinship that deepened their relationship. Moses moved from being a stranger to being blood. The narrative notes that from this incident, the assault of God was relinquished. "God let him go." Moses proceeded from there to encounter Aaron, who was also sent by God, and met him on the Mountain of God, "and kissed him."

Prophetic ministry is not a work to be engaged in with a band of strangers. We need people who are covenant connected in the work against imperialistic powers. Over 20 years ago, on the front pew of my first pastorate, I covenanted with Reverends Raymond Bowman and Joseph Warren Walker, III. We pledged to be brothers for life in the work of ministry. I have been privileged to pick up a few more brothers and sisters along the way, but I mark that moment 20-plus years ago when the importance of authentic kinship became vital to prophetic ministry. I pray no one goes at prophetic ministry alone. It would be like being on a journey and your strongest ally, God, is trying to kill you.

Can you claim any sisters or brothers in prophetic kinship? Or, is your involvement in ministry a work where it seems like serving God is killing you?

PRAYER:
God, I pray for all of those who are engaged in prophetic ministry. May my brothers and sisters be given soul mates and prophetic kindred to travel this journey where death looms imminent. Hope us, I pray, and bless my brothers and sisters with people who kiss them with such kinship depth that they experience being on the mountain of God. AMEN.

Exodus 4:28-31

"On Being Remembered"

Prophetic engagement facilitates the process of the oppressed being remembered. The late African American prophetic mystic, Howard Thurman, once noted that nothing is more dehumanizing than to be ignored. Dehumanization is essentially the process of being systematically ignored. Prophetic engagement enables the ignored to experience being remembered and recognized, and, as a consequence, to be valued.

The prophetic tandem of Moses and Aaron collaborated in an experience where the people of God dared to believe. Moses obeyed the strategy of God and shared with Aaron what God had shared with him. Aaron furthered the message by sharing it with the leaders of the oppressed community. Moses confirmed Aaron's words by using the rod of God to demonstrate and validate what God was up to. I believe that the most powerful moment during this prophetic discourse was the response of the oppressed people. The Bible says, "The people believed, when they heard that the Lord (Adonai) had remembered the people of Israel…"

One of the most powerful objectives of evil is to perpetuate despair. Evil maintains its oppressive grip as long as a people dawdle in despair. A few years ago, a scrappy basketball team overcame limited talent and exceeded expectations because the fan base cheered them on with the slogan, "We Believe." The improbable was attempted and achieved because people dared to believe.

The current plight of the poor, the disenfranchised, and the suffering multitudes is largely the result of a lack of belief. A recent jobs report painfully indicated that thousands of employable people have given up on finding employment. Millions of once-proud homeowners do not see themselves ever owning another home because of the lingering trauma of our nation's worst economic downturn since the Great Depression. There are areas upon areas where people have given up. Unfortunately, many have given up on the church as a viable community for the restoration of their humanity.

The need is great for a prophetic community to facilitate and cultivate a powerful sense of being remembered. There needs to be a collaboration of Word and signs that allows people to experience the presence of God. What our text reveals to us is that people who experience being remembered respond through worship. I wonder what kind of worship we would have if more of our people realized that God does remember the plight of the oppressed?

Who represents the forgotten within your community? Who is ignored? How are you validating the existence of the historically forgotten?

PRAYER:
O God, I know we often forget You, and our forgetfulness causes us to not experience You. Hope us, I pray, to believe more strongly in a God who always remembers. AMEN.

Exodus 5:1-21

"Prophetic Aggravation"

Prophetic engagement aggravates before it liberates. Oppressive powers never relinquish control without an aggravated response. It should never be assumed that those who hold power will surrender it on demand. Evil never gives up a good thing when it is more profitable to leave things as they are. Likewise, it should never be assumed that those who are oppressed will not suffer more once liberation is demanded. The aggravation of prophetic engagement raises the ire of the oppressor and intensifies the pain of the oppressed.

Moses and Aaron boldly confronted Pharaoh. Their confrontation was framed by "Thus says the Lord…" They did not make personal requests. They gave to Pharaoh what God had given them. God wanted His people to be released from bondage so that they might share in a feast. Noteworthy is the fact that the request was to be released from labor to feast, from consumption-based activity to community-based activity, or from work to worship. They were being released to participate in something totally opposite from what was necessary to maintain the oppressive status quo. Such a request aggravated Pharaoh to initiate a "bricks without straw" policy. The people were ordered to continue producing what they had always produced, but without adequate resources. Pharaoh's new policy caused an additional hardship upon the people. Consequently, it triggered an organized protest, not against Pharaoh, but against Moses and Aaron.

It is no easy thing to subject the people you love to additional pain and duress. I suspect that the reason why prophets are so few in the land is because too few possess the prophetic perspective, or capacity for aggravated responses. Most of us would rather have the people admire and adore us than resent and reject us.

As I write these lines, I revisit the harsh images of Billy clubs raining down upon unprotected skulls, and unleashed canines ripping at soft flesh. So many people suffered for civil rights because of aggravated responses. Currently, the seduction of consumption has numbed the masses to the extent that we don't even feel deeply the pain of "bricks without straw" policies. We are at risk of losing multiple generations to policies that expect continued production without the benefit of adequate resources. Who feels the pain of people who have to work for less than a minimum wage, or who struggle without the benefit of an adequate education? Why are we so numbed to apparent injustices?

PRAYER:
Merciful God, Your ways of liberation are never free of painful aggravation. Hope us, I pray, to be diligent to Your call for festive liberation, even in the face of painful aggravation. May we be consumed with passion for communion and community over the idols of competition and consumption. AMEN.

Exodus 5:22-6:13

"The Burden of Bondage"

Prophetic engagement inevitably faces resistance accompanied by the burden of bondage. There will always be resistance when confronting the obstinate forces of organized oppression. Resistance should be expected from those who oppress, and, ironically, from those who are oppressed. In fact, creative tension should be expected from those who engage in prophetic ministry.

Moses directed his angst toward God. From his perspective, the initiative of God to liberate his people had caused added grief and pain. The evil had intensified and liberation had not come. To make matters worse, the people had rejected Moses's message of God's liberation. The burden of bondage deafened the ears of the oppressed people. The resistance was so intense that Moses's fragile ego collapsed and he despaired that "the children of Israel had not heeded me. How then shall Pharaoh heed me, for I am of uncircumcised lips?" God's response to those who collapsed under the burden of bondage was to offer the assurance of deliverance.

To Moses's credit, he directed his frustration toward God. When our frustrations are directed toward the One who calls us, then the burden is shifted from us to God. I repent the times, too many to enumerate, when my frustrations were misdirected. The times when I saw no discernible movement in God's plan of redemption, I took it out either on those I love or those I serve, or both. And, like Moses, I've had moments when my ego collapsed and I sank into despair. Yet, it was in those times where the assurances of God have meant so much. Nothing lifts the burden of bondage more than the timely assurances of God's Word.

Are you having prophetic frustrations? Who is bearing the brunt of your frustrations? What's in the way of you hearing the assurances of God?

PRAYER:
O God, I repent the times when what I should have brought to You I misdirected on to the people I love and those I serve. Yet, how grateful am I for Your timely assurances. You did not hold my folly against me and continued to assure me. Hope me, I pray, to trust You in the midst of frustrations. AMEN.

Exodus 6:28-7:13

"Swallowing Serpents"

Prophetic engagement must be prepared to demonstrate the capacity to overcome trickery. We can never underestimate the power of the oppressor. The powers of domination exist because of their capacity to utilize deception. Tricks and deception are tools of oppression. Being "wise as a serpent and gentle as a dove" is a call to understand the serpentine dimensions of oppression. Moreover, there will come times in every prophetic undertaking where we must out-serpent oppressive serpents.

Moses did not take up the prophetic mantle easily. He struggled with issues of competency, one of which was being a convincing speaker. God's response to Moses's reluctance was to complement him with Aaron. The presence of Moses was to be a representative of God to Pharaoh, and the complementary ministry of Aaron was to strengthen the witness. Pharaoh's response was to seek a convincing sign of the power and presence of God in Moses. At that point, Aaron was to demonstrate power by putting forth his rod. Aaron's rod transformed into a snake. However, Pharaoh's cabinet included people who could also put forth snake-turning rods. Aaron's snake, however, devoured the snakes of Pharaoh's sorcerous emissaries. Of note in this pericope is that Pharaoh was not impressed.

Being a voice for God in the service of the oppressed is challenging. Our biggest challenge is our sense of inadequacy in the face of ominous power and resources. We should never be surprised by the resourcefulness of evil. In fact, be prepared for the powers to counter our demonstrations of power with comparable demonstrations. Although our initial engagements will not be well received, we have to be able to swallow some things and proceed.

I recall a serious boycott of black students at Tennessee State University. I was a young pastor and chose to ally with the students. During a tense confrontation with school officials, the riot squad was brought in to remove the protesting students by force. With no armor or protection, we shielded those students with our bodies and led them to safety. We swallowed the serpents of oppressive power and helped to position the students for an eventual victory.

What is your default response to ominous power and unlimited resourcefulness? Can you identify an experience in ministry where you had to swallow the serpent?

PRAYER:
Lord, I don't always feel comfortable confronting well-resourced evil. In fact, I have had moments of serious doubt and trepidation. Hope me, I pray, to use what You provide to swallow up the inept tricks of oppressive evil. AMEN.

Exodus 7:14-25

"Blood in the Water"

Oppressive powers are never receptive to prophetic engagement. The resistance of evil to God-initiated concerns is inevitable. No matter how convinced we may be of God's concern, such a concern is never shared by oppressive powers. Therefore, we should never assume an easy go in bringing about change to an oppressive system. The only power that power respects and responds to is a greater Power.

It is noteworthy that Moses, the one drawn from water, was led to confront Pharaoh by the water and performed the first plague on the water. Moses made clear to Pharaoh that God had sent him to demand the release of God's people so that God's people may worship God. Pharaoh refused to release the people under his power in order to worship another Power. Moses response to Pharaoh's refusal was to strike the water, "and it turned to blood." God commanded Aaron to strike all the water tributaries, rivers, canals, ponds, and reservoirs. Water represented life and the Nile was the life of Egypt. Likewise, blood represented life, but blood in the water destroyed the life-forces of the water. Everything within the water, the Egyptian's primary source of life, was killed by the blood in the water. Pharaoh's magicians duplicated Aaron's demonstration, thus stiffening the resolve of Pharaoh to not release the children of Israel.

For some time I have struggled with the intent and process of integration. Integration was intended to allow African Americans access to the same privileges as white America. I considered the process of integration as being flawed from its inception. As proposed in America, integration was always about black people going to where white people were. Integration meant black people going to white schools, black people being allowed to live where white people lived, and so on and so on. It was never about whites going to where black people were.

Metaphorically, integration never had the impact of pouring blood in the water. Integration never killed off the life-forces of white supremacy or segregation. White America has found ways to bypass the intent of integration by gerrymandering enclaves of white privilege. In effect, there has been a stiffening of the resolve of white supremacy to maintain its illusions of power. The challenge of modern day prophets is to continue the work of showing how plagued these systems of power really are. The Nile of white supremacy and male patriarchy is not sustainable.

How have you experienced the resistance of oppressive power? What are the economic life-sources within your community? What are your thoughts on integration?

PRAYER:
O God, there have been some sincere efforts to liberate people to authentically serve You. May those who engage in this work, not get weary in well doing. Hope us, I pray, to have Moses-like resolve in the work of prophetic ministry. AMEN.

Exodus 8:1-15

"Frogs in the Bed"

Truth telling and promise keeping is not a part of the character of oppression. Oppressive powers are maintained and sustained by deliberate practices of deceit and dishonor. The ability to hold people down and limit their lives is the result of narcissistic ingenuity. The legacy of oppression is replete with lies and broken promises, all of which are acceptable to those who oppress. Oppressors have a way of justifying any behavior that sustains oppression.

The plagues of the frogs represent an expression of what was normally harmless becoming disturbingly disruptive. The ancient Egyptians were not inclined to destroy frogs, thus, the invasion of the frogs represented a disruptive inconvenience. What was once limited to the water invaded every arena of human existence, including the bedroom. The magicians of Pharaoh were able to duplicate this plague, consequently intensifying the population and presence of the frogs. As harmless as the frogs were, them not being where they were supposed to be caused unwelcome disruption.

One of the major tasks of prophetic engagement is to agitate. We are called to stir things up, to make trouble and to make things as uneasy as they can be. We are to create moments where the narcissistic ingenuity of the empire experiences discomfort. A few years ago, students at the University of California-Berkley staged a protest by climbing in trees. A seemingly harmless act became quite disruptive and attracted huge media attention, thereby assisting in getting out the grievousness of their message. Whenever things start showing up in places where they should not be, things are more prone to cease being what they have always been.

Has your ministry ever called you to show up in places where you were not supposed to be? When was the last time you became a frog in the bed of the oppressor? What disruptive ideas can you create, organize, and implement?

PRAYER:
O God, sensitize us to Your use of small things. Hope us, I pray, that we will not be disempowered by our lust for big events, but help us to use small things in creative ways for Your grand purposes. AMEN.

Exodus 8:16-19

"The Finger of God"

The ultimate goal of prophetic engagement is to demonstrate the power of God. Until the powers of oppression are rendered impotent, the practices of oppression remain and are sustained. Somehow, both the oppressed and the oppressor must be faced with the reality of the intervening power of God.

What is unique and interesting about the third plague is that it was brief and unannounced. The text suggests that Moses and Aaron were commanded to simply strike the dust so that it would become lice. Lice are not indigenous to Egypt, so perhaps because the Nile River is so prominent, the insects were mosquito-like in expression. Their presence was biting! Of equal interest is that the lice plague was not duplicated by the Egyptian magicians. The magicians tried, but they could not duplicate the lice plague. They thus replied, "This is the finger of God."

For God to be on the side of the oppressed, there must be evidence of God's powers. There must be some manifestations of power that only God can do. Without the aid of overwhelming armies, military prowess, or economic influence, women's voting rights were secured and the socially accepted structures of racial oppression came tumbling down. It has been interesting to observe that certain segments of white America try to duplicate the strategies of the civil rights movement to advance white nationalism. Even in the name of the Christian faith, their efforts to bring forth any noteworthy advances have failed. Noteworthy is that Pharaoh's heart is hardened, even after his trusted advisors testify to the "finger of God."

While God may act on our behalf, we should not expect an immediate softening of the powers of oppression. Oppressive powers are not committed to faithful obedience. We must continue the work of prophetic engagement until pestering realities can no longer be ignored. America will not repent until overwhelmed by life-depleting forces that bring a stinging rebuke to oppressive behavior and unjust constructs.

Can you identify a moment when you witnessed the finger of God? How did the oppressor respond to an obvious manifestation of God?

PRAYER:
O God, only You have the power to bring forth life from dust. Hope us, I pray, to be committed to faithful obedience, even when the empire hardens its heart. AMEN.

Exodus 8:20-32

"Corrupted by Flies"

The pervasiveness of social inequity and racial injustice has corrupted the very fabric of American life. It appears that, as many laws are passed to support and enforce justice, someone finds as many ways to continue the perpetuation of injustice. White privilege has a way of subverting any claims that people of color make toward social and economic equality.

The fourth plague was pivotal in the liberation process of God's people because of God's directives to "let my people go, that they may serve me." God's threat to unleash flies upon the entire oppressive regime represented the pervasiveness of evil in the land. Like flies, injustice and inequity are nagging nuisances to the plans of God. Yet God promised to provide a place of sanctuary for the oppressed from the swarming flies "in order that you (Pharaoh) know that I am the Lord in the midst of the land." While the flies would pervade the land of the oppressed, the absence of flies in Goshen would distinguish God's people from the oppressor.

After over 60 years of life, all of which has been lived as an American, in America, I am not convinced of America's commitment to justice and equality. It sounds good in song and creed, yet the ubiquitous nature of racial inequality and economic injustice cannot be avoided. Racial injustice and economic inequality swarms the American landscape with infectious intensity. Even with the election and re-election of an African American president, there is no fly-free zone, a Goshen, that distinguishes God's people from the oppressor. The flies of racial and social injustice have infected the oppressed with their toxic evil.

Why are there no fly-free zones within the communities of the oppressed? What has happened to the black church that it can no longer insulate its people from the corrosive influences of an oppressive society?

PRAYER:
O God, You Who yearn to distinguish Your people from the corrosive influences of oppression, hope us, I pray, to create Goshen-like sanctuaries so that Your people can legitimately serve You. AMEN.

Exodus 9:1-7

"A Set Time"

The issue of time is an important variable in prophetic engagement. Time is critical to what is done and how it is done. There must be a consideration for time in order for prophetic engagement to be impacting, as well as how a prophetic intervention unfolds. Clearly, the gatekeepers of the empire will resist engagement at all times, because the maintenance of oppressive constructs exists out of a static sense of time. For everything to remain the same, there must be a widespread belief that every day is the same.

The fifth plague targeted a longstanding economic asset: the commoditization of livestock. Moses was directed to demand the people's freedom, with the threat of the destruction of the empire's livestock. The empire's continued monopoly and control of livestock powerfully substantiated economic advantage. According to the ministry of Moses, it was time for the destruction of a pillar of economic advantage. It was time for economics to be used as leverage for the demand of the release of God's people, so that they might serve God. Of note was the fact that the livestock of the oppressed was to be spared, and this would even be verified by Pharaoh's inspectors.

I believe it also important to note the religion, or idolatry of livestock. Cattle have long held a sacred place in many ancient, as well as some modern communities. The very fact that the children of Israel would build a golden calf (Exodus 32:1-8) reflects the religious prominence of the position of the cow. The striking down of livestock threatened the legitimacy of an economic and a religious stronghold of the oppressive power.

Today, the United States of America and the world honor and celebrate the life of Martin Luther King, Jr. He represented a prophetic presence that boldly confronted both the economic and religious claims of America. The life of this bold prophet was violently cut short during an organized protest against unjust economic policies and practices. Ironically, as our nation celebrates his life and legacy, policy makers and economic institutions are fiercely rejecting all efforts for a livable wage. Politicians will give speeches to honor Martin Luther King, Jr. on Monday, but for the rest of the week will angrily deny the raising of a livable wage, as well as the extension of unemployment benefits for those who have been unable find work. It is time that the sacred cows of economic oppression die for justice to be a reality.

What sacred cow in your life needs sacrificing for you to be truly free? What are the sacred cows of American oppression?

PRAYER:
O God, may we continue the bold work of Dr. Martin Luther King, Jr. Hope us, I pray, to believe that it is now time to be courageous enough to identify and denounce the legitimacy of any and every economic and religious injustice. It is past time for us to defraud the prophetic ministry of Martin Luther King, Jr., through weak domestication or exploitative commoditization. May his work move us beyond the limits of social events and into the work of social transformation in our time. AMEN.

Exodus 9:8-12

"Ashes in the Air"

Prophetic engagement must always include the grief process. Grief represents the healthy process of integrating losses into life and living. The loss of a sense of right and wrong, justice and injustice, is a serious and grievous affliction of those who oppress. Ashes are symbols of the grief process. Ironically, the rejection of the grief process potentially causes greater harm than the experience of the loss itself.

The plague of the boils is a powerful symbol of the empire's insensitivity to loss, its own loss of a sense of justice. Moses and Aaron were ordered to throw into the air a handful of ashes in the face of Pharaoh. Pharaoh and his oppressive minions were to be eyewitnesses of this act. The dust of the ashes spread throughout the land and caused infectious sores on people and animals. Symbolically, the whole of the empire was infected with the grievous loss of a sense of justice, which was basically a loss of their collective humanity. Pharaoh's magicians were powerless before Moses and Aaron, and they too were infected with the sores.

One of the most troubling venues of oppression is religion. It's troubling when that which is supposed to advance the highest ideals of human compassion loses its way. Religion in America has historically been infected with the same oppressive ideals as the empire. Religion has either been complicit with oppression, or silent in the face of oppression. The current pope has raised eyebrows and caused consternation as a result of his bold statements about the historical injustices of capitalism. He has thrown "ashes in the air" for the opposition to consider the world's injustices and has created an infectious outcry. From the houses of statehood to the houses of worship, voices of objection have been lifted.

We are called to throw up in the faces of empire the grievous nature of oppression. We have no control over the response, but we do give witness the fact that "ashes in the air" will either affect or infect.

What part does grief play in your faith community? How so? Identify some key sources for community lament.

PRAYER:
O God, we consider Your feelings about the grievous impact of oppression on the oppressed and the oppressor. Hope us, I pray, to recover our highest sense of humanity and justice. May we evolve into a wholesome people who practice the healthy processes of grief. AMEN.

Exodus 9:13-35

"Nothing Like It"

Oppressive realities result in the creation of unprecedented phenomena. When social and economic forces are being unfairly tilted to the benefit of a few, an environment is created for strange and bizarre happenings. Prophetic engagement serves as a catalyst for the unusual. The static perspective of time upheld by the empire loses control and relevance when challenged by the newness of prophetic engagement.

The plague of hail is noted as something never experienced by Egypt. God's word to Moses was to declare the onslaught of hail that would bring further destruction to livestock, as well as upon people, plants, and trees. The economy of Egypt was severely disrupted by the unprecedented environmental phenomena. The wheat and barley, a feast-producing commodity, was totally devastated. There would be no feast of economic prosperity for the wealthy. Likewise, the traditional ideologies that normally supported and sustained the Egyptians proved powerless. Meanwhile, the humble props of the Israelite economy were spared from the destruction of the hailstorm.

Of interest was the response of Pharaoh. It seem that the magnitude of this plague was so incredible that it moved him to acknowledge his sin and plead that the hailstorms stop. Once the hailstorms stopped, Pharaoh persisted in his inhumane practices and refused to let God's people go.

As I write these lines, America is experiencing unprecedented weather phenomena. An Arctic front has gripped the northern part of the nation with unprecedented cold and snow, while causing unprecedented warmth in the western United States. The weather has created unprecedented chaos, inclusive of the disruption of the transportation economy. Of note is the news revealing that 1% of the nation is experiencing unprecedented growth in wealth, while the 99% are stuck in an economic slump. The rationalistic lens through which the world is viewed blinds even the prophetic community from making any connection with the weather and the economy. No one is making a claim of divine intervention; as a result, no one is making any confession of sin. Can even the church not see that we have never seen anything like this before?

PRAYER:
Most merciful God, forgive us for our blindness to the relationship between unprecedented environmental phenomena and unprecedented wealth disparity. Hope us to recover our prophetic sensitivities and give voice to what we have never seen before. AMEN.

Exodus 10:1-20

"Driven Out of Pharaoh's Presence"

One of the primary goals of prophetic engagement is to understand how what is important to the oppressor adversely affects the oppressed. The more we understand the value system of the oppressor, the better we can help the oppressed. The late Kelly Miller Smith, Associate Dean of Vanderbilt Divinity School and professor of preaching, informed us that we should know as much about the oppressor as we know about the oppressed. Information about the oppressor demands critical objective research and analysis.

A common response to the demands of Moses was Pharaoh hardening his heart, or becoming more and more resistant. Each plague intensified Pharaoh's objections. The plague of the locusts is prefaced with God observing the hardhearted responses of Pharaoh. Of note, God takes credit for hardening Pharaoh's heart: "I have made him and his servants hardhearted…" The plague of the locusts clearly threatened what was extremely important to the empire, to the extent that Pharaoh's cabinet advised that he let the people go to worship.

Throughout the biblical text, locusts represented a serious threat to agriculture. The book of Joel focuses its prophetic agenda around a devastating experience with locusts. Pharaoh's response to Moses's demands was to modify them. Instead of letting all the people go, as well as the Israelites' livestock, Pharaoh insisted that only Moses and his men be permitted to go. The request of Moses resulted in him and Aaron being "driven out of Pharaoh's presence."

During the recent financial crisis, I participated in numerous protests against the banks. The concern was for the massive and widespread foreclosures inflicted upon minorities. We were always nonviolent, but always persistent. At one of our many protests against Wells Fargo, the highest-ranking officials refused to see us. They sent out low-ranking employees to turn us away. Our refusal to be turned away provoked Wells Fargo into calling the police. No one was arrested, but the message was clear: we were being driven out of Pharaoh's presence.

The issues, or, better stated, the gods of finance, are extremely important to the empire. I can comfortably say that most the effective campaigns for justice will do well to follow the money. The economic variables of oppression are certain to raise the ire of the oppressor, and will surely provoke response. However, the responses to the disruptions of economic variables inevitably carry great risk. God will certainly be needed when facing the gods of finance.

What do you consider of ultimate importance to America? How have you attempted to disrupt any icon of oppression? What are your thoughts on the idolatry of money?

PRAYER:
O God, we need You to be viewed as God of all life. Hope us, I pray, to be mindful that there is no One greater than You. Empower us, we pray, to go forth, even at risk of being driven away. AMEN.

Exodus 10:21-29

"The Feel of Darkness"

Prophetic engagement is an adventure into darkness. Just as evil is antithetical to life, darkness is symbolic of the limitations of life. Darkness limits sight, therefore limiting life's possibilities. Plants grow in response to light, and vision is most effective during the light. As the prophetic seeks to enliven and enlighten, it must do so in the midst of ominous darkness. We are up against a "darkness so ominous that it is felt throughout the land."

God commissioned Moses to direct his rod toward the sky. The sky represented the throne room of the sun god of Egypt. The eclipsing of the sun represented a serious challenge to one of the prominent symbols of Pharaoh's power, the symbol of the sun. The effect of darkness severely limited the movement of the people: "People couldn't see each other, and no one went anywhere for three days." The number of days of darkness signaled how pervasive the darkness was. It was so pervasive that it was felt. It was existentially overwhelming. Yet, it was noted that "Israel had light in their homes."

Pharaoh's response was to again reject the request of Moses to release the people for worship. Moses wanted the complete liberation of the people, so that the people could freely decide how they would worship. Pharaoh would not release the livestock. This was an attempt to control or influence the depth and quality of their worship. Moses's insistence that all of the livestock be released enraged Pharaoh to the point where he declared that Moses would never see his face again.

The impact of oppression has severely affected the depth and quality of worship in America. So ominous is the darkness of pervasive injustices and inequity that its impact is felt throughout the land, even within our places of worship. God-centered worship enhances human community and progress. Conversely, idolatrous oppression perverts community and sabotages progress. Perhaps the epidemic of violence in our communities is because people can't see the common humanity in one another. We also don't seem to be moving forward as a country, or as a people, because the darkness is so great. As a voice for justice and equality, it is necessary that we feel the darkness.

How do you feel about adventuring into darkness? What expression of darkness have you identified in worship?

PRAYER:
O God, You, who experiences the darkness and the light, hope us, I pray, to be conduits of light in a world of darkness. Encourage us to brave the darkness in spite of its ominous feel. AMEN. AMEN. AMEN.

Exodus 11

"Pharaoh Will Not Listen to You"

Prophetic engagement inevitably faces resistance. In fact, we would be safe to assert that authentic prophetic activity exists because of resistance. The empire's hold on the lives of the oppressed is never easily surrendered. In the Star Trek series, the Enterprise's most difficult challenge was the Borg. By brutal force, the Borg assimilated all life forms into an oppressed collective by declaring an intimidating cadence: "Resistance is futile."

God's insistence on liberating the people from the oppressive and idolatrous arrangements of Egyptian bondage was met with obstinate resistance. The more Moses demanded freedom, the more Pharaoh resisted. God's final plague upon Egypt would create a clear distinction between the children of Israel and Egypt. Although Pharaoh's servants were amenable to the release of God's people, Pharaoh resisted. Moses's status had grown within the Egyptian community and Pharaoh was not ready to validate Moses's leadership because it clearly would diminish his.

The cadence for Pharaoh's resistance was "The Lord hardened Pharaoh's heart." The hardheartedness of Pharaoh represented a response to the intention of God, which radically opposed the intention of Pharaoh. What God wanted done was against what Pharaoh was doing, so Pharaoh resisted.

I have never heard of or witnessed an easily capitulation to a liberating demand. Oppressive powers, and the representatives thereof, have very little motivation to listen to people who they consider beneath them. The narrative of white supremacy shapes the response of minority demands for equality. From the perspective of the empire, there is no motivation to respond favorably and with equity to a people who have historically been considered inferior. Thus, we should never be surprised that Pharaoh is not listening to us. Yet, be assured that God has heard from us.

What are your feelings about resistance? How has resistance kept you from opposing known injustices? How does the reality of God sustain you?

PRAYER:
O God, for years we have been raising our voices in protest against obvious injustices. Our voices seem to have fallen on deaf ears. Hope us, I pray, to be assured of the ear that matters -Your ear. AMEN.

Exodus 12:1-28

"A Holy Convocation"

Prophetic engagement needs the energy of ritual. The process of liberation must have a ritualistic cadence in order to sustain momentum and provide meaningful reflection. People who have experienced severe oppression benefit from established rituals of liberation. Likewise, without established rituals, the potential for repeated or sustained oppression is likely.

The Exodus story sets Passover before liberation. Moses and Aaron were commanded to speak to the congregation of Israel and establish the dynamics of the Passover. The date was established, so that Passover could occur at a set time in the future. The sacrifice was specified, which gave opportunity for every family to participate, regardless of economic status. Instructions on how to prepare the sacrifice and how to apply the blood on the doorposts provided symmetry throughout the community. Everyone was doing the same thing the same way. There was a ritualistic process and program for the execution and celebration of Passover. The meaning of the Passover was to secure in the collective consciousness of the people that the Lord "passed over the houses of Israel in Egypt when He struck down the Egyptians and delivered our households."

While living in Brooklyn, I observed the Jewish community engaging in the annual ritual of Passover. One year I noted smoldering piles on the sidewalk throughout the Jewish neighborhood. I inquired about the source and meaning of the smoldering piles. I was told that they represented the bread that had been brought out of the Jewish homes and set afire. I further inquired about the meaning from a Jewish brother who was dressed in the attire of Judaism, and in addition, had the haircut of a very conservative sect of Judaism. He either chose not to, or could not tell me the meaning of the smoldering mounds beyond the fact that it was bread. I was finally told by a Jewish merchant that burning the leavened bread represented the destruction of pride. Pride was viewed as a detriment to the process and the celebration of Passover.

I am intrigued by the Passover because the African American community is bereft of rituals of liberation. Dr. Johnny Ray Youngblood established the MAAFA in Brooklyn to address the absence of rituals of liberation. In California, where I now live, I see brothers and sisters who wear the look, but don't know the meaning. Christians partake of the Lord's Supper, but few can make a connection between it and the liberation of oppressed people.

Have you any rituals that set cadence to your struggles? How has your faith community responded to the adventures of liberation?

PRAYER:
Lord, You are ever mindful of all that it takes to liberate a people. Forgive us for our callous forgetfulness. Hope us, I pray, to provide responsible ritual to the meaning of our salvation. AMEN.

42 STATIONS OF THE EXODUS

> **NOTE:** *The next phase of my meditative journey takes me into an adventure that is personally unfamiliar and further highlights the limitations of traditional Christian academia. As a seminarian, and even a post-graduate student, I was not encouraged to learn or to appreciate the incredible perspective Judaism provides the Christian faith. There were certainly opportunities to learn Hebrew and the Old Testament, but at no point in my academic journey was I ever informed about the 42 Stations of the Exodus, a staple in Jewish biblical studies. I do not suggest that my seminary education was not good. In fact, it was great! I am merely citing it as a gross oversight to exclude what had to have been a primary experience in the life of Jesus – those experiences that represent the defining observations of his faith and community.*

The Stations of the Exodus, like the Christian Stations of the Cross, represent the citing of significant moments in Israel's redemption. The stations are noted as 42 sites that the Israelites visited following their exodus from Egypt. They are primarily located in the book of Exodus, Numbers and Deuteronomy, with them being crystallized in Numbers 33. I suspect some will latch quickly on to the number 42 and seek numerological significance. I am not convinced that the numerological value of these sites will mine for us the most meaningful contributions. I do believe, however, that the depth of meaning of the sites can be significant for those who view the Bible through the lenses of liberation theology, or for issues of social justice.

It will be in that vein that I will reflect upon the 42 Stations of the Exodus. I want to consider them for what might be the most difficult challenge of social justice and the consequent liberation of a people, namely, process. The 42 Stations of the Exodus perhaps provide clues to the significance of process for those who would engage in the work of prophetic ministry.

Exodus 12:29-42; Numbers 33:3,5

"Otherwise We'll All be Dead"

The work of prophetic engagement must impact the lives of both the oppressor and the oppressed. In order for oppressive arrangements to be significantly altered, it must be viewed as advantageous to the oppressor and for the oppressed. A recent movie rendition of the life of Nelson Mandela demonstrated that before the evil of apartheid was dismantled, white South Africans had to be convinced that it was in their self-interest to dismantle the existing social arrangements. Oppressors need to realize their vested self-interest in survival, even at the expense of loosening their oppression.

The final plague brought Egypt to its knees. The painful horror of the death of the firstborn sons was more than the people could bear. The text indicates that a "horrendous wailing" could be heard throughout Egypt. Pharaoh relents and declares the total liberation of the Israelites, inclusive of livestock and symbols of wealth procured from the Egyptians. Pharaoh even entreats Moses and Aaron for prayer. Yet, it was the pressure applied by the Egyptians that carried the day. The Egyptian people feared for their survival, because firstborn sons symbolized the potential of a future. With no firstborn sons, Egypt's very existence was at risk. Thus, they pressed to send the Israelite people on their way, "otherwise we'll all be dead."

Ramses is the starting point of Israel's journey out of Egypt. Every act of social transformation must have a starting point. Perhaps the slow progression for African Americans is because we've lost sight of our starting point. We can't seem to sustain progressive movement because it feels like we are always starting all over again. The deluded promises of would-be leaders fill this gap with faulty Messianic claims. Perhaps we could benefit from having a Ramses perspective that points us back to the starting points of our liberation. There has to be a place in our history where the oppressors declared, "Otherwise we'll all be dead."

Where did you begin making a prophetic difference? Are there places and people who represent your Ramses perspective? What point of self-interest has historically motivated a change in the heart of white America?

PRAYER:
O God, You have always been our starting point. Hope us, I pray, to always consider You as the starting point of our liberation. AMEN.

Exodus 12:43-51

"In One House"

Prophetic engagement involves an arduous process. It is never an easy endeavor. It is not a one-night affair, or a twenty-four hour journey. There is a tendency to overlook the traumatic impact of oppression upon the oppressed. People who have been subjected to oppressive realities are uniquely ill-prepared for the long journey of liberation. Thus, the work of liberation must take into account the process of preparation.

In the early stages of the Exodus, Moses was commanded by God to establish the Passover. The Passover ritual was to be instituted within each household, making the heads of households responsible. There was to be order in the partaking of the Passover and it was to include only those who identified with the Exodus movement. Thus, the first stop in the Exodus was Sukkoth, which means "shelters" or "booths." God provided a shelter, and the people of Israel were to shelter all who identified with the Exodus movement.

There is rarely a day where the residual of oppression is not expressed within the African American community. The trauma of a long night of oppression continues to adversely impact the progression of the people. It requires a high level of compassion to negotiate communal trauma, lest one become frustrated and despair.

The lesson of Sukkoth is the need for shelter. Communities of oppression must organize spaces and places of shelter to incorporate all who would participate in the drama of liberation. We cannot assume that just because people are in the community they know the story of the community, or the goals of the community. There is a need for each house to become equipped and accountable for assimilating all participants into the process of liberation. Sukkoth reminds us that freedom is a long process that requires intentional assimilation.

What do you do in ministry to assimilate others into the work of the prophetic? Or, is your ministry all maintenance and institutional upkeep? How is liberation being processed within your community?

PRAYER:
O God, I am grateful for Your process. I confess to ignoring the need for redemptive assimilation. Hope me, I pray, to be ever mindful of the need for shelter in the processes of redemption. AMEN.

Exodus 12:37, 13:17-20; Numbers 33:5-6

"On the Edge of the Wilderness"

Being truly led by God is to be ok with living on the edge. The presence of real danger seems to always lurk near those who obey God. While such an arrangement bodes better with individuals, it can be extremely unsettling for a community. Perhaps this is why prophetic engagement is rarely welcomed and embraced, because living on the edge is too tenuous for communal consensus.

The journey from Succoth to Etham was a circuitous route. The text notes that God chose to lead the people around by the Red Sea, avoiding the land of the Philistines, which was noted as being war-filled. The activities of war might prove to be too much for the freshly liberated nation and might have provoked a back-to-Egypt campaign. Of further note is the presence of Joseph's bones. Joseph's ministrations brought them into Egypt, but not even the privileged Joseph wanted his legacy to remain in Egypt.

It was in Etham, at the edge of the wilderness, that we are introduced to the Exodus symbols of God's abiding presence. The abiding presence of the Lord was symbolized by "a pillar of cloud" in the day and "a pillar of fire" by night. During the day Israel would be protected from harm and during the night Israel would be able to see. While journeying on the edge of the wilderness, Israel would be able to progress in the day and the night. There would be no limiting the people's journey just because they were living on the edge.

A major obstacle for progressive adventure is the reluctance of the oppressed to live on the edge. I have noted that African Americans support liberal politics, but embrace a conservative theology. The painful practices of slave religion espoused by misinformed preachers harmfully infect most of our religious communities. The brilliant young African American scholar-pastor, Raphael Warnock, labeled it in his book, The Divided Mind of the Black Church. As an emerging mental health clinician, such double-mindedness is a sign of mental dis-ease. From a biblical perspective, we are not given to living on the edge. Etham-like arrangements are unsettling for us. Yet, the realization of God's abiding presence is for those who dare journey with God on the edge.

Can you deal with the unsettling moments in life? How? Would realities mark out for you the presence of God?

PRAYER:
O God, Who would lead us by day and by night, please don't forgo Your abiding presence. We confess with being unsettled, and sometimes unfaithful to Your liberating agenda. Hope us, I pray, to develop an awareness that we can't move into Your progressive future without following You on the edge. We need Your abiding presence. AMEN.

Exodus 14:1-9; Numbers 33:6-8

"Camping by the Sea"

Obeying God's liberating instructions will not only have us living on the edge, but will also make our steps seem aimless. The unsettling arrangements of living on the edge can be disturbingly exacerbated by perceptions of aimlessness. The strategies of God, although unsettling for the oppressed, are designed for the destruction of the oppressor. As long as the oppressive mindset exists, the intent of oppression remains. God's ultimate goal is to destroy oppressive thinking.

The Fourth Station of the Exodus was to camp at Pi-Hachirot. The journey from Egypt was considered somewhat circuitous. God ordered Moses to turn around and set camp in Pi-Hachirot. It was a channel-like opening by the sea. Camping at Pi-Hachirot was a ploy to draw Pharaoh out, or to raise in him his true intention. The Bible notes that, "The people did as ordered." However, Pharaoh believed that Israel was aimlessly wandering and decided to pursue them and return them into servitude. As a ploy, God's intention was to prove to Pharaoh and the Egyptians that there was only one God. Of note is the fact that proving the supremacy of God was for the Egyptians and not for Israel. It seems that who most needed to know God was supreme were the Egyptians, the oppressors, or the regime of the empire.

I find this text quite challenging because it upsets a major theological assumption of oppressed people, at the least within the community that I am most familiar with. The African American community holds strongly to the belief that everything God does is for us. We have assumed that the intention of God is to demonstrate to us that God is God. Yet, the ones who most need to realize the supremacy of God are really not the oppressed, but the oppressor. The demagogues of white supremacy are the ones most in need of a theological shift.

The oppressors, or the upholders of the empire, need to realize the presumptuousness of their godly delusions. Oppressed people have a need for God's deliverance from the wrongness of oppression, whereas the oppressor needs God's deliverance from what they believe right about oppressing. The irony of prophetic engagement is God's ultimate intention of upsetting the kingdom of the oppressor.

What is it about your ministry that upsets the arrangements of the empire? Do you believe everything God does is for you? Why? How would your God-thinking change if you considered God's intention for white supremacy?

PRAYER:
O God, forgive us for not always understanding Your intentions. Hope us, I pray, to become more aware of what You are really trying to do, even when You are using us to do it. AMEN.

Exodus 15:22-26; Numbers 33:7-8

"Bitter With the Sweet"

During the early stages of the civil rights movement, Martin Luther King, Jr. noted the tensions between those committed to nonviolence and the student movement that was not. To intensify the tension, powerful movements like the Black Panthers and the Nation of Islam were also gaining attention and adherents. All of the groups wanted the same thing, but they were not all in agreement about the best process of getting there. It was truly a time where the movement toward freedom had to take the bitter with the sweet.

The Fifth Station of the Exodus is Marah, where Moses encountered a serious challenge to the liberation movement and his legitimacy as a leader. The movement was only three days in the wilderness and they encountered a serious challenge to their physical wellbeing: the lack of water. There was water there, but the water at Marah was unfit for human consumption. The response of the newly liberated slaves was to project their bitterness upon Moses, the leader. Moses cried out to the Lord and was shown what was necessary to change the water from bitter to sweet.

Moses was told to throw a certain piece of wood into the water and the water became sweet, or fit for human consumption. It was at Marah where the Lord began establishing the protocol necessary for a liberated people. Obedience, no matter how strangely constructed, was primary for the community of the recently enslaved. That protocol, when followed and obeyed, would demonstrate the healing presence and power of God.

What are the common responses to challenging situations? Most people seek alternatives, or solutions. Some might even give up, surrendering to the difficulties. In the process of leading a people into a new way of life and living, the tendency is to project one's bitterness upon the most visible target – the leader. Any leader who leads a liberation movement should not be surprised or discouraged by bitter projections. Prophetic engagement demands being able to take the bitter with the sweet, and use bitter experiences to establish liberation protocol.

What has been your normal response to challenging situations? Have those responses worked for you? How have those responses showed up in your community or church?

PRAYER:
O God, Who leads us in the ways of liberation, hope us, I pray, to deal wisely with bitter experiences. May our bitter moments be opportunities for creative interventions, thereby sweetening the bitterness. AMEN.

HOPE US, LORD!

Exodus 15:27; Numbers 33:8-9

"Wells and Palms"

My pastoral predecessor and academic benefactor, Dr. A. H. Newman, used to say, "God takes a great risk when He blesses us." His observation suggests that being given what we want puts us in position to compromise the total journey of faithful living. For some, getting to where we want to be places us in danger of not going where God wants us to go. For others, having what we want shuts us down from getting all God wants to give us. There are dimensions of the faith journey where the good can get in the way of the better, and the better eclipses the best.

After the very difficult time in Marah, where water was bitter and the complaints intense, the children of Israel arrived at Elim. Unlike Marah, which was characterized as having no water, Elim is noted as having twelve wells of water and seventy palm trees. There was plenty of water and there were plenty of trees. It was a healthy place. It was a good place to be, so "they camped there by the waters."

Noteworthy in the text is "no grumbling" and no need to establish new protocols for faithful living. Of equal interest is the fact that they camped. They did not settle. With plenty of water and the most useful trees on the planet, they set up temporary living quarters.

As a child, I recall my parents loading us up in the car and travelling back to a place they described as "home." For me, home was California, but for them home was Louisiana, the place of childhood memories and communal formation. Home, for them, was marked by the painful challenges and experiences of the Jim Crow South. As challenging as was the Jim Crow South, California and its oceanic waters, sandy beaches and palm trees was equally challenging. The losses we have experienced in California are probably far more grievous than anything we would have lost in Louisiana. The loss of healthy community, family centered living, personal accountability, and Bible rooted faith have been costly to our survival as a people. It's been over 70 years since my family migrated to California, and perhaps we have stayed too long. Perhaps we were only supposed to camp here and not settle here. Prophetic engagement has to address our tendency to settle in places meant for camping.

Are you in a place of settling? Or, or you at a place of camping? What has where you are been like?

PRAYER:
O God, keep us mindful that we are pilgrims travelling through a "barren land." Hope us, I pray, that we do not confuse temporary dwellings with our eternal destiny. AMEN.

Exodus 14:13-31; Numbers 33

"At the Expense of Pharaoh, his Chariots and his Calvary"

A major objective, as well as strategy, of prophetic engagement is to make oppression too expensive for the oppressor to sustain. In a world shaped by bottom-line thinking, the thing that matters most is the bottom line. Oppression profits from the devastating cost of human suffering. Its systems and structures are designed to make money more important than people. As a result, oppressive constructs have been designed to dehumanize a people from birth. The ministry of prophetic engagement views cost from the perspective of human suffering.

The Seventh Station of the Exodus is the Red Sea epic. There is clearly a numerological aspect attached to this experience. The number seven is the biblical number for fullness, or perfection. As the number of fullness, or perfection, the Red Sea epic represents a pivotal and decisive moment in the deliverance of God's people. The impossibility of the Red Sea before them and the death-dealing machinery of the empire closing in from behind portray a pivotal and decisive moment in the journey to freedom. An irony of the story is God's statement to Moses informing him that he would never again see the Egyptians as he sees them today. The decisiveness of God's victory over the expensive machinery of the empire would radically change how Egypt was perceived in the eyes of the recently released slaves. Israel's ability to walk through the Red Sea on dry land and the complete conquest of Pharaoh, his chariots, and his horsemen demonstrated the awesome power of God. Adonai is God, and not Pharaoh, and Moses was firmly established as God's leader.

There is probably not a better known story in biblical folklore than the Red Sea epic. This epic has been used to fuel the freedom aspirations of the oppressed, for it demonstrates two things: the possibilities to overcome overwhelming odds, and the cost of trying to hinder people destined for freedom. I believe we have focused exclusively on the former, and not utilized the potential of the latter. We believe in God's ability to make a way for freedom, but have not always seen the wisdom of making oppression too costly.

As I write these lines, the nation is fixed upon the vacillating trends of the stock market. The up and down dynamics of the stock market dominate societal conclusions about the health and welfare of our country. So much of American life is shaped by the idolatrous claims of the market. Perhaps when oppressed people begin to utilize the strategy of making oppression too expensive, there are some forms of oppression we will no longer see. God is still able to bring freedom at the expense of Pharaoh, his chariots, and his cavalry.

What market realties do you focus upon? Are there any market realities that you know support oppression? How can we make those realities too expensive too maintain?

PRAYER:
O God, we are grateful for Your decisive interventions. Hope us, I pray, to be strategic in our struggle for freedom. Give us victories so decisive that the idolatrous image of the oppressor will be altered forever. AMEN.

Exodus 16:1-15, 17:1, Numbers 33:12-13

"He Has Heard Your Complaints"

The work of the prophetic must be sensitive to the conversations among the oppressed, even when those conversations sound negative. Such conversations among the oppressed can be extremely helpful in determining prophetic direction. There are moments in the process of liberation when what the people are saying determines what needs to be done next.

The Eighth Station of the Exodus is at the Wilderness of Sin, which is noted as being "between Elim and Sinai." Between a pleasant place and a pivotal place lies a place of serious challenge. At the Wilderness of Sin, the provocations of the people are aroused by the lack of life's most basic need – food. The lack of adequate food supplies triggered a serious volley of complaints against Moses and the folly of their exodus from Egypt. The people compared the sustenance of oppression with the life-threatening reality of their wilderness state. In the minds of the people, they were at a place and state where death by starvation was imminent.

God responds to the complaints of the people by providing a food supply of quails and bread. The intent of the food supply was not only to sustain life, but also to recognize Who was engineering the liberation adventure. A quota of food was established as a "test" as to "whether or not they will walk in My law or not." For a liberated people, even food served as a barometer of faithfulness to God. The question raised in verse 15, "What is it?" in the Hebrew is "Man hu?" It is a play on the word "manna," bread from heaven.

In my years as a pastor, even as a child of a pastor, the complaints of the people have always been viewed in a negative light. In fact, preachers have viewed complaints as being tools of the Devil. A closer look at this text reveals that the people's complaint served as the catalyst for God to intervene in a manner necessary for the journey. There is no mention of demonic influence or negative subversions. What can people do without bread? It might be time for us to listen more to the complaints of the people, for in their complaints we might get clues as to what God is about to do next. If God listens to complaints, we surely need to listen to complaints.

What do you do when people bring you complaints? What was the nature of the last community complaint you heard? What happened next?

PRAYER:
O God, we are so grateful for Your listening ear. You hear what we don't want to hear. Hope us, O God, to be more attentive to the complaints of Your people, so that we might be more attentive to You. AMEN.

Numbers 33:12-13

"They Camped, They Departed"

What is important, and what is not? Where we put our time, resources, and energy is determined by what we consider important. Unfortunately, the values we place on things are often arbitrarily determined. Prophetic engagement must be discerning in determining the best use of time, energy, and resources. There are some places, although important in and of themselves, that are not the places where God wants us to expend too much time, energy, or resources.

The Ninth Station of the Exodus is Dophkah. Dophkah is only mentioned twice in the Bible, and nowhere in the book of Exodus. It is cited in the Book of Numbers, and in two successive verses. It merely states that they camped at Dophkah, and in the next verse, "they departed from Dophkah." Whatever happened at Dophkah fell through the cracks of biblical significance. Although the name, ironically, suggests pressed hard, or thrust, there is nothing in the biblical text that informs us about what was so pressing, hard or thrust at Dophkah.

The significance of Dophkah seems to be that it was noteworthy to mention as a place where the children of Israel did camp and then departed. February has been set aside as Black History Month. It is a time where the contributions, contributors, and experiences of being black in America are highlighted and celebrated. I have always enjoyed Black History Month, because it allows a people whose history has been historically diminished, to celebrate and validate it. Its importance looms large when we consider the Dophkah nature of the black experience in America. Much of our history has been lost because of the exigencies of white supremacy, combined with the negligence of black culture. The dominating ideology systemically erased our history, while we virtually ignored our history.

If the Jewish story tells us anything, it tells us that the prophetic progress of a people demands that they be mindful from whence they have come. All stations and places have meaning, even when noted, "They camped, and they departed."

Where are the places that have been ignored and minimized in our history? Can you locate a place in your ministry that was minimized because of your own oppression? How do we recover the significance of places we camped and departed from?

PRAYER:
O God, help us to value all the places You have brought us through to get us to where we are going. Hope us, I pray, to discover the importance of knowing from whence we have come. AMEN.

HOPE US, LORD!

Numbers 13:33

"Alush"

The process of liberation is a winding undertaking. It involves a journey through places and spaces that serve to deepen the significance of the liberation experience. We do not get to the Promised Land of freedom without adventure. There are moments when divine dependency overrules human certainty.

The Tenth Station of the Exodus is Alush. It is another one of those briefly mentioned, nondescript places where the children of Israel camped and departed. There is no mention of it within the Book of Exodus, or anywhere outside of the Book of Numbers. Alush's significance is neither detailed nor explained. There are no speeches given at Alush, or any mention of divine intervention.

Perhaps its Hebrew meaning provides some insight into its significance. Alush means "wild place," or "desolation." It is also referred to in Jewish symbolism as "I will knead." As a part of the wilderness journey, Alush accentuates the risky and adventurous nature of transitioning from a context of oppression to an experience of liberation. The process of liberation is likened to being kneaded, or prepared for the tough journey. As evident in the previous Stations of the Exodus, freedom from the illusions of comfort in Egypt involved risk, adventure, and moments of uncertainty.

A recent award-winning movie entitled, 12 Years a Slave highlighted the painful adventure of Solomon Northrup. Solomon Northrup, a free black, was kidnapped from New York and sold into Southern slavery. The drama of the movie was intended to highlight a neglected part of the slave experience: of free blacks being violently subjected to slavery because it was easy to do so. The color of one's skin made him easy prey to the profit-driven motives of chattel slavery, outlawed in parts of the nation, but vigorously sustained in other parts.

The journey to freedom has been a wild one for African Americans. Even now, the warehousing of black men in prisons illustrates the continuing predatory nature of white supremacy. Because of our slave experience, black men have become easy prey to the profit-driven motives of the prison industrial complex. Perhaps we are living out an Alush moment, where the illusions of oppression are being stripped away that we might better see freedom. Perhaps we are being further kneaded for the Promised Land of authentic liberation.

What are your thoughts on the difficulties of obtaining freedom for all in America? How have the challenges of inequality prepared us for freedom? Are there risks you are willing to encounter for the sake of freedom and equality?

PRAYER:
O God, I pray that we remain open to the risks involved in the liberation process. Hope us, I pray, to more wholly trust You during times of risk, adventure, and uncertainty. AMEN.

Exodus 17:1-16; Numbers 33:14-15

"Testing and Quarreling"

The journey of liberation can be a contentious undertaking. The internal opposition can be as contentious as the external. Leading oppressed people into a life of freedom, justice, and equality is not easy. Developing healthy collaborations among oppressed communities remains difficult. It appears that the dependency nature of an experience of oppression is not easily overcome or resolved. Oppressed people are known to struggle with the challenges of freedom. Internalized oppression is a difficult reality to overcome because the perverted dependency on the empire has a tendency to be incredibly strong.

The 11th Station of the Exodus is Rephidim. Metaphorically, Rephidim means "to rest." However, Rephidim presented the newly liberated slaves with multiple challenges, none of which were restful. There is nothing restful about Rephidim. The challenge of a lack of water precipitated a challenge to Moses's leadership, and then there was the surprising and vicious assault of the Amalekites. Moses identified the challenge to his leadership as a challenge to the Lord. He viewed the contentiousness as tempting the Lord. In desperation, Moses cried out to the Lord, "What shall I do with this people? They are almost ready to stone me."

God's response to Moses was to direct him to use his rod to strike the rock in Horeb, thereby producing an adequate water supply. Moses obeyed God and named the place Massah and Meribah, symbols of testing and quarreling. The battle with the Amalekites is a surprising development, for it is not stated in the text when the tension developed with the Amalekites, nor when and where Israel secured weapons to fight. Nonetheless, the Amalekites were defeated, as Aaron and Hur upheld Moses's hands.

As we face overwhelming challenges in the journey to freedom, I am constantly exasperated by the constant contentiousness among oppressed people. The point of contention seems to always center on the inadequacy of resources. Something about oppression seems to always focus oppressed people on what is lacking versus what is available. Could it be that the effects of internalized oppression draw their power from the perspective of lack?

What has been the source of contention within your community? How have such contentions been resolved? Have such contentions led to experiences of restfulness?

PRAYER:
O God, I am often at my wits end over the internal contention among oppressed people. Hope us, I pray, to see more opportunities to cooperate and collaborate, rather than more experiences of quarreling and testing. AMEN.

Exodus 18

"Wearing Yourself Out"

The personal toll upon those who engage in prophetic ministry is legion. The self-sacrifice, and the loss of health and healthy home life is a constant cost to those who commit themselves to prophetic ministry. It has become much too common for those on the frontlines of freedom end up on the front pages of personal tragedy. Ironically, those who are compassionately concerned for people in the freedom movement rarely practice good self-care.

The text for today is not a part of the Stations of the Exodus, but it is one I believe critical to prophetic reflection. Chapter 18 provides a rare snapshot into the family life of Moses. Zipporah and sons had not been heard from since that dramatic episode in chapter 4, verses 24-26. Other than the constant presence of Aaron, Moses's family had gotten lost in the dramatic busyness of the Exodus.

Chapter 18 brings Zipporah and the sons back into the story, as well as Moses's father-in-law, Jethro. It appears that some form of marital separation had taken place between Moses and Zipporah. In fact, the text suggests that Moses "sent away his wife." "Sent away" is a statement of divorcement. However, when Jethro listened to the Exodus story, he sent word that he was bringing back Moses's wife and sons. Jethro celebrated the Exodus pilgrimage and contributed to its wellbeing. He then observed Moses's daily transactions and interactions, and inquired about the wisdom that informed the leadership style Moses was using. Upon reflection, Jethro asserted that Moses's leadership style was not healthy for him, the people, and clearly not for his family. Jethro provided Moses with an alternative model that reduced the stress on him and the people, and the consequent drag on freedom's progress.

I love this text. The Jethro-epic seems pivotal to the progression of the Exodus story. Jethro allows us to see the need for abandoning unhealthy leadership styles that basically mimic the practices of the oppressor. We, too easily, overlook how pervasively the tentacles of oppression exist within ourselves. We may be free from the oppressor's presence yet not from the oppressor's influence. Without a Jethro-like intervention, we risk sabotaging our own movement and our family's health, as well as our own health. Of interest in this text is the fact that Jethro's intervention precedes Sinai.

Could it be that healthy self-care is a necessary prelude to greater revelations from God? How are you at taking care of yourself? How is your leadership style impacting your family?

PRAYER:
> *O Lord, help me to help myself. Forgive me for the pain I have inflicted in the name of good. Hope me, O God, to see clearly when I am sabotaging myself. Send me a Jethro to point out self-perpetrating oppressive residuals. AMEN.*

Exodus 19:1-9; Numbers 10:12; 33:15-16

"Shaped by God's Voice"

Communication is an indispensible dynamic to liberation activities. Communication is critical in getting people from one place to another. The voice that is heard is the one that will usually shape behavior and outcomes. The work of prophetic engagement must be diligent in communicating desired outcomes and behavior.

The 12th Station of the Exodus is the Wilderness of Sinai. The text notes that the wilderness was "before the mountain." The people camped in the undisciplined, uncultivated context of the wilderness as a prelude to the God-centered, covenant-making, community-building experiences of the mountain. God spoke to Moses and reminded Moses of the new-life defining experience of the people, which was deliverance from Egypt. God informs Moses that the life and wellbeing of the people depended upon their faithful adherence to God's voice. God's voice would shape the lives of the people so profoundly that they would "be a special treasure above all people."

Moses conveyed God's message to the people and they declared, "All that the Lord has spoken we will do." A consecration ritual was performed that designated the place and limits of the people, all of which was a response to God's voice.

In these times of endless media bombardment and technological stimuli, the worth and significance of the voice gets minimized. We would-be prophets and would-be preachers can be threatened and intimidated out of using the only tool we have – our voices. Our voice is often minimized as one among many, and the intentions of God lose their impact on the people's lives. However, the voice of God has a way of being heard in the midst of the noisy hum of our daily lives. The apostle's words ring true and demand our faithfulness: "How shall they hear without a preacher?"

How convinced are you in the power of your voice? In what ways has your voice been compromised and minimized? How does such compromise and minimization make you feel?

PRAYER:
O God, help me, I pray, to be faithful to Your Word. Hope us, I pray, to be assured that what You say is eternal and everlasting, and that what You say matters. May the lives of Your people give evidence of being shaped by Your voice. AMEN.

Numbers 11:35, 33:16-17

"Graves of Lust"

Prophetic engagement must always factor in the wandering ways of human experience. The vicissitudes of human experience are often magnified, intensified, and sometimes distorted when viewed through the lenses of oppression. Small things have a way of becoming big, normal becomes abnormal, what's abnormal can quickly become normal, and what's immoral conveniently becomes moral.

The 13th Station of the Exodus comes immediately following the Sinai experience. The 13th Station is a place called Kibroth-Hattavah. Although the biblical text does not detail the narrative dynamics of Kibroth-Hattavah, Jewish tradition gives meaning and attention to it. According to Jewish tradition, Kibroth-Hattavah was the place where a large contingency was buried because they complained about the monotonous diet of Mannah. It was the place where physical appetites consumed and sabotaged God's liberating perspectives. The children of Israel longed for the spicy variety of food experienced in Egypt. In fact, the name Kibroth-Hattavah means "graves of longing" or "graves of lust."

In his book, The Journey to the Common Good, Walter Brueggemann writes about the "anxiety of scarcity," which he describes as the pyscho-social response to the belief that there is not enough. The paranoia created by oppressive exploitation feeds widespread anxiety about the availability of adequate resources for all people. Kibroth-Hattavah is a further corruption of the "anxiety of scarcity," because it suggests that what is available is not good enough.

As I observe the economic dynamics of oppressed people, there is a need to bury all that causes us to lose perspective. Our insatiable obsession for the consumption of the very products that fuel oppression distorts the long-range process of freedom. Perhaps the prophetic agenda should include a curriculum for wilderness survival. It's hard to keep a people focused on freedom with a one-course curriculum called trust, yet trust in God remains a constant criterion.

Consider ways in which you might want to add to the abundance perspective of people gripped by the "anxiety of scarcity." What experiences have you had where the focus was more on what wasn't available than on what was available? How might we enhance people's perspective on the adequacy of what's available?

PRAYER:
O God, our hope for freedom is located in our unwavering trust of You. Hope us, I pray, to maintain our focus so that no one needs to die in a grave of lust. AMEN.

Numbers 11:35, 12:16, 33:17-18

"Places"

An often-overlooked part of life is the significance of places. The commoditization of land has ironically cheapened the significance of land, while, at the same time, increased its market value. The places we occupy possess spiritual value, which is far more significant than market value. Prophetic engagement values spiritual value over market value.

The 14th Station of the Exodus is Hazeroth. Hazeroth is one of those places that gets lost in the narcissistic proclivities of modern Christian practices. We, Christians, engage in self-impoverishment by ignoring the rich Jewish symbolism of place. Hazeroth, in Jewish symbolism, means "villages," or "places." Hazeroth was the place where Miriam and Aaron spoke against Moses having married a Cushite, who was an African woman. It was a place where xenophobia raised its ugly head among oppressed people. Consequently, Miriam was stricken with leprosy. The people had to remain in Hazeroth until she was healed.

This morning I listened to the late Curtis Mayfield's "We the People who are Darker than Blue," a song that addresses, among many things, the deadly issue of "colorism" among African American people. Mayfield noted that our tendency to make distinctions among ourselves could eventually destroy us all. It's astounding what oppression does to a people! When we start making distinctions among ourselves, we unconsciously repeat the behavior of the oppressor.

Prophetic engagement must responsibly address oppressive behavior within the delivered community. We must be mindful that any behavior that separates us perpetuates the fragmentation of our humanity. It is a place, where, like Miriam, we become diseased and need to be healed. We can never move forward until we move from the place(s) of our disease.

I challenge you to note the places of disease within your faith community. What will your response be? How has oppression diseased our people's self-perspectives?

PRAYER:
Lord, You Who have created us as one flesh, hope us, O God, to acknowledge the place of our dis-ease. May we move from this place among ourselves so that we might move forward in embracing our global family. AMEN.

Numbers 33:18-19

"A Place of Cleansing"

We continue our reflection on the significance of place. We are multidimensional in life experiences. Consequently, we are people of time, place, and culture. A significant, but often overlooked dimension is the significance of place. Not every place has the same value, or impacts us the same way. In the journey toward freedom and wholeness there are places in life that are distinguished for their cleansing effect. There are places known for assisting in the process of purging unhealthy, unclean, and unproductive behavior and thought patterns.

The 15th Station of the Exodus is Rithmah. Although the Christian community values cleansing and purging, we do not connect the experience to a place. For us, it is an activity, an event, or a process. In Jewish symbolism, Rithmah is noted as a place of cleansing, or the "broom" place. It is a place where some critical aspect of oppression was swept away. Perhaps it was the place where the Hazeroth syndrome, the dis-ease of racial separation, was decisively dealt with. We have no details of its specificity. All we know is that they camped there and moved on.

In his groundbreaking experience and consequent book, Black Like Me, John Howard Griffin chronicles what it felt like to be a black person in the South in 1959. After going through a process of darkening his skin, Griffin spent six weeks in the South as a black man. Prior to the experience, he had been stricken blind, and the recovery of his sight heightened his appreciation for the gift of sight. In blindness, he was not bound by the limiting physical presentations of people. All he experienced was people, and not black or white people. During his experience as a black man, he noted, "The gift of sight becomes a curse when used to perpetuate segregationist behavior."

As I write these few lines (during the presidency of Barak Obama), I think of the fact that America is being led by one of the most brilliant men in our world. After eight years of a president of obvious intellectual challenges, the office is being distinguished with admirable wisdom and thoughtfulness. Ironically, instead of the intelligence of the president being applauded and appreciated, he is constantly being criticized, demonized, and dehumanized. Why? He is African American. He is black.

Clearly, America is in need of a Rithmah experience. We need a place where the dis-ease of racism can be purged from our consciousness. Prophetic engagement in our context must locate the place where cleansing can transpire.

How has racism poisoned your view of yourself? Other people? Are there any places where the dis-ease of racism can be purged from our collective psyche?

PRAYER:
O God, we love You for loving us just the way we are. Yet, we love You more for loving us enough to not leave us the way You find us. Hope us, I pray, to journey to the places of cleansing. And where those places don't exist, give us the courage and imagination to create them. AMEN.

Numbers 33:19-20

"Pomegranate Faith"

A major work within any transformative undertaking is productive analysis. How we view a matter, or understand a reality, largely determines how we will respond to the matter or reality. In the work of prophetic engagement, there are a lot of forces at work to support oppressive realities, as well as resistant forces designed to dissolve oppressive constructs. It is folly to expect radical change without any analysis of what it is we are up against.

The 16th Station of the Exodus is Rimmon-Perez. Rimmon-Perez is another of the many Exodus experiences that is exclusively cited within the Book of Numbers and strangely absent in the Book of Exodus. The absence of Rimmon-Perez does not diminish the significance of it. Rimmon-Perez, referred to as "the place of pomegranates," in Jewish symbolism means "breaking up." A pomegranate is a fruit of many seeds, with the essence of it, or the fruit of it, being the substance around the seeds. We have to break up a pomegranate to enjoy its fruit.

Rimmon-Perez represents a place in the journey where some stuff was broken up in order to move closer to the Promised Land. We are not told what was broken up, but perhaps it was some deep inner residual of the planted seeds of oppression. It could have been some self-defeating tendency or behavior that did not serve well a liberated people or just cause.

As a people, African Americans shy away from analysis. We are not a people who welcome any kind of work that exposes something about us. Although we are subjected to endless analyses, our oppressive legacy resists being subjects to further pathological exposures. I suspect it's the result of the barrage of negative stigmatization that has accompanied the pathological results of oppressive analyses. It should be understood that it's difficult to accept some new ways to be told that something is wrong with us. Yet, many of the obsolete practices and traditions of the African American church are the result of an unhealthy resistance to productive analysis.

However, before we can move beyond some of our self-defeating practices and behaviors, some things need to be analyzed and broken up. The pomegranate symbol suggests that there is fruit in the breaking up. Prophetic engagement must assist oppressed people in seeing the fruit of productive analysis. We have to know what's within us, what's around us, and what's going on with us to get where God wants to take us. Blind faith is not biblical faith – it's stupid faith!

How do you use the tools of analysis in ministry or community activism? What are those tools? What has been the result of such analysis?

PRAYER:
O God, You are a God of truth, and You have declared that "the truth shall make us free." Hope us, O God, to accept certain harsh truths, as we journey to become more like the people You intend for us to be. Create for us spaces and places where we can expose ourselves to our greater selves. AMEN.

Numbers 33:20-21

"Clarity"

I have always placed a premium on building capacity. In fact, I consider a crucial aspect of the work of "making disciples" as building capacity. People need to possess a sense of capacity, or agency, to navigate the shifting sands of life. It's extremely difficult to get liberating results from incapacitated people. Thus, the work of capacity building is vital to the work of prophetic ministry.

The 17th Station of the Exodus is Libnah. After departing from Rimmon-Perez, the place of "breaking up," the congregation of freshly liberated slaves arrived at Libnah, the place of "clarity." Libnah is not detailed in Scripture, yet it holds a significant place in Jewish symbolism. It is symbolized as the place of "clarity," or "brilliance." It is viewed as the place where the congregation experiences clarity of thought, or clearness of mind. After the breaking up of stuff, or the analysis of their reality, the congregation of Israel started seeing things clearly.

Of interest to me is the meta-meaning of the word "brilliance." "Brilliance" can be viewed as the sparkling clarity of a costly jewel, or it can define someone with high intelligence, or keen acumen. Could it be that the true mark of high intelligence, or keen acumen, is the capacity to see reality with clarity? When people can see things with a greater sense of clarity, their intellectual, psychological, and social capacity is considered brilliant. The results of healthy analyses logically build capacity for people to see things clearer. That's brilliance!

A stimulant for oppressed people to reconsider healthy and productive analysis is to build capacity for brilliance. When we begin seeing our reality in all of its related components, we are better equipped to start making the right decisions for our freedom. Freedom is more than a slogan, a desire, or a rhetorical passion. Freedom is about being able to coordinate the disparate realities of human existence into a cohesive, compassionate, just, and meaningful whole. We must see the connections of all the parts, including economics, political, educational, social, legal, moral, and military in producing a more humane society. To view life with clarity is a sign of brilliance!

What are you doing in ministry that develops prophetic brilliance within your community? How is it validated? If not, what do you need to further the capacity of the people you serve?

PRAYER:
O God, we who were made in Your image and likeness often diminish ourselves by living lives that are empty, void, and dark. Hope us, I pray, to be more like You and initiate our creative capacity by speaking forth Your word of clarity. AMEN.

Numbers 33:21-22

"Ruins"

The obstacles we overcome often measure us, shape us, and define us. Who we are is often the result of what we've overcome. There is something to be said about a people who demonstrate resiliency in the midst of overwhelming obstacles.

The 18th Station of the Exodus is Rissah. The experience of Libnah had provided some clarity about the deeper meaning of the Exodus. Rissah symbolized "ruin," or "devastation needed to be overcome." I am not clear if the camp at Rissah was a ruin, or if the experience of Rissah provided a perspective of the "ruin" needed to be overcome. Oppressive constructs destroy significant aspects of humanity. People lose valuable components of what it means to be human when oppressed.

Perhaps Rissah provided the recently liberated slaves an opportunity to consider the ruins of Egyptian oppression. The inability to differentiate who they were, apart from the exploitative arrangements of Pharaohic oppression, would have been a challenge to the ex-slaves. The sense of community, the sense of connectedness, and the worth and value of person represent collateral damage of an experience of oppression. Upon arriving at Rissah, they began to see clearly the extent of the ruins of oppression, as well as what devastation needed to be overcome.

During Black History Month, African Americans nationwide engage in some form of celebration around the historical contributions of African Americans. It is a time for even the nation to consider the historical significance of African Americans. Much of that time is spent considering the contributions and highlighting significant African American personalities. I am always somewhat miffed by the perfunctory nature of it all. However, as mentioned above, I appreciate the prophetic promptings of Dr. Johnny Ray Youngblood, who called attention to the MAAFA, the "great suffering" of the Middle Passage. During my time in Brooklyn, New York, Dr. Youngblood called on African Americans in Brooklyn to consider and collectively grieve the "ruins," the "devastation we had to overcome." I discovered this ministry effort to be profoundly necessary for our collective healing and forward progress.

Can you think of any way in which your ministry facilitates the "devastations we had to overcome?" What's in the way of creating spaces for discerning the "ruins" of our experience?

PRAYER:
O God of all of our life experiences, I acknowledge You as God of the good, the bad, and the ugly dimensions of life. Hope us, I pray, to be mindful of the "ruins" and all of the "devastation we must yet overcome." AMEN.

HOPE US, LORD!

Numbers 33:22-23

"The Assembly"

The most fundamental or basic necessity for community is for people to be together. Being in community means more than sharing geographical space, or being ethnically, culturally, or racially connected. Being in community is a state of being where people sense a profound connectedness. It is the work of being in assembly. Prophetic engagement includes the work of building community and holding people together for the long haul of liberation.

The 19th Station of the Exodus is Kehelathah. In Jewish symbolism, Kehelathah means "assembly." It is the station within the Exodus where the significance of assembly is emphasized. The two previous stations called for clarity and ruins. An obvious ruin that needs to be overcome is isolation, or the lack of connectedness. While in the wilderness, as well as in the Promised Land, the need for assembly was critical to the self-identification, growth, and survival of the ex-slaves. The Exodus was not a solo experience. It was an experience of a people who needed one another to realize the blessing of the Promised Land.

There is probably no challenge as difficult as building a prophetic community. To get a people beyond the fragmented existence of oppression is an arduous undertaking. A significant part of the work of prophetic ministry is for the purpose of building a people fit for the Promised Land of liberation. I recall the words of the late Dr. C. A. W. Clark, who noted that when "you see a group of preachers working together, you will see a miracle." His words came after long years of ministry, countless efforts in clergy collaboration, and an extensive tenure as a pastor and denominational leader. After a long life, Dr. Clark had concluded that it would take a miracle to build a working collaboration among those who hold the most significant leadership roles in African America.

Gathering in assembly can unite people for good or evil. On the one hand, people can get together for evil. I have witnessed and read of people getting together for the wrong reason. I've witnessed Klan marches. I've seen groups gang up on an individual and inflict needless pain. Our history is fraught with instances and incidents where the herd instinct, fueled with bigoted claims of privilege, has been painfully executed. On the other hand, I have witnessed the beauty and the power of people working together. The political campaign of Barak Obama provided America with one of the most beautiful testimonies of people working together the world has seen. The tears he shed upon being re-elected testified to the beauty of people working together. I can say that there is nothing more rewarding than to witness people perceive and embrace the value of collaboration.

What are the collaborations that identify your ministry? If there are no significant collaborations, why not? How do you feel about collaborations?

PRAYER:
O God, we acknowledge and embrace You in oneness. Hope us, I pray, to perceive and embrace the value of redemptive assembly. AMEN.

Numbers 33:23-24

"A Perspective of Beauty"

What is the beauty of prophetic engagement? Prophetic engagement, by nature of its callings, deals with what's ugly in the world. Its focus is upon the unbecoming effects of oppression. The disfiguring inhumanity of human beings inflicted upon other human beings is what drives prophetic engagement. So, what does the oppressed community see that bespeaks beauty?

The 20th Station of the Exodus is Mount Shapher. In Jewish symbolism, Mount Shapher referred to "beauty." Combining the reference of "Mount," which has to do with a perspective, Mount Shapher speaks of a "perspective of beauty." It is what the congregation perceived, or perhaps what Moses saw. The previous stations provided such a "beauty" perspective. When oppressive realities are broken up, or overcome, as in Stations 16 and 18, and the brilliant assembling of a people in pursuit of the liberating purposes of God, as in Stations 17 and 19, such a reality can create a perspective of beauty. Clearly, where the people were, was a long way from where they had begun. The progressiveness of the people was indeed a beauty to behold.

As painful as the journey of the last generation's participants in civil rights was, and the ugly dynamics of the previous generations of South Africans' African Nation Congress, the long lines of first-time voters were a beauty to behold. Seeing formerly oppressed people get to a place of noteworthy development is beautiful. I will forever hold in my heart the beauty of standing out in sub-freezing temperatures as the United States swore into office the first African American president. The beauty of a little white girl being hefted upon the shoulders of an African American man so that she might witness history was a beauty to behold.

Although I am far from being satisfied over the direct impact of Barak Obama's presidency, I did catch a fleeting glimpse of what a color-blind America would look like. Obama's policies, at least the ones he's been able to implement, have not had the anticipated impact upon the lives of the people who love him the most. African Americans need a Mount Shapher moment to crystallize the beauty of America's first African American president and shield us from the ugly divisiveness of the current president. Prophetic engagement needs to include moments where a perspective is given that we have come a long way from where we were. A constant litany of prophetic aspirations can corrupt the beauty of praiseworthy gratification.

Consider ways in which you can highlight beauty among so many ashes. Identify from whence we have come and where we are. What would be beautiful in the place of our collective ashes?

PRAYER:
O God, You Who have been known to turn beauty from ashes and mourning into dancing, give us a perspective of beauty. May we see with appreciation the beautiful distance we have travelled and from whence You have brought us. AMEN.

Numbers 33:24-25

"Moving Beyond Fear"

The fluctuating moods of people continue to be one of the most baffling dynamics of leading them in liberating adventures. It is astounding how people can be in such a beautiful mood one day and in a completely different mood the next. Although the moods of people can be baffling, it should also be expected. People doing something that they have never done before is an unsettling experience, which leaves them vulnerable to mood shifts. Yet, moods, good or bad, should never be mistaken as the goal. Freedom is the goal; moods are experiences of the journey.

The 21st Station of the Exodus is Haradah. Jewish symbolism identified Haradah as a place of "fear" or "trembling." Haradah is a place where the mood of the people shifted from beautiful to fearful. For some inexplicable reason, a deep trembling seized the hearts of the recently freed slaves and a fear-filled drag temporarily slowed the movement. Of note in the text is the fact that they "moved from Haradah." In other words, the fear did not stop the movement.

As inexplicable was the fear, the determination to keep moving was also inexplicable. They moved to the next place in the journey because fear did not have the last word. A movement of God was not sabotaged by the vacillating moods of an unsettled people. I would assert that the leadership of Moses and Aaron steadied the people and empowered them to move forward in spite of their fears.

Prophetic engagement is a call forward. It is a call to proceed beyond the places of our fears. Fear represents a constant foe to liberating and progressive movements. The inexplicable power of fear to ambush the hearts of people should not surprise us. The late drum major for justice, Dr. Martin Luther King, Jr., once stated, "The only thing we have to fear is fear itself." Our Lord Jesus repeatedly called for the disciples to not allow fear to diminish, distort, or detract them from the power of God.

I can hardly imagine where we would be as a people, as a nation, and even as a church if we did not tend to get stuck in Haradah. Much of what plagues us as a people, a nation, and a church is fueled by fear. Racism, sexism, homophobism, militarism, and the whole host of dehumanizing "isms" are propped up by fear. Personally, I can see where fear has prevented me from being a better person, parent, friend, lover, pastor, and professional. Yet, the presence and power of God has strangely and inexplicably moved me forward. Haradah must be the place where God moves us in spite of our fears.

What are your greatest fears? List them. Do you know where those fears come from? What are you doing to get beyond identified fears?

PRAYER:
O God, You Who call for faithful engagement and obedient response, deliver us from our fears. Hope us, I pray, to continue following You in spite of our fear. AMEN.

Numbers 33:25-26

"A Place of Assembly"

The work of building community is an arduous and endless task. It is probably one of the most constant quests of prophetic engagement. It is challenging because the people who benefit most from transforming a community must themselves work toward becoming community. The splintered and disparate consequences of oppression ill-affects the noble processes of community building.

As the people moved from the fear-filled episode at Haradah, it became obvious that there was a need for community building. Although we are not given the particulars of what caused such fear at Haradah, the next stop, Makheloth, indicates it must have been quite challenging. The 22nd Station of the Exodus, Makheloth, was a place of assembly. Jewish symbolism depicts Makheloth as a place of assemblies, or convocations. The plurality designated to the place suggests a number of assemblies, or moments of convocations. Perhaps Moses and Aaron saw the need for a number of assemblies to quell the damaging impact of Haradah.

I am actually intrigued by the suggestions of Makheloth. Makheloth provides an interesting response to the work of community building. Firstly, Makheloth acknowledges. It acknowledges the fact that something adversarial impacted the health of the community. Secondly, it acknowledges the need to give attention to the health of the community. Thirdly, it does something specific about building up the health of the community. The health of the community became a primary cause for a camp and convocation.

As I reflect upon the many civic and denominational meetings I have attended, I am struck by the absence of a sense of intentionality toward community building. The denomination that has dominated my life, the National Baptist Convention, USA, Inc., has never just acknowledged. The wide array of adversarial realties that have negatively impacted, and sometimes traumatized the people, have never been significantly acknowledged. We have allowed people to sit in unhealthiness without providing healthy interventions. Perhaps we would do well just to acknowledge, or meet, for the sole purpose of community cultivation.

What about your ministry cultivates community? How has your faith community acknowledged trauma? If not, why not?

PRAYER:
O God, Who calls us into meaningful and redemptive community, forgive us for our failure of acknowledgement. Hope us, I pray, to give attention to the incredible work of building community, so that we might more healthily embody the redemptive community. AMEN.

Numbers 33:26-27

"Immersed"

We are never just one thing. We are never in just one space or place. We are a number of things, often all at the same time. We occupy many spaces and places. Life is about integrating our many and disparate experiences and then moving forward to the Promised Land of completion. Monitoring the moods and movements of community life is an important aspect of prophetic engagement. We must be sensitive to where a people are at all times.

The work of convocation had to have been a solemn assembly. Camping at Makheloth lingered in the spirits of the people, because when they arrived at the next camp, something of noted significance settled upon the people. In fact, the 23rd Station of the Exodus, Tahath, symbolized "settled," "immersed," or "inclined." One translation suggested "under the authority of." The implications are that something of great significance came upon the people. We are not told what it was, but we can be assured that it had to do with who they were on this journey with God.

The issues of community, journey and God are basic and indispensable to the Exodus journey. It is aptly stated that "what brings a fresh future into being is when citizens are willing to self-organize." There must be an intentional, purposeful, and powerful effort to build up agency within the redemptive community. Community is essential to what God wants to do, because community always implies relationships. The journey represents the process by which God prepares a community for redemptive living. A people engage in self-discovery while on the journey and come to realize life beyond oppressive realities. Moreover, the God who calls the community to live life beyond the oppressive idolatries of Egypt is experienced and verified.

We cannot successfully move a people beyond oppressive constructs without them having a weighty sense of community, journey, and God. It is within the context of community where justice and righteousness are realized. It is within the process of journey where people experience and realize the potential to live as healthy and wholesome human beings. Finally, for people of faith, the awesome reality of God imposes and impacts the quality of both community and journey.

Perhaps what has contributed to the current apathy within many oppressed communities is a lack of burden, or a powerful sense of being weighed with the significance of community, journey, and God.

What are you doing to address the apathy within our oppressed communities? How has your community embraced a sense of journey? Or, is your community stagnated?

PRAYER:
O God, we look to You to deliver us from the loss of the significance of community, journey, and You. We are aware of our proclivity to live lightly, not wanting anything to weigh upon us. Hope us, I pray, to connect, to evolve, and to worship. AMEN.

Numbers 33:27-28

"Lagging Behind"

Planes, subways, trolleys, buses, trains, and other forms of mass transportation are often technologically identified as people movers. Technological people movers are big business, and necessary components of the lives and lifestyles of millions of people. While visiting China and parts of Europe, we witnessed the technological wonder called the bullet trains. This is technology at its best, and is strangely missing in America. America is technologically lagging behind the rest of the world because the people are lagging behind. The people will have to move before the technology moves.

The 24th Station of the Exodus is Terah. Although it bears the name of Abraham's father, nothing suggests any historical connection to him. Symbolically, however, there are connections. Terah died in Haran, at the crossroads, because he chose to not go any further. In Jewish symbolism, Terah means "lagging behind." After leaving the camp of heaviness, where something weighed upon the people, they arrive at a place where they are inclined to lag behind.

Perhaps Terah represented a moment where the weight of the journey proved too much. The difficulties of the journey may have taken a toll and there arose a spirit that caused the people to lag behind. Moving ex-slaves into liberating realities is an onerous task. Living beyond the spirit of Terah and embracing the spirit of Abraham does not come easy. Thus, we see included in this journey a moment where the people lagged behind.

I am often baffled by what seems to be a lack of evolving in America. It appears that the more things change, the more we remain the same. In the area of human equality, economic equity, and racial justice, America seems to be lagging behind. We have witnessed major advances in technology, but little movement in sociology. America remains a nation largely defined by homogeneity, where people are most likely to live, work, and worship among people just like them. Prophetic engagement must serve as a catalyst for movement among a people who have a tendency to lag behind.

What movement do you discern among your people? Does the issue of evolvement shape your ministry? Or, are you content with spiritually lagging behind?

PRAYER:
O God, You are a progressive God and seek to shape a progressive people, forgive us for our tendencies to lag behind. Help us, I pray, to embrace Your progressive vision as revealed in Jesus Christ. AMEN.

Numbers 33:28-29

"Refreshed"

No matter how difficult and challenging the journey, there are always moments of joyous sweetness. We can never allow challenges and difficulties to blind us to life's sweeter moments. Just because we engage the unpleasant forces of evil, we should not allow evil's unpleasantness to shape who we are. We should stay open for the refreshing moments that even struggle provides.

Israel did not stay at Terah. Israel moved from the heaviness of Terah and arrived at Mithkah. The 25th Station of the Exodus is Mithkah. Mithkah symbolized "sweetness," or "pleasantness." It was a place where the people of God were refreshed, quite possibly from the sweet waters of a fountain or stream. The heaviness of Terah was washed away by the pleasantness of the fountains of Mithkah. The people were invigorated, inspired to move forward and face the glory of a future with God.

My Brooklyn pastor, Dr. Johnny Ray Youngblood, brilliantly highlighted the possibility of us becoming that which we detest. While exploring Psalm 23, he noted the possibility of our missing out on the table God prepares by focusing too much of our attention on the enemy. As the prophetic community, we must not allow the contrivances of the enemy to make us miss the blessed refreshments of divine pleasantness. We need to stay open to refreshing experiences and allow our spirits to be energized for the journey.

Can you note some time when your attention was so focused on the struggle that you missed out on God's refreshments? Even prophets can become jaded and sour of spirit when all of their time and energy is consumed by the struggle. As I write these lines, the faces and dispositions of a number of powerful men and women of God run across my mind. I see men and women who have lost the capacity for authentic happiness. They seem to have missed the moments in the journey where God wanted to refresh them.

What have you found refreshing in ministry? How do your cultivate freshness in your life? If not, why not?

PRAYER:
O God of still waters and refreshing streams, continue to offer the pleasantness of Your presence. Hope us, I pray, to be aware of the moments when You want to refresh us with Your presence. AMEN.

Numbers 33:28-29

"Fruitful Possibilities"

We are not always in a state of crisis and struggle, nor is it healthy to be so. Prophetic engagement does not mean to be in perpetual crisis mode. Such an approach to life and living is not healthy, nor is it likely to fuel hope. There are moments when some expression of the bounty of justice, fairness, and equity are experienced.

The 26th Station of the Exodus is Hashmonah, which in Jewish symbolism means "fatness," "fruitfulness," or "fat soil." Another meaning of the word is "ambassador." Nonetheless, Hashmonah was probably not a place, but an experience, or a development in the people's perspective. The text does not indicate any specific reason why the congregation of ex-slaves experienced Hashmonah. Could it be that Hashmonah provided the people a moment to experience the fruitful possibilities of being agents of the liberating directives of God?

Perhaps the further they moved from the exploitative realities of Egypt, the more the prosperous opportunities of freedom began to shape their perspective in some unique ways. Such a movement in consciousness can have an amazing effect on community life, and certainly upon the worship experience.

Prophetic engagement has an undeniable economic dimension. No one should deny the economic realities of liberation, or try to cloak freedom in religious exclusivity. The bondage of Egypt was an economic bondage, and so was the slave experience of America. If oppression and exploitation has profound economic implications, then liberation should carry with it an agency of economic prosperity. People are freed from something, but are also freed to something.

As I consider the acute wealth disparity in America, particularly as it is expressed in racial distinctions, the meaning of today's reflection is sobering. So much of the energy of poor people is expended in basic economic survival, there is no time to consider one's self as an agent of prosperity. What kind of movement would we have in our communities if people began seeing themselves as agents of a more prosperous reality?

How is economic freedom incorporated into your ministry? What are the barriers to economic prosperity?

PRAYER:
O God, Who is concerned about the economic wellbeing of Your people, empower us with a sense of economic agency. Hope us, I pray, to become more conscious of the economic dimensions of freedom. AMEN.

Numbers 33:30-31

"A Strong Admonition"

We are never at a place where discipline is to be avoided or where correction is not necessary. There is nothing we can do that cannot be enhanced with discipline, or any status we can attain that exempts us from correction. The work that God wants to complete in us demands discipline, and for us to be all God wants us to be requires that we stay open to correction.

The 27th Station of the Exodus is Mosoreth. Mosoreth, interestingly, is the camp that follows Hashmonah. As you recall, Hashmonah was the place of "fatness," or "fruitfulness." It was a place where the ex-slaves experienced a prosperity perspective. Mosoreth, however, also symbolized "discipline," or "strong admonition." The need for discipline and strong admonition was closely attached to the experience of prosperity. The journey to the Promised Land provided a context where the people of God would understand that longstanding prosperity demanded discipline, and reckless indulgence in the place of prosperity required admonition.

We are not given any detail of reckless indulgence or thoughtless consumption. It was understood that the blessings of God were not to be carelessly appropriated and thoughtlessly consumed. When a people's resources had been meagerly regulated by an oppressive economic system, it would have been easy for them to squander the Lord's blessings.

Perhaps the most difficult challenge of developing a prophetic community is to develop patterns of discipline. The most recent economic downturn savagely devastated black wealth. Homes which had been in families for years and had represented the primary symbols of black wealth were lost and will never be recovered. People of color were more vulnerable to the pipe dreams of subprime lenders and the loose lending practices of mainstream banks. As a consequence, financial losses among African Americans will have long-term impact.

Prophetic engagement in economically vulnerable communities must not forsake the work of establishing patterns of discipline. We must include in the work of liberation strong admonitions when waste and graft are easily practiced. Clearly, our journey is not complete, nor have we arrived. Let's embrace the fact that people who have never had much need to learn the value and discipline of holding on to something once we get it.

I'm not convinced that we cultivate discipline in our respective communities, are you? What tools might we employ to cultivate greater discipline?

PRAYER:
God, we avail ourselves of Your discipline and correction. Hope us, I pray, to be open to correction and creating patterns of healthy community discipline. AMEN.

Numbers 33:31-32

"Children of Perversions"

The twisting of the truth is a constant challenge to any liberating endeavor. It does not take much to veer a people from a truthful path when lies start sounding like the truth. Purveyors of fake news use seats of power to disperse litanies of lies. A longstanding strategy of evil has been the use of propaganda, which rarely is used to support the causes of the oppressed.

The 28th Station of the Exodus is Bene Jaakan. Bene Jaakan is also mentioned in Deuteronomy 10:6, even being mentioned as the place where Aaron died and his son assumed priestly responsibilities. The significance of Bene Jaakan is probably found in what it symbolizes. Bene Jaakan means "children of Jaakan," or "children of the perverter." An encounter with descendants of those who pervert truth presented an obvious challenge for those who were seeking truth. Pharaoh's Egypt was upheld by lies, and lies supported Egypt's ability to control the people within an oppressive context. As they progressed toward the Promised Land, an encounter with those who supported oppression was inevitable. The challenge depended upon their response to Bene Jaakan.

We are not told how the ex-slaves of Egypt responded to Bene Jaakan. What is clear is the recognition of where they were. To recognize a lie, or the place of lies, is an important work in prophetic engagement. In the work of prophetic engagement, we will encounter those who pervert the truth. It's important to know that the children of Jaakan are not always foreigners, or outsiders. Jaakan's children can rise up among us. Although the greatest perpetrators of untruths have been oppressors, the promulgation of untruths is known to come from those among us.

I am a strong advocate against racism. I perceive racism as a perversion of truth, which uses skin color to advance political and economic advantage. Yet, it disturbs me when racism is distorted, or twisted into something other than political and economic advantage. Most disturbing is when those among us twist ignorance into racist constructs.

Have you any social perversions that cause you angst? How have you responded to obvious untruths? What are some of the dominant lies that shape your reality?

PRAYER:
O God, help us to recognize where we are. Grant us discernment to separate truth from lies. Hope us, I pray, to not be enslaved by twisted truths. AMEN.

Numbers 33:32-33

"The Inward Journey"

A helpful space and place is when we are called inward. The busyness of life often robs us of opportunities for going inward. So much of what we do is external. We are always living on the surface, rarely being summoned into the deep caverns of our subconscious. Much of what God really wants to do through us must come from within us. Life is more rewarding when lived from the internal rather from the external.

The 29th Station of the Exodus is Hor Haggidgad. It is another one of those places that received no detailed description. It is commonly believed to be the same campsite as Gudgodah in Deuteronomy 10:7. In Jewish thought, Hor Haggidgad symbolizes a cave, or the "hole of the cleft." The journey of the ex-slaves led them to a place where they had to go inward.

Hor Haggidgad seems an obvious place for people who were leaving a place where the truth was twisted. We are not told which truth was twisted, but it must have had something to do with their sense of self, purpose, and God. Pharaoh denied the people a clear sense of self and purpose, as well as opportunities to worship, which is the critical time for self-understanding. However, the journey provided them an opportunity to respond from twisted truths by going within.

As I reflect upon the many experiences when efforts to achieve justice were hindered by twisted truths, a time to pause and reflect was critical. Unfortunately, oppressed people are not given to deep reflection. The issues of survival preoccupy the mind and consume most of the energy of oppressed people. Yet, the work of prophetic engagement demands moments when the process of liberation needs to be reflected upon. A needed space and place is for oppressed people to consider what oppression has done to them, as well as the opportunities freedom suggests. Liberation is actually a healing process that must take place from the inside. It is a good time to adventure on what the amazing mystic, Howard Thurman, called the inward journey.

What time and attention do you give to the inward journey? What have you discovered about you and the world when journeying inward? How has the inward journey impacted your outward experiences?

PRAYER:
O God, hide us in the cleft of Your truth that we might consider the nuances of liberation. Hope us, I pray, to carve out moments where we can go within and assess what You are doing with us, to us, as well as for us. AMEN.

Numbers 33:33-34

"Priestly Health for Prophetic Hazards"

What is healthfulness for those who engage in the urgency of the prophetic? Are there spaces and places where we can have healthful experiences? Certainly, we must recognize that living in a perpetual mode of urgency cannot be healthy. Always being under extreme stress does not promote healthy living, healthy thinking, or healthy ministry. Finding healthful places and spaces is essential for those who engage in the urgency of the prophetic.

The 30th Station of the Exodus is Jotbathah. Jotbathah interestingly and naturally followed Hor Haggidgad, the place of inward reflection. We could even assert that Jotbathah was the result of inward reflection, or coming out of a cave experience. In Jewish symbolism, Jotbathah represents healthfulness. It was a good place. In Deuteronomy 10:7, it is characterized as a place of many waters. It was a refreshing place where the presence of God was distinguished.

A common affliction among those who engage in prophetic ministry is the experience of burnout. It is a time where loving and concerned people can no longer give, because they have nothing to give. Tragically, many have become ill and prematurely died as a result of always living in the urgent. The creation story informs us that even God rested. Sabbath represents a restful place, a time for refreshment. Built into the rhythm of creation is a time for refreshment.

We would do well to synchronize the prophetic with the priestly, which would allow us healthful spaces. The priestly provides an opportunity to be attentive to life. We cannot serve well or long without being attentive to healthful experiences of life. I have had to work hard and be extremely intentional about carving out spaces and places where I can experience the healthful. I have learned the hard way that being eternally strapped into the urgency of the prophetic is not healthful.

What are you doing to create healthy spaces and places in your life? Is your ministry a complement of the prophetic and the priestly? How so?

PRAYER:
O God, You Who created us in goodness, continue to provide for us healthful experiences. Hope us, I pray, and deliver us from the slavery of urgency and allow us to appreciate the rhythm of the sacred. AMEN.

Numbers 33:34-35

"A New Way"

We are always looking for a way to achieve something, go somewhere, or a way to accomplish something. To have a way is to be given access, and to not have a way is to lack access. A major frustration in life is to not have access, to be denied, or to not be privileged for one reason or another. Civil rights struggles and deliberations usually are fought on the grounds of denial of access to assumed social privileges. Prophetic engagement seeks to gain access for those who have been unjustly denied.

The 31st Station of the Exodus is Abronah. In Jewish symbolism, Abronah was understood to mean a "way." After leaving the place of fruitfulness, the people arrived at Abronah. Abronah provided an experience where the ex-slaves of Egypt enjoyed greater access to the privileges of promise. We are not provided any details of the experience, but some aspect of God's promise opened up to them in a profound and memorable way. Perhaps a profound realization that God could and would provide a way for ex-slaves to realize a liberated and fulfilled life settled upon the people. Realizing the growing possibility of a new way of living would mean much to a once oppressed people.

A constant struggle among those who seek to provide prophetic leadership is to awaken the consciousness of oppressed people. It is a huge accomplishment to get those being subjected to oppressive constraints to begin realizing that there is a way to a more liberating reality. The civil rights struggles of African Americans began as isolated events. There was not an initial widespread quest for civil rights because the Jim Crow South was generally accepted as the norm and inequality assumed to be just. However, when the movement began awakening the consciousness of the oppressed masses, the Jim Crow arrangements became universally unacceptable and adamantly denounced.

Currently, millions of young men of color are trapped in deep cycles of despair. They literally see no way for their lives to be anything other than a cycle of street corner economics, violence, and incarceration. President Obama's My Brother's Keeper initiative, and other urban initiatives, seek to address this tragic blight on America's self-image. Yet the challenge remains for us to awaken within our young men the vision that there is a way to live beyond the limiting confines of their oppressive realities.

Are you aware of those within your community who are being denied access? What part of your ministry provides people access to justice and equity? How so?

PRAYER:
O God, awaken within us the possibility of living life in more liberating ways. Hope us, I pray, to see beyond the limiting constraints of oppression in any form. May we believe in You enough to pursue life in a new way for all who have been unjustly denied. AMEN.

Numbers 33:35-36

"Moral Backbone"

A journey represents an experience of movements. It is more than a casual trip, or a vacation. A journey defines how those movements profoundly impact life and living. Each moment holds special meaning for the journey, and each moment should impact the lives of those on the journey. The journey of liberation necessarily includes impactful experiences.

The 32nd Station of the Exodus is Ezion Geber. Ezion Geber was an experience described in Jewish symbolism as the "backbone of a man." Apparently, the previous stop, Abronah, which bespeaks a way, provided a perspective that would promote "the backbone of a (hu)man(ity)." This symbol has to do with a distinct characteristic, perhaps a moral one that would be revealed within the people. Perhaps Ezion Geber was an experience that set forth the distinction that a truly liberated people are an upright people. The commandments given by God provided a framework that promoted moral uprightness. A liberated people were to be distinguished by their witness to the just nature of God and how it shows up in community.

One need not look far to locate the moral depravity that accompanies oppression. While our media predominately directs attention to the indiscretions of the lower class, we all know how widespread is the moral turpitude of the upper class. In fact, the greatness of America can never be accredited to an unwavering commitment to justice and equality. America has been built on one of the most oppressive economic systems in history. The only thing worse than a capitalist society is a totalitarian one. The fact of slavery, the genocide of native Americans, the oppression of women, and other exploitative realities are the pillars of American wealth. Even now an incredibly wealthy few hold surreal economic sway over the masses.

The work of prophetic engagement must be ever mindful of its commitment to moral uprightness. The goal is never seeking to replace one system of oppression with another system of oppression. We who seek justice must live just lives, and promote just interactions within the being-liberated community.

What is your commitment to justice among the people you serve? How is it facilitated? How does morality play into your work or ministry?

PRAYER:
O God of mercy, justice, and equality, keep us mindful of Your liberating ideals. Cause within us a desire to seek, promote, and live out lives of uprightness. Hope us, I pray, to not become "so drunk with the world" that we "forget Thee." May we be bearers of light, and not just another form of darkness. AMEN.

Numbers 33:36-37

"Set Apart"

I return to the thought mentioned yesterday. A journey represents an experience of moments. It is, indeed, a series of moments that profoundly impact life and living. As those moments and experiences impact us, they also define us. We become who we are as a result of our journey. Our experiences have an indelible impact upon who we are in the world.

The 33rd Station of the Exodus is called the Wilderness of Zin, which is Kadesh. Kadesh is mentioned in Deuteronomy 20:7-12 as the place where Miriam died and where Moses struck the rock. However, in this context, or experience, Kadesh represents being "set apart." The previous experience provided the journeying ex-slaves with backbone, or the moral fortitude to become what Kadesh implies. As a people of moral fortitude, they are set apart, they are distinguished as a special people with a special assignment. They were delivered from one experience in order to be delivered into another more just one. They have moved from being slaves to becoming a special people.

The making of a prophetic people is not an easy task. To get people to the place of seeing themselves differently, however, is an essential part of the prophetic. Who we are determines what we will do. Tragically, we cannot get to our royal assignments when we allow the definitions of others to define us. As long as we see ourselves as being defined by our oppressors, we can never fulfill liberating possibilities. Being set free must lead us into the moment of being set apart.

I am currently struggling with the distinctions of African Americans. I am not convinced that we collectively have a sense of being set apart. Too much of what we do reacts to our pathologies rather than our possibilities. I guess my struggle is with how do we move beyond the pathological distinctions into the possibility distinctions? Any thoughts? How might we further distinguish ourselves as a "special people?"

PRAYER:
O God, Who liberates and calls us into a special work, grant us a greater sense of not only Whose we are, but who we are. Deliver us, I pray, from the limiting confines of oppressive definitions and direct us into more positive perspectives of self-awareness. Hope us to become what You desire of all people – distinct, distinguished,

Numbers 33:37-38

"Thinking High"

As we continue following the journey motif of our meditative invitations, we learn that the possibilities of self-definition are endless. The self-defining impact of the journey causes us to not only view ourselves differently, but enables us to see the world differently. A more comprehensive perception accompanies self-reflection. In order to see beyond ourselves, we must first begin to accurately see ourselves.

The 34th Station of the Exodus is Mount Hor. Mount Hor symbolizes the capacity "to conceive," " to think," or "to be high." It was a mountainous experience where former slaves were able to actually conceive of life in a different way. As the "set apart" people, they distinguished themselves by seeing the world in a different way. Perhaps they began to see life through different lenses, lenses free of the dehumanizing stains of oppression and the toxicity of exploitation. A new world opened up to them from the vistas of their journey with God. Although it is noted that Aaron died on Mount Hor and the priestly garments were placed on his son, Mount Hor provided the people with a moment to conceive of life in a new way.

A well-used euphemism declares that "old habits are hard to break." In the world of the oppressed, longstanding biases and bigotries are visceral. They have been intuitively embedded. The perspectives we have on the world are often limited by the way we view ourselves. It's hard to get a new vision of life when we are clinging to an old paradigm of self. We must begin the ascent of a liberated self-understanding to see the world in a new way.

What are some of your community's favored biases and bigotries? How are you addressing them? Does your ministry feed or starve your community's longstanding biases and bigotries?

PRAYER:
O God, we are privileged to know You and see ourselves in a new way. Enable us to ascend to the heights of new thinking about the world. Hope us, I pray, fresh opportunities to conceive of hopeful possibilities in the world. AMEN.

HOPE US, LORD!

Numbers 33:41

"A Heavy Weight"

We can never underestimate the value of living with a sense of being covered, or overshadowed. The weight and worth of having some noted presence or power overshadowing our lives provides much needed perspective and focus. Without a sense of an overshadowing presence and power, we risk drifting into self-driven illusions and fantasies. What overshadows us connects us and grounds us.

The 35th Station of the Exodus is Zalmonah. Zalmonah naturally followed Mount Hor, the place of "thinking," or "conceiving." We are not privileged with the particulars of Mount Hor, other than Aaron's death and Elezar's priestly promotion. The experience does, however, seemed to have been significant. Perhaps the cumulative experience of the Exodus began to weigh heavy upon the people, causing them to sense an overshadowing. The weight and worth of God's purpose being worked out in their lives could have rested heavily upon the people.

I would assert that the most significant presence and power would be God. To be shadowed by the awesome presence and power of God weighs heavily upon a thinking people, especially those who are experiencing life in new and liberating ways. The realization of God's continued protection and provision, attached to God's liberating purposes, can rest heavily upon the spirit of a people.

If there is a need among those who currently aspire to engage in liberating activities, it is a need to live with a sense of being overshadowed. Too many are claiming leadership and initiative in the liberation of our people, without a defining sense of God or history. It just seems to me that the best intentions are doomed to failure without a defining presence and power. Along with the shadow of divine presence, there is also the need to sense the "cloud of witnesses," a gathering up of ancestral support. We would do well to cultivate a sense of being overshadowed by God and our ancestors.

What weighs heavily upon the people you serve? Is it worthy of the weightiness it bears?

PRAYER:
O God, You Who are with us even when we are unconscious of Your presence, hope us, I pray, to cultivate a greater sense of You in all that we do. May our need and awareness of You enable us to sense the presence of our faithful ancestors. AMEN.

Numbers 33:42

"A Troublesome Darkness"

To live with a sense of being overshadowed is a noteworthy experience. The experience of having a sense of being covered or overshadowed has been known to enhance perspective and focus. Yet, when that which overshadows blankets our perspective, darkness is imminent. Ironically, the same presence that overshadows can become so overwhelming that it can cause perplexity, which is the loss of perspective and focus.

The 36th Station of the Exodus is Punon. Punon represents perplexity. In Jewish symbolism, Punon signified a "darkness." It was not a friendly darkness, or a comfortable one. It appears to be a darkness that was troublesome. Punon caused a serious agitation to seize the people, perhaps due to the previous encampment, where the experiencing of serious thinking opened up to them the gravity of their journey. Being overshadowed by the awesomeness of God could have possibly triggered a sense of darksome dread. The reality of God is not always a comfortable thing to live with.

I live in the San Francisco Bay Area. It is an area noted for overcast and fog. When we have overcast, we can see the world quite clearly. Overcast is not a hindrance to visual perspective. However, when the overcast drops down and becomes fog, vision is challenged. The same element, but different positions cause different realities. It all depends upon where the elements are situated: above or upon.

The awesomeness of God's power and purpose can be a source of joy or dread; it all depends on how it is being experienced. When people are participating in the liberating work of God, the reality of God providing perspective and focus can also become weighty with gravity. The same God who brings the joy of freedom also brings the gravity of communal responsibility. When we seriously consider what all liberation entails, it can become a sobering reality.

I am not always convinced that worship and preaching within our communities is sobering. We have become praise intoxicated. We promote spiritual highs and never spiritual gravity.

When was the last time you heard a sermon that you found prophetically sobering? What was said that made you realize the gravity of life? Did you share the experience? With whom?

PRAYER:
O God, continue to provide us with a powerful sense of Your presence and purpose. Hope us, I pray, to accept the gravity of freedom with the same reception for the joy of freedom. AMEN.

HOPE US, LORD!

Numbers 33:43-44

"Waterskins"

One of the continuing challenges of our lives is self-awareness. We are not always mindful of who we are and the capacities we possess. Our sensate culture of heroism/sheroism has a tendency to discount the rest of us. We don't always see ourselves as having something of worth and significance to contribute to the greater good. As a result, we suffer from the lack of widespread communal involvement and acceptance.

The 37th Station of the Exodus is Oboth. Oboth, interestingly, followed a place of darkness. From the place of darkness they arrived at a place symbolized as "waterskins." Oboth represented a place where the significance of skin-made water bottles became apparent. We are not privileged with what brought waterskins to the forefront of the experience. Yet, waterskins provided the defining experience of Oboth. For the agrarian people, we are mindful that water represented the essential source of human existence.

While waterskins represent vessels that provide for the transport of the essential source of human existence, perhaps Oboth became a place of communal awakening. As a people who were active participants in the liberating processes of God, they became containers of the experience. What God was working out through them could be used to refresh the freedom aspirations of all people. The Abrahamic promise of being a blessing to all nations (Genesis 12) carried with it the responsibility of being a resource for others.

As active participants of the liberating processes of God, it behooves the prophetic community to become more positively self-aware. The continuing legacy of black oppression, sexism, homophobia, and other xenophobic residuals has taken a horrendous toll on the collective psyche of the American people. Even now many of us find ourselves engaged in an unending struggle to overcome a plethora of negative definitions of who we are and what we represent. For the sake of our progeny, we must see ourselves as waterskins of God's liberating purposes. Such a powerful sense of self-awareness can only serve us well as we continue this journey to the Promised Land.

Oppressed people are convenient sources for the dumping of the toxic. How are we reshaping the paradigm into becoming containers of refreshment and resourcefulness? What resource of renewal does your community carry? How are they being distributed?

PRAYER:
O God, You have poured so much into our development as a people and in our experience with You. Hope us, I pray, to become containers of the refreshing source of life and liberty. AMEN.

Numbers 33:44-45

"Displaced"

I am convinced that the only One not surprised by the vacillating, often confusing thought patterns and behavior of human beings is God. The Bible's portrait, and the witness of current affairs, surely reveals that we can be astounding creatures. We are not locked into instinctual patterns of animalistic behavior, nor are we bound to the noble expectations of the Divine. We are just outright astounding creatures! We even surprise ourselves.

The 38th Station of the Exodus journey is quite startling. It is startling because it comes after such a powerful experience of self-awareness. Leaving Oboth, the ever-evolving ex-slaves arrived at a camp called Ije Abarim, or the "ruins of Abarim". Ije Abarim is startling because it literally symbolizes a state of displacement. How is that a people who had travelled so far and experienced so much, arrive at a place where they feel displaced? Were they still conflicted over the loss of their familiar oppression? Ije Abarim implied that they had arrived at place of feeling disconnected, lost, and aimless.

Ije Abarim is a troublesome state. It is troublesome because it speaks of an astounding truth. The astounding truth that it speaks of is that people can be on an extended liberating journey and still hold a connection to their oppressive state. Internalized oppression is portable. It travels with us.

We witness it daily in the lives of the African American community, when significant numbers lack initiative for liberating independence. The further down the road of freedom we travel, the more creative we get in finding ways to stay bound to oppressive realities. The current loss of a loving community has created a displaced psyche that intensifies our self-hatred. Even with the experience of a re-elected African American president, followed by the confusing election of a white megalomaniac, a state of communal displacement persists. We still need to be diligent in building up the capacity of our people.

Can you identify ways in which we hold on to oppressive realities? How has internalized oppression surprised you? What are you doing about it?

PRAYER:
O God, I know our behavior toward You, others, and ourselves is astounding. Hope us, I pray, to steady our journey with a determined sense of purpose and power. AMEN.

Numbers 33:45-46

"Wasting Away"

Where there is no sense of connectedness, opportunities are lost. People must possess a sense of belonging to begin the process of maximizing their potential. Without a sense of belonging, endless opportunities and possibilities are wasted.

The 39th Station of the Exodus is Dibon Gad. Dibon Gad seems a natural place to stop, following Ije Abarim. From a place or state of displacement, the energy and the potential of the people is severely challenged. Dibon Gad means "wasting away a fortune." After all the community had experienced, they seemingly had not become comfortable at being home in God. It seems as if the Promised Land was more important than the One who made the promise. While lacking a powerful sense of connectedness to God, the potential of the people apparently began to waste away.

The work of prophetic engagement has the awesome assignment of keeping the community connected. The connection of the community must be based on that which transcends the objects of accomplishments, momentary successes, and perceived objectives. The connection of the prophetic community must be firmly based on their relationship with God.

I recently listened intently to the prophetic scholar, Dr. Cornell West. Dr. West aptly states that the failure of the civil rights generation was in not connecting the consequent generation to God. Too many of us believed that the civil rights struggle was merely about giving us opportunities to be successful. The greater testimony of the civil rights struggle was not for my generation to be successful, but to be faithful. Prophetic engagement must keep before the people the true focus of our liberation, lest we waste its prophetic intent.

How are the people you serve living beneath the mantle of the civil rights victories? What is the God connection that holds the people together? Are they successful, or faithful?

PRAYER:
O God, Who promised us the blessings of land, family, and just opportunities, hope us, I pray, to reconnect with You, the "Promise-giver," lest we faithlessly waste away. AMEN.

Numbers 33:46-47

"Hidden Fig Cakes"

A vision that connects a people to all of the seemingly disparate parts of an experience can be incredibly motivating. When we can find meaning in all of our many and diverse experiences, tremendous possibilities are birthed. Prophetic engagement must seek to connect and provide meaning to the seemingly disparate components of the liberation journey.

The 40th Station of the Exodus is Almon Diblathaim. In some interpretations of the Exodus Stations, this is the final camp, although Numbers 33 provides us two more stops. It is also the camp where Moses was given a vision of the Promised Land, and became resigned to the fact that he would not enter therein. Almon Diblathaim means the "hiding of two fig cakes," or "hiding of trouble." Biblically, figs represent plenty, or prosperity. Because of the seediness of the fruit, it was also symbolic of fertility.

Following the previous camp, where life's fortunes were wasting away, the possibility of not perceiving the prosperous possibilities of the Promised Land is conceivable. While Moses may have seen the prosperous possibilities of the Promised Land, this does not mean the people saw them. Perhaps the fact that Moses would not enter the possibilities of the Promised Land were concealed or hidden from the majority of the people.

I am not always convinced that African Americans, or Americans as a whole, see completely the possibilities of the United States of America. Because of the nation's imperialistic tendencies, I don't think we always see the powerful possibilities of a true democracy. The prosperous possibilities of America are hidden by the continuous racist rhetoric, political demagoguery, xenophobia, and insatiable capitalistic greed. Martin Luther King, Jr. proclaimed that he saw the Promised Land, and then he was assassinated. How can we see when those who do see are discredited and killed? Perhaps what God really wants to do with America is hidden by the distortions of democracy and the contortions of injustice and inequality.

Prophetic engagement must facilitate visions of our possibilities. How are you shaping vision within your ministry or community? Who stands at the center of the vision? Have the people captured the vision? If not, why not?

PRAYER:
O God of mercy, open up our eyes to the powerful possibilities of our witness. Hope us, I pray, to embrace a vision of what it means to live out the meaning of a true democracy, particularly one that is theocratically enhanced. AMEN.

HOPE US, LORD!

Numbers 33:47

"The Regions Beyond"

The capacity to see beyond where we are often requires assistance. Philosophically, and even sociologically, we are a nearsighted people. We cannot see distant realities without assistance. We struggle to see that what brought us here won't get us there. The work of prophetic engagement is to assist a philosophically and sociologically nearsighted people to see distant realities. What people cannot perceive, they will never conceive.

The 41st Station of the Exodus is Abarim. Abarim represented the "regions beyond." In Jewish symbolism it was known as the "passages." It was considered a mountainous region that provided the people "passage," or vision to the "regions beyond." From Abarim, a perspective of Promised Land possibilities formed within the collective consciousness of the people. We are not provided the details of what experience brought about this heightened awareness. Perhaps it was the physical heights, or the accumulative experiences. Nevertheless, the journey's end and ultimate meaning became known at Abarim. They were able to see from the "regions beyond," the goal of their meandering journey.

I claim no clear perspective on the ultimate destination of our journey. However, I do know we have not arrived. We are yet a significant distance from where God wants us as a people, a nation, or as a world. I do know that what little I do see would never have been possible without assistance. I have in the library of my life a huge collection of persons and personalities who provided me assistance in shaping a prophetic perspective.

A couple of years ago I attended the funeral of my primary theological mentor, Dr. John Dee Mangrum, former Dean of the Chapel of Bishop College. Dr. Mangrum, as articulated by the eulogist, Reverend Frederick D. Haynes, III, was used of God to help his students see beyond their nearsighted theological perspectives. Dr. Mangrum began a long procession of incredible men and women who have assisted me in seeing the "regions beyond." Even now I continue to gain assistance from a range of sources and resources to provide me assistance in shaping prophetic vision. Some are persons who now populate the "cloud of witnesses."

Who are the people who helped shape you to see the "regions beyond?" How do you manifest this within the community you serve?

PRAYER:
O God of sight and vision, continue to move us forward to the places of vision and higher consciousness. Deliver us from any and every notion of arrival. Hope us, I pray, to access and appreciate those who lift us upon their shoulders and assist us in seeing the "regions beyond." AMEN.

Numbers 33:48-49

"Flowing from the Father"

What we make of where we are is largely up to us. God can bring us to a great opportunity, but we must make it happen. Just as Eden can be marred, the Promised Land can be missed. Gifts are only as good as they are received.

The 42nd and final Station of the Exodus is Moab. Moab has a rather complex biblical perspective. It is often referred to as a people birthed incestuously by Lot and his eldest daughter (Gen. 19:37). (I suspect such a perspective is the result of a Western hermeneutic that imposes moralistic distortions upon the text. Westerners impose their moralistic disdain for incest upon the text to the extent it misses its prophetic point.) Symbolically, Moab means "seed of the father," or "flowing from the father." Moreover, the incestuous complex is neutralized by the noble legacy of the Moabites in Ruth. The final station of the Exodus seems to represent a perspective where the Promised Land was ambivalently considered.

Where we are as a people is often determined by who we ask. On the one hand, some would probably view our current plight as progressive and full of promise. Such a perspective can be statistically substantiated. The data would suggest that we have made considerable progress. For instance, I know of no small number of people who died with a tremendous sense of accomplishment upon the election of the nation's first African American president.

On the other hand, some would diminish our progress by citing the obvious and pervasive pathologies within our communities, and the obnoxious return of an apparent white hate backlash. Just as the progressive perspective is supported by data, this view would likewise be data supported. There are volumes of statistics that indicate that America is as racist, sexist, classist, fascist, and imperialist as ever. The growing economic inequity would represent the most striking statistic, along with the massive number of incarcerated people of color. Prophetic engagement must provide a clear assessment of where we are, free of the distortions of a power-controlled media.

What is some obvious reality that has been prophetically clarified in your life? How are you responding? Are you prepared to correct the distortions with a prophetically inspired narrative?

PRAYER:
O God, You Who bring us to where You want us, grant us clarity about where we are. Leave us not to our own machinations. Hope us, I pray, to be clear that we are where You want us and it us up to us to make it what You desire. AMEN.

The 42 Stations of the Exodus are complete. Admittedly, I was drawn to them as an attempt to hear better the intent of the people who crafted them as liturgical expressions of their experiences to note and highlight God's liberating activity. I am not so presumptuous to believe that I did anything other than scratch at the surface of their full meaning and intent. Considering it took me a journey of over 36 years of Christian ministry before I discovered their existence, I am convinced that I will be considering them for the rest of my life. At best, the few words I applied to them will serve as an interesting indicator of what Christian seminary training unfortunately overlooks when its academic focus is exclusively Christian. The people with whom the Christian faith was birthed and nurtured have much to add and to enhance our spiritual longings. I return now to more traditional prophetic texts, and, hopefully, to consider them in nontraditional ways. I bring my thoughts back to Moses, and allow the Moses tradition to further shape my prophetic meditations.

Exodus 16:19-30

"Sabbath Perspective"

I am sure that I owe this insight to Walter Brueggemann. Brueggemann argues that a debilitating anxiety created by an oppressive construct is the overstated belief in scarcity (Journey to the Common Ground). This belief in scarcity creates enormous anxiety that causes a relentless restlessness within us. When we don't believe there is enough, we never rest from trying to make sure we have some, whatever some might be. We live in an eternal state of anxious acquisition.

The episode in our text illustrates how the anxiety of scarcity served as the basis for disobedient behavior. The Lord had commanded that the people would only gather food or bread for the day, but on the sixth day gather enough for two days. The seventh day was to be a day of rest, when the people would rest from the pressing demands of gathering sustenance. It was also a day when the people would nurture faith in the provisions of God.

However, the anxiety of scarcity prompted many to disobey. They gathered more than was necessary for a day. They hoarded, and the results were that that which was hoarded was spoiled. God responded angrily to the people being more responsive to anxious living than to faith living. Moses insisted that the people honor the seventh day, thereby honoring the all-providing character of God.

I am not sure how long it took for the people to get to the place where the seventh day would be respected. If the journey was, in fact, a 40-year journey, they had a number of seventh days to get it right. As I consider the hoarding tendencies in America, a nation that boasts to be the richest country in the world, it appears that we lack a Sabbath perspective. In fact, those of us who attend church on Sundays never hear anything about a Sabbath perspective. If we are to lead people into authentic experiences of freedom, we must not neglect cultivating a Sabbath perspective and rhythm. A Sabbath perspective is critical to people who have been subjected to an oppressive system that promotes scarcity anxiety.

In my faith community, the busiest day is often Sunday. How is the Sabbath observed in your community? Your life? What could a Sabbath perspective add to your community?

PRAYER:
O God, we know that everything we have, You have provided. We have not been neglected by You, nor do we believe it possible. Hope us, I pray, to regain a respect for the Seventh Day. Let us not settle for being eternally captive to the idolatry of scarcity. AMEN.

Exodus 17:1-7

"Questioning God's Presence"

There are some indispensible variables to prophetic ministry. We can get by without some things, but there are some things within the repertoire of the prophetic ministry that we cannot do without. We cannot go very far without life's essentials and relevant leadership, and we can go nowhere without a powerful sense of God.

The journey to the Promised Land was noted as being a journey with camps. We considered the 42 Stations of the Exodus, and Rephidim in particular. It was the place where the lack of water became a dominant focus and concern. It was also the place where Moses was contentiously confronted. There is a tone of not only anger in the text, but outright disrespect. Moses responded by literally crying out to God. He sensed that his life was at risk, thus, his position of leadership would be lost.

Moses was instructed by God to go to Horeb and strike a rock, "and water will come out of it, that the people may drink." The contentiousness of the people was so pronounced that the place was called Massah and Meribah. The behavior of the people seemed to have been so insulting that they even questioned whether the Lord was among them.

There is no prophetic movement without leadership. Someone, or some core group, must be looked to and depended upon for prophetic direction. I mention some core group as an alternative because the day of a solo leadership may well be past and gone. Peter Block suggests that leadership is convening. "Community building requires a concept of the leader as one who creates experiences for others – experiences that in themselves are examples of a desired future." However leadership is expressed or provided, leadership is essential to a prophetic cause. Nonetheless, leadership is at risk of suffering insulting behavior when people lack a sense of God.

An interesting phenomenon is happening within the African American community. American individualism has distorted our perspective of leadership to the point that many leaders are emerging who are insulting and insulted. We have leaders who insult the intelligence of the people with presumptuous posturing and profiling. (Donald Trump has insulted America's collective intelligence with a deluge of lies and he is totally devoid of a God concept.) Strangely, we have good leaders who are insulted when they offer clear goals and means to pursue them. I hold that both responses are the result of a loss of a sense of God. People who question the presence of God will probably question the legitimacy of leadership.

What is the model of leadership being shaped in your ministry? When you stand, who do you want people to see, you or God? How do you handle insults?

PRAYER:
O God, Who is always present, we acknowledge You in the name of the One who became flesh. Hope us, I pray, to be more mindful of Your presence and Your promise. AMEN.

Exodus 18:1-27

"Family Matters"

We look more closely into the things that are indispensible to prophetic engagement. As previously mentioned, the need for leadership and the need for God are indispensible. We do not go far without leadership, and we go nowhere without God. I would add that what we do is not worth doing without some personal and passionate context to envision its value. That context is the family.

The Jethro narrative is initiated by an observation that he had heard about what God had done in the life of God's people. The next verse, interestingly, notes Jethro sending back the wife of Moses, as well as his sons. Sending them back? He actually escorted Zipporah and Moses's sons back into the camp of the Israelites. The implication is that Zipporah, who was Moses's wife and Jethro's daughter, had returned to her father's house unexpectedly. He stayed long enough to observe Moses's leadership dynamics. His consequent observations led him to provide invaluable leadership suggestions to Moses, which would result in the "people going to their homes in peace."

I have long viewed this scene as an apparent breakdown in Moses's marriage and family. The actions of Jethro, who dominates the chapter, indicate that Moses's manner of leadership was not good for family life. Perhaps he had failed to incorporate his family in meaningful ways to the process of liberation. Without an intentional approach to leadership, which would empower more people within the liberation process, the family life of all would be strained and tested. Jethro provided Moses with an approach to leadership that enhanced family life for his family and everyone else's.

A tough and challenging project for those who engage in prophetic engagement is to balance ministry and family. Unfortunately, many of us destroy our families before we realize it. We do well to locate some Jethro personalities to observe, evaluate and assist us in shaping ministry in ways that support family life. I suspect that our inability to incorporate family into prophetic ministry is our unconscious commitment to the family arrangements of the oppressor. We cannot shape a people for liberation when we are blindly loyal to oppressive family constructs.

Slavery did not give us a healthy model of family. Where did you get your model of family? Is it working for you? What alternative family constructs have you considered?

PRAYER:
O God, Who created us for relationships and provides us suitable helpmeets, we give thanks. Hope us, O God, to free our families from the bondages we seek to free others from. AMEN.

Exodus 18:13-27

"Justice Matters"

Today we look further into the indispensables of prophetic engagement. Again, leadership is an indispensable. Likewise, a powerful sense of God is irrefutably indispensable. And family can never be discounted and minimized as an essential context for why we do what we do. Yet, the matter of justice among the prophetic community is a critical indispensable. Justice has to do with how we treat one another. How we treat one another provides integrity to our journey toward an equitable society.

The Jethro narratives have often been used as a model for church leadership. We have gleaned from the suggestions of Jethro to Moses a model for the formation of boards, committees, ministry teams, etc. However, a closer look at the story reveals that the primary issue that prompted Jethro's outrage was Moses's cumbersome and exhausting manner of dispatching justice. The matter of justice represents a fair and wise process whereby people can receive relief from the normal discords associated with living in community. As a people who had been subjected to a legacy of oppression and exploitation, the potential for lapses in judgment was great.

Therefore, Moses was correct in providing a forum whereby the issues of communal justice could be heard and resolved. It is inevitable that people within a community will have disagreements that need objective mediation. Where Moses was wrong, according to Jethro, was the belief that he needed to be the sole dispatcher of justice. As a product of the Pharaohic leadership community, Moses mimicked the model of leadership to which he had been exposed. Just as everything was brought before Pharaoh, everything was being brought before Moses.

The Jethro plea needs to be heard within most oppressed communities. We have a tendency to mimic the leadership models of the dominating culture. If we are to create a more equitable society, we must begin by creating one within our respective communities. As necessary as leadership may be, it does not need to be the leadership of rugged individualism that mimics the style of the dominating culture. We don't need anyone narcissistically deluded to believe that "I alone can fix it."

I have witnessed egregious oppression from African American clergy, particularly male clergy. If we are to be God's transformative agents for justice, we need to demonstrate justice in our models of leadership. We need a Jethro announcement for men and women who are reverent, firm, fair, honest, and who share a passion for justice within and without the redemptive community. We can never have justice for some of the people and deny it to others.

Is there anyone in your life who you allow to be honest with you? What blind spot for justice do you maintain? Why?

PRAYER:
O God of justice, righteousness, and fairness, we bless You for demonstrating to us that justice matters. Hope us, I pray, to be mindful of the leadership models we provide. May we be led by You, and the voices of the wise, to construct new models of leadership for a new people of freedom. AMEN.

Exodus 19

"Consecrated Liberation"

A further look into the indispensables of a liberating engagement has to do with how the people see themselves. Knowing who we are, or at least some sense of who we are aspiring to be, is essential to the work of liberation. In fact, how we view ourselves is a major determinant in how we treat ourselves, as well as others. We can never be truly liberated when we treat others better than we treat ourselves.

The Sinai experience was critical to the self-understanding of the once-enslaved community. It was at Sinai where the people were provided a self-understanding based upon how God saw them. It was a theologically grounded self-understanding, based upon the liberating interventions of God, who bound himself to them. The covenant dynamics of a God-centered relationship provided the people with a sense of who they were in the world, as well as how they would function in the world. Identity and function went hand-in-hand: "Then you shall be a special treasure to Me above all people; for all the earth is Mine. And you shall be to Me a kingdom of priests and a holy nation."

Of interest in the text is the consecration response to their self-understanding. The people were called upon to consecrate themselves "and be ready for the third day." Who they were in their relationship with God was cause for consecration. To be consecrated was to give reverence, or a sense of sacredness as to who they were as a people. Noteworthy is the fact, that their clothes were included in the consecration process. External presentation would line up with internal consecration.

A painful consequence of communal trauma is essentially the severance of a people from their identity. In the African American community, the trauma of a legacy of slavery has had a horrendous impact on our self-understanding. We not only carry with us the names of our oppressors, we wear within us a deep sense of the loss of self. The self-hatred among us is painfully evident in the constant violence we inflict upon ourselves, and our refusal to distance ourselves from self-denigrating labels. Perhaps a major consideration of prophetic engagement is to engage in identity work, an intentional ministry devoted exclusively to shaping a theologically grounded self-understanding. Such an approach would assist us in connecting identity and function, both needed assets in our community.

How do the people of your community view themselves? Are their efforts being pursued that correct the legacy of self-denigration? What are they?

PRAYER:
O God, we are clear on who You are. You are the God of our ancestors, and the God of our Savior. Hope us, I pray, to take seriously our need for an identity based upon our relationship with You. AMEN.

THE TEN COMMANDMENTS IN PROPHETIC PERSPECTIVE

The Ten Commandments have often been viewed as a litany of prohibitions. This perspective has caused them to be read and heard as moralistic bans, or the top ten things we are not to do. Moreover, the "Thou shalt not" cadence in each of them has given them a negative reputation, as well as provided scriptural fodder for the punitive and judgmental perspective of the church. The Ten Commandments are rarely heard or seen in a positive light. My traditional Baptist upbringing did not give me a positive view of the Ten Commandments, and they stood so tall that they did not provide me a liberating perspective of the church. In some ways, they drowned out the liberating voice of Jesus and the power of grace.

However, while attending Vanderbilt Divinity School, the late Walter Harrelson shared with me a more hopeful perspective of the Ten Commandments. His book on the Ten Commandments and Human Rights afforded me a refreshing perspective on the Ten Commandments. Also while in Brooklyn, I was blessed to hear Dr. Johnny Ray Youngblood preach a remarkable series on the Ten Commandments. His imaginative preaching gave the commandments a positive function within an oppressed community. Dr. Walter Brueggemann has also challenged and enhanced my understanding of the Ten Commandments, as he has for so much of my understanding of the Old Testament.

I want to use the battery of my academic and ministerial influences to contour my reflections upon the commandments through the lenses of the prophetic. I want to prayerfully invite those amazing and liberating influences to impact the next several days as we meditate on the Ten Commandments.

Exodus 20:1-3

"The God-Factor"

For oppression to be sustained and justified, it needs ideological and theological sanction. The values espoused by government and the tenets upheld by religion often serve as the primary forces of an oppressive culture and society. Some form of religious perspective is always behind the brutal exploits of politics and policies.

A critical development in the shaping of the liberated community of ex-slaves was the gift of the Commandments. The Commandments provided the band of ex-slaves with the fundamental values necessary for the creation of a new community, a community that would be distinct from the one they experienced in Egypt. The first and foremost value would be the God-factor. God was to be recognized as the One who delivered the people from the oppressive arrangements of Egypt, which is identified as "the house of bondage." The God of deliverance was to be acknowledged as primary and prominent in the lives of the people.

Walter Brueggemann noted this announcement and value as "regime change." The God of deliverance would be the primary reference point for how the community would see itself and how it would be arranged. What would make the community radically different from what it was in Egypt, or within "the house of bondage," would be Who they considered as worthy to be worshiped.

The undeniable complicity that the Christian church has had with oppression makes it difficult to distinguish the God of the biblical text and the god of the empire. The historical arrangement that the church has had with the government, beginning with Constantine's decision to embrace and sanction Christianity as the religion of the empire, complicates the God-factor. It behooves the oppressed community to learn from the biblical text. Community values that shape liberation are forged in the wilderness of community development and not within the tangled arrangements of "the house of bondage." We cannot accept the theological tenets of those who historically oppress us as being value-free. We must unequivocally acknowledge that the god who oppresses can never be upheld as the same God who liberates.

Prophetic engagement has the responsibility of dismantling any and every oppressive construct of God. Prophets must distinguish the god of oppression from the God Who liberates.

How is God perceived within your community? Whose construct of God dominates and shapes how you do ministry? Are there any oppressive constructs of God that you perceive?

PRAYER:
O God, we acknowledge You as the One who liberates. We thank You for Your liberating interventions. Hope us, I pray, to maintain You as the primary focus of our adoration and praise. AMEN.

Exodus 20:4

"God-Perversions"

Theological constructs are fortified through images. The way we conceive God is easily perverted when reduced to some projections of our own imagination. The gods of oppression are normally constructs that support oppression. When these gods are mass-produced, they tend to perpetuate internalized oppression. Self-inflicted oppression is usually because oppressed people buy into oppressive images.

The experience of Egypt provided the ex-slaves with a perspective from which to view images. They saw how images served to support oppressive realities. As cited earlier in our meditative journey, the plagues were often assaults upon images that supported the social and economic oppression of the people. The golden calf experience provided a lived experience that highlighted the potential of deluded projections becoming idolatrous prostrations. Consequently, the Second Commandment supports the First. The Second Commandment recognized the human tendency to project itself into the place of God by way of images. The God who creates and recreates was not to be supplanted by oppressive human projections. This commandment guarded the ex-slaves from borrowing anything from the creation and making it a substitute for the Creator.

I grew up with two pictures proudly displayed across the mantle of our aspiring-to-be-Christian home: a picture of a white, blue-eyed Jesus and a white president, John Fitzgerald Kennedy. My father, a Christian pastor, believed that these two white images represented the loftiest ideals of America: a Savior and a political judicator. Therefore, he proudly imposed these two images upon the collective psyche of his family. We would all later come to understand that this was far from true, but the damage to our psyche would remain. The white Jesus was a social construct that was supported by a distorted perception of an assassinated president, who really had no interest in supporting the civil rights agenda of protesting blacks.

What has been your experience with images? Have you any longstanding images that literally support the oppression of the empire? I suspect that most African American churches yet hold to oppressive images.

PRAYER:
O God, You are more than any image we could ever project or select. Hope us, I pray, to cleanse our environment of the toxins of oppressive images. May our children not be deluded or seduced into believing anything other than You is worthy of our worship and praise. AMEN.

Exodus 20:5-6

"Habits of Homage"

The dominant focus of our lives usually represents our deity. In some ways, even the agnostic and atheistic end up bowing to something. The challenge for us, however, is in our willful intentionality to bow to what oppresses us. Without being willful and intentional, idolatry can be a subtle and sinister takeover of our will and ways.

Verses 5-6 provided further support to the First and Second Commandments. The God-factor seems to be so critical that it needed to be nuanced and extrapolated. Clearly considering the depths of the God-factor would only heal the trauma of oppression and lead to authentic liberation. Thus, the issue addressed is that of the behavior of idolatrous beliefs. Idolatrous beliefs are evident in willful prostrations, or habits of homage. In other words, the people were informed that a core value was to not give their time and attention to anything that displaced God.

A contrast is made. Those who willfully and intentionally displaced God exhibit hatred toward God, and those who do not displace God give evidence of loving God. Moreover, those who displace God engage in behavior reminiscent of the oppressors, and those who do not, reflect the love of God in the world. Interestingly, idolatry backfires upon succeeding generations, whereas faithful homage to God multiplies the love of God in the world.

I find this commandment particularly challenging. Its insight into the subtle and sinister seduction of idolatrous behavior is striking. It strikes me because the false claims of the American empire parallel the claims of the Egyptian empire. We have been so seduced by the false claims of the idolatry of the American dream that we have normalized making bricks without straw. Painfully evident is that the people who are most vulnerable to economic inequity and exploitation tend to be the most faithful to the false claims of the American dream. As a consequence, we prostrate ourselves to the idolatry of invidious and insatiable consumption. I challenge you to monitor your time and see where it is spent, and look at your checkbook and note where all your money goes. Our schedules and checkbooks are accurate barometers of our true worship and adoration.

What has seduced you into giving your best time and best energy? What behavior is evident in your life that you may not be as worshipful to God as you would like to be? What is it that we willfully and intentionally focus upon?

PRAYER:
O God, You Who are irreplaceable. We confess to moments of being seduced by the subtle and sinister. Yet, we know that You alone are worthy of our praise and worship. Hope us, I pray, to be vigilant in our love and loyalty to You. AMEN.

Exodus 20:7

"The Name Game"

Names identify us. Our society has been structured by the use of names, as well as the misuse of names. Names also identify who we know and what we are all about. The use of names has had historic impact on social perception and access. By the use of names we are profiled and privileged, or denied privileges. Without question, we have organized our lives around the name game.

The Third Commandment placed value on the name of God. Although the Jewish tradition refuses to name the One who cannot be named, there was the use of the Tetragrammaton, YHWH, signifying the Hebrew name "Yahweh." Jewish tradition considers "God" to be too holy to pronounce. However, the value placed on God's name could be used in an empty way, where what God is all about is completely ignored. Using God's name in vain was to engage in activities of using the name of God without substantiating those activities according to the character of God. Such behavior can be demonstrated in broken promises made that were based upon illegitimate assumptions about one's relationship with God. This would be largely seen in the business arena where promises were broken using God's name, thus demonstrating an outright irreverence for the holy character of God. A good assumption is that people coming out of slavery were very much concerned with how God can be used to justify economic oppression and they were not interested in repeating that practice.

I grew up with the flawed belief that to use God's name within the context of profanity, or in a "swear" word, was to use God's name in vain. Words like "God-damn" were considered to be using the Lord's name in vain. My Brooklyn pastor, Dr. Johnny Ray Youngblood, powerfully suggested that "God-damn" was not a curse, but a prayer. In an attempt to demonize the candidacy of Barak Obama, Dr. Jeremiah Wright's use of the same phrase was taken out of context to suggest that he was cursing America.

The truth is, there are some things in this world that we should prayerfully ask God to damn from the face of the earth. There are some practices and behaviors within the American society that have been used to dehumanize and discriminate, often through twisted and illegitimate usage of the name of God. Racism would be one such reality that I, too, prayerfully ask God to damn from the face of this earth. I passionately desire that God damn any and every xenophobic belief and practice. I further hold that people most likely to take God's name in vain are those, like the Israelites, who claim to be in a relationship with God. Who can deny the fact that people who use God's name as a password are justifying much of today's economic exploitations?

Is it possible that much of what we have witnessed with the prosperity gospel is the taking of God's name in vain? What practices and behaviors have you witnessed, or perpetuated, that literally use God's name without representing God's character?

PRAYER:
Most holy God, holy be Your name! Grant us a greater sense of the reverence of You in all that we say in connection with You. Hope us, I pray, to be more mindful of our use of Your name. AMEN.

Exodus 20:8-11

"Sacred Rhythms"

I have long heard that too much of anything is not a good thing. The "anxiety of scarcity," however, seduces us into an endless pursuit of production and consumption. As a result, we have become addicted to constant busyness, believing that our busyness will somehow give us something that will satisfy us. We have a profound need to recover from the dangling discords of busyness and embrace a more harmonious rhythm for life and living.

The Fourth Commandment provided the ex-slaves a reprieve from the endless demands for labor and production as experienced within the Egyptian empire. A Sabbath, a weekly pause from the demands of labor and production, would provide the people with a cadence conducive to healthy living and communal appreciation. Moreover, the call for Sabbath was to be extended to all who were a part of the community, including servants and strangers. No one was to be subjected to endless demands for labor and production, which would only be a duplication of the systems and policies of the empire. Everyone was expected to participate in the Sabbath, for in the Sabbath, the people could recalibrate and reconnect with the communal rhythms of the sacred. The Sabbath provided opportunity to consider the holiness of life and living that would only be found by being liberated from the constant challenges of competitive production.

Although this commandment has the longest commentary, there is strangely no call to worship. The call is for a cessation of labor. It is a call to honor the sacred rhythm that is expressed within the creation narrative, which is a day of rest. As a pastor, and the son of a pastor, Sundays were never days of rest. In fact, Sunday within the family of the clergy is labor intensive. As I look at the current dynamics of church life, the act of worship has become a production of labor. A lot of people engaged in the drama of worship are now necessary to maintain the institution. There are high-priced church seminars that boldly tout the need to shift our worship paradigm into that of a well-planned production. I know pastors who frown upon any talk or thought of shifting from the marketing model that dominates American church life.

A careful and thoughtful consideration of the Sabbath commandment provides for us the basis for prophetic engagement. We engage the prophetic as a critique of any and every system, thought, or practice that exists for the purpose of chewing people up for the sake of greedy production and consumption. Perhaps the primary target for Sabbath correction should be the church, as the marketing model aids and abets the perpetuation of scarcity anxiety.

How are you celebrating the Sabbath? Is the goal of cultivating and enhancing community of primary concern for your church? Has worship become work rather than enjoyment?

PRAYER:
O God of the Sabbath, we acknowledge Your desire for sacred rhythm. Hope us, I pray, to prioritize community wholeness and wellbeing. Deliver us from the mindless obsession of production and consumption, especially in what is supposed to be worship. AMEN.

Exodus 20:12

"Parents Matter"

Who we are in life is largely determined by who parented us. Parents represent the primary structure of family life. Any benefits, privileges, or the lack of are usually reflections of the advantages or disadvantages afforded by parents. The parents who loom large in a person's life have an indelible impact on how he or she parents. None of us can deny the fact that parents matter.

The Fifth Commandment, the honoring of parents, follows the God Commandments and the Sabbath Commandment. The priority of parents was considered a matter essential to the development of a liberated community. Parents represent the basic structure of family and give us our primary witness of community life. I find this commandment interesting in light of Moses's hybrid parenting arrangements. During his childhood, we hear nothing of his father's role in his life. We only know him as of the house of Levi (Exodus 2:1). His mother served in a surrogate role in the service of his parent of adoption, who was a daughter of the oppressive regime (Exodus 2:7-9). Perhaps such a complex parenting arrangement gave him opportunity to witness the significance of parents, even those subjected to exploitative arrangements.

I believe the honoring of parents represents the essential dynamic for healthy families, particularly for families that have been devastated by oppression. When families are subjected to exploitative economic realities that are driven by oppressive policies, the outcomes are traumatic. It's difficult to hold parents in esteem when they are viewed through the lenses of daily acts of oppression and dehumanization. Yet, the vision of the liberated community was to reshape family life by giving value to the primary structure of the family – parents.

To love and honor our parents we have to see them through the lenses of their cultural experiences. My parents were children of the Jim Crow South. As a result, they carried within them the psychic wounds of oppression and dehumanization. The work of prophetic engagement must responsibly include a compassionate critique of family life, particularly the manner in which we parent. We honor our parents when we understand that to do so brings honor to family, even honor to God, Who provides us a context in which to be loved, nurtured, protected, and cared for.

What cultural construct shaped your parents? How did that construct show up in their parenting approach? Are you repeating it, or rejecting it?

PRAYER:
O God, the Mother and Father of us of all, hope us, I pray, to recover the honor for our parents, even those who were shamelessly victimized and violently dehumanized. Give us love and respect for them, so that we may love and respect ourselves. AMEN.

Exodus 20:13

"Life Matters"

The devaluing of human life finds its most horrendous expression in murder. When one person takes it upon him or herself to kill another person, he or she violates the most fundamental understanding of life in community. Life is a gift from God that should be treasured and respected. None of us have been privileged with a more valuable life than another, thus, none of us has the right to deprive another what has been gifted to all.

The Sixth Commandment provided a critical value to community. Community is an expression of life, and to kill was to assault the essence of community. Egypt was a context where human life was merely a means to an economic end. Life, for certain people, held no sacred worth and was expendable. In Egypt, a person's life was considered as valuable only to the extent of the contribution he or she made to maintain the machinery of oppression. For instance, Pharaoh's eagerness to kill male children served as a vivid reminder of how demagogic powers considered the lives of the oppressed. This commandment allowed the liberated community to hold life in an honored space that was more valuable than money, production, and consumption. The respect for life was based upon an understanding that life is a gift from God, not an expendable cog for economic efficiency.

Violence is as American as apple pie. Killing is a prelude to every major social movement in America. I am not sure where one expression of American violence is going – the senseless killings of black males by black males and by law enforcement. But I do know that the epidemic of violence within our communities powerfully illustrates the adverse effects of killing on community life. In the African American community, every time a life is lost, and a chalk line is drawn, we lose something. Every time a family has to bury a child, a victim to violence, the community loses. We lose a sense of giftedness, our sense of being connected to one another. The violence perpetuated by our nation against other nations, in the name of protecting American interest, has the eerie sound of killing for the sake of the oppressive machinery. We do well to challenge all acts of violence within our community as a responsibility of prophetic engagement.

How has violence affected you? Your community? Your practice of faith and family?

PRAYER:
O God of life and living, we acknowledge You as the source of all life. Hope us, I pray, to recover the sacred worth of life as You deliver us from the demon of violence. Give us holy boldness in the manner of Your crucified Son. AMEN.

Exodus 20:14

"Marriage Matters"

The deluge of love songs that flood our airwaves, and occupy so much space in our treasuries of artistic expression, seemingly would protect marriage from the brutal intrusions of adultery. The emotional energy invested in loving another should be protected space. However, no institution has been as violated as marriage. We witness marriage being violated from the annals of biblical writ to the literary tomes of our most esteemed classics, and even in the relationships of the revered and respected.

The Seventh Commandment focuses upon the sanctity of marriage. It is the second of the Commandments that is tersely stated and provides social boundaries. Marriage, as the primary expression of community, had boundaries that were to be honored and protected. While Egypt did not honor and respect boundaries in the relationships of the then oppressed community, the now liberated community was expected to do differently. Adultery and idolatry hold in common the feature of misplaced affections, and one often fed the other (for example, Hosea). Just as idolatry supported oppression, adultery feeds exploitation

Unfortunately, this commandment was aimed primarily at women. While the sexual activities of men were not limited to marriage, women were held to a different sexual standard. Women were severely scrutinized and penalized for adulterous activity (John 8:1-5). Perhaps the dowry given for women influenced the sexual mores of the community, but men were given greater latitude in sexual relations. Nonetheless, the sexual relations within marriage were to be honored and respected.

Prophetic engagement must recognize the value of boundaries within marriage, and its consequent effects upon community. It was common knowledge that noted men within the movements for social justice often violated the boundaries of marriage. In many instances, the violators of the marriage boundaries were lightly reprimanded and their ministries and marriages remained intact. However, the adverse impact on community is always felt.

What are your thoughts on marriage? How has marriage been honored within your community? How has marriage been violated? What have the consequences been?

PRAYER:
O God, we know You to honor loyalty and fidelity. Hope us, I pray, to hold marriage in high esteem. Grant us a greater sense of the connection between idolatrous prostrations and adulterous violations. AMEN.

Exodus 20:15

"It's Not Yours!"

I grew up with a television series, entitled "It Takes a Thief." Alexander Mundy, played by Robert Wagner, was a skilled thief who bargained with the government to stay out of jail. He plied his thievery skills in the service of national security. What a thought! The government has need of thieves.

The Eighth Commandment focused upon another major threat to community. This particular threat had to do with the corruptive process of unlawfully and unjustly seizing what belongs to another, with no intention of providing compensation. Although stated tersely, stealing was being viewed in a much bigger light than stealthily taking some inanimate object that did not belong to you. Walter Harrelson states, "When anyone or any institution takes away the life, the selfhood, the honor, or the goods of others, that is stealing." The "Thou shall not steal" sought to provide the community an alternative to the unjust exploitation of enslavement. As a free people, they were to hold person and property rights in ways that honor community. Harrelson concluded by adding that stealing "is any activity that damages or destroys a person's or a community's opportunity for a tolerable life in community – consisting at least of adequate food, shelter, work, and hope for the future."

This is a challenging commandment for those who would prophetically engage. So much of what we must address has to do with theft. If the above television series suggests anything, it suggests that even government has used theft to advance its causes. We could easily state that empire exists by stealing. America, with all of its claims of democracy and nobility, exists by way of legislative and contrived thievery. This land was stolen from the Native Americans, developed on the backs of stolen Africans, and constructed on legislation that allowed some people the legalized right to steal from others. We are yet reeling from one of America's most blatant thefts, where millions lost homes to legalized thievery.

Name instances where legal thievery devastated your community. How has such thievery been communally conceived? Are there any movements in place for restitution?

PRAYER:
O God, You Who provide us with enough to live comfortably and equitably, we bless and honor Your graciousness. Forgive us for our continued ways of contrived thievery, and even our attempts to rob You of Your glory. Hope us, I pray, to be vigilant in our communal aspirations to be theft-free. AMEN.

Exodus 20:16

"Talkin' and Testifying"

How we are perceived in the world is often determined by longstanding assumptions and well-constructed social projections. Many of these assumptions and projections are based upon the biased and bigoted interests of those in power. There are forces that benefit from the way people are perceived. Thus, billions are spent each year shaping perceptions to maintain the status quo. We make huge investments to keep things as they are.

Although tersely stated, the Ninth Commandment holds immense value for the quality of life within a liberated community. The prohibition against bearing false witness had to do with the words used to misrepresent a person, community, or entity. Such words were often cleverly constructed attempts to undermine a people, community, or entity for political and economical reasons. As a community of slaves and exiles, Israel had little influence on how they were perceived and represented. They were at the mercy of those who possessed the power and the means to effectively propagandize. When this Commandment is reduced to individual lies, it essentially sterilizes its primary intent. The Ninth Commandment sought to assure all people of the privilege of accurate and just representation.

Years ago, a noted psychoanalyst provided the seminal essay on propaganda. His analysis was used by the Nazis to advance one of the most effective campaigns of community misrepresentation. Unfortunately, the community that was victimized by Hitler's horrific campaign was the same community that offered us the Ninth Commandment. The horrors of racism, sexism, ageism, homophobism, and other xenophobic projections are cleverly contrived violations of the Ninth Commandment. The ease with which politics and religion contort misrepresentations has been legion. Prophetic engagement will find a formidable foe in the systems and constructs that perpetuate misrepresentation.

In what ways have you witnessed the Ninth Commandment being violated within your community? What responses have been given to the widespread misrepresentations of vulnerable communities?

PRAYER:
O God of truth and honor, we acknowledge You as being our source and inspiration for truthful representation. You created us in Your image and likeness, nothing more, nothing less. Hope us, I pray, to be deliberate in our representations of our brothers and sisters. AMEN.

Exodus 20:17

"Other People's Property"

A few years ago, the youthful rhymes and rhythms of the hip-hop genre focused attention upon a critical source of community disruption, OPP. OPP is an acronym for Other People's Property. Other People's Property had been identified as cause and effect for much of our community's disruption and destruction. Too many of us were channeling our energy into unreal and unhealthy desires for that which belonged to another.

The Tenth Commandment provided the final moral value intrinsic to shaping community for a liberated people, another tersely stated prohibition that has immense social implications. As with the other commandments, this one provided an alternative to the exploitative practices of Egypt. This commandment deepened the need for boundaries to be honored and respected with regard to the property of other people. The exploitation and violation of what belonged to another was not to be replicated within the liberated community, for it adversely affected the soul of the community. The issue of coveting is strongly stated by Walter Harrelson when he noted "that it is an action within the soul, the self, the inner being of persons who are sickened with longing for that which others have."

I personally struggled with the inclusion of "wives" as property. The objectification of women has had dire effects upon the soul of our nation. It appears that this soul sickness has affected us in ways that are yet to be fully understood and/or alleviated. The proliferation of sensate commercialism consumes us by creating within us insatiable desires to want what belongs to others, even their person, body, and soul. Who can ignore the constant grandstanding of overindulged celebrities, and the reality shows of lust and greed? The most admired are usually the most immersed in debaucherous lifestyles. Prophetic engagement must seek ways to spiritually inoculate the oppressed from the soul sickness of the oppressors.

What is your ministry doing to inoculate your community from covetousness? What about the widespread objectification of women's bodies? Or, has your ministry being consumed by a "deep longing for that which others have"?

PRAYER:
O God, You Who give each of us according to our need, we give You thanks. Hope us, I pray, to protect our souls from being consumed by wanting what belongs to others. AMEN.

Numbers 27:1-11

"Daughter Rights"

As previously observed, the inclusion of wives as property in the Tenth Commandment caused me serious textual consternation. The sexism implied by reducing women to property provoked concern for how even the Bible can contribute to the objectification of women. Admittedly, there are many biblical passages and stories that cause me to cringe. I am acutely aware of the social distance between my world and the world of the text, as well as my limited grasp of the redactor's intentions. However, where there are texts that illuminate and magnify attempts toward justice and equality I am gratified. The texts that highlight the daughters of Zelophehad are worth noting.

The fair and equitable distribution of land was included in Moses's prophetic assignment. Who would get what was determined by family lineage, and allocations were normally awarded to male descendants. As the inheritances were being awarded, an interesting development occurred. We are told that the daughters of Zelophehad addressed Moses. They informed him of the fact that their father had died in the wilderness struggle and had no sons to which to award an inheritance. They insisted that their father's legacy continue and that they be given rights to his inheritance. Moses consulted the Lord and was informed that Zelophehad's daughters were right in their claim. Furthermore, what Zelophehad's daughters were claiming were to be the rights of all daughters whose fathers had no sons. Of interest in the text is that each time the daughters of Zelophehad are mentioned, all five of the sisters' names are provided. The daughters' protest seems to have been so impacting that their names were not to be forgotten.

The rights of women must remain critical to any and every prophetic engagement. Too often male-driven crusades suffer from sexist blind spots. Martin Luther King, Jr., with all of his brilliant passion for justice and equality, suffered from serious sexist blind spots. Although some strides have been made in providing women equal access to privileges, there is still a long ways to go. Sexism remains firmly entrenched in most churches and still shapes the landscapes of American business and politics. Moses's wise consultation with the Lord ought to be a model for those entrenched in sexist practices. A consultation with the Lord delivers us from the restraints of patriarchy and allows us to hear the voice of Justice say, "The daughters are right."

In what ways do we continue to slight women on the bases of male privileges and prerogatives? How important are the voices of daughters in your church and/or community?

PRAYER:
O God, Who created us male and female, we are humbled by Your creative genius. Hope us, I pray, to become more mindful of what You consider just as it relates to our sisters, daughters, and mothers. May we not leave any daughter vulnerable to the predators of the empire. AMEN.

Deuteronomy 18:15-22

"Raising Up a Prophet"

I started this journey considering Moses, who represented the primary paradigm of the biblical prophets. His shadow looms large over the entire Bible and provides us invaluable insights on the voice, vision, and value of prophetic ministry. Even when Moses is ignored, his prophetic absence speaks. As I have probed the Exodus, which is also the primary narrative for grounding prophetic ministry, I was in awe of the immensity of the Mosaic tradition. However, my interest in the consequent reactions to the Mosaic tradition calls me to consider some other texts. Yet, before I proceed to other biblical texts, I want to meditate on a few more critical junctures of the Mosaic tradition.

I want to briefly consider a few of the transitional texts from Moses to those who follow. The first of these is the Deuteronomic acknowledgement that the prophet who follows Moses will be just like Moses. Deuteronomy continued the tradition of a prophet coming from among the people, and, like Moses, will be God's voice. The prophet who will be raised up from among the people will be noted as a representative of God, who speaks God's truth. Conversely, any prophet who does not represent God, and speaks the truths of another god, shall not be heard. Presumptuous prophecy would result in the death of the prophet.

Again, the paradigm of Mosaic prophecy represents a notable standard. Prophets, today, should come from among the people who are most affected by oppressive realities. Unfortunately, the prophetic mantle has become so eschewed that so-called prophets are coming from without rather from within. The presumptuousness of the prophetic has basically killed off the impact of the prophetic tradition. Although people remain religious, most people do not align their faith practices with prophetic engagement. With the aid of the idolatrous empire, too many of us, including preachers, see church and the world as being separate. We have become content in doing what my friend, Dr. Elliott Cuff, calls maintaining "status quo spirituality."

PRAYER:
O God, Who yet speaks, we need to hear from You. Hope us, I pray, to be susceptible to prophetic voices. Rise up from among us new prophets, so that we can more faithfully serve You. AMEN.

Deuteronomy 31:1-8

"Passing the Mantle"

John Maxwell, a prolific mentor of Christian leaders, noted that true success is in having a successor. Maxwell was concerned with the incredible works of impactful leadership continuing beyond their lifetime. If what we do really means something, we should give serious thought to it having legacy. In other words, legends provide legacy. The fact that we are going to die, often much quicker than we think, we would do well to consider preparing others and ourselves for our demise.

Moses's tenure of leadership was supposedly forty years, which was the time of the wilderness wandering/development. As dramatic as it began, it would end as dramatically. Moses faced the fact that he would not enter the Promised Land. He embraced the fact that his leadership was for a certain time and period in the development of Israel. As pivotal as his leadership was, Moses understood that the real leader was God. God brought the children of Israel out of Egypt. God provided for them in the wilderness, and God protected them from their enemies.

Moses had prepared another to assume the leadership mantle. He had chosen and nurtured Joshua, and before the people, he passed the mantle on. His words to Joshua were "to be strong and of good courage," and the Lord would bring them into the Promised Land. Moses bid farewell knowing that all that was done was really because of God, and Joshua would continue being an instrument of God.

I see few pastors passing the mantle, and I suspect it is very difficult. How does a person get so close to the goals of his or her life, and accept the fact that he or she will not reach them? What does it mean to a person, who has worked hard for something, to know that he or she will not reap any reward? Martin Luther King, Jr. announced that he had seen the Promised Land of black equality, but embraced the fact that he wasn't going to enter it. Is there anything in your life that you have worked hard for and are willing to turn over to another?

PRAYER:
O God, who gives us life, assignments and the time to complete our assignments, we understand that all that we do is ultimately because of You. Hope us, I pray, to accept our limited roles and embrace our mortality. May we be visionary enough to prepare others to work with You. AMEN.

HOPE US, LORD!

Joshua 1

"Always in the Shadow"

Those who are content to stay in the background often make the greatest contributions. While we are motivated and inspired by those who dare to stand up and speak out, the momentum needed to move an initiative forward is usually from those in the shadows. This is not always a celebrated position, but it is indeed a necessary position. We will only go as far as those who are behind us are pushing us.

We consider the Joshua narrative only briefly. It is not because Joshua is not a major player in the prophetic tradition. We consider Joshua because he is the immediate successor to Moses, who functions primarily as an extension of Moses. He was tutored and nurtured by Moses, and, more importantly, he assumed the mantle of Moses free of the theatrics of resistance and excuses. We never see anything halting or hesitant about Joshua's willingness to serve Moses.

In the opening chapter of the book of Joshua, he is introduced as Moses's assistant, and everything he is to do is a continuation of Moses's leadership and ministry. Joshua would not be distinguished as Joshua. His existence in ministry was to further the work begun by Moses. Even God speaks to Joshua as an extension of Moses. "As I was with Moses, so shall I be with you." Joshua was to even gain his strength and courage on the basis of God's allegiance to Moses. Moses literally dominates the book written in deference to Joshua.

The Joshua scenario intrigues me because it counters the egomaniacal drives of ministry in America. Perhaps we could learn a worthwhile lesson from Joshua, who models for us the power and efficacy of functioning from the shadows. We do not all have to blaze new trails to affect prophetic transformation. We might do better walking in the trails already blazed by Frederick Douglas, Sojourner Truth, Martin Luther King, Jr., Fannie Lou Hamer, Cesar Chavez, Nelson and Winnie Mandela, and the grand host of sisters and brothers who have gone before us. The inefficacy of prophetic ministry in our communities may well be the result of a diluted message created by too many wanna-be trailblazers. We might recover our relevance and significance if more of us would be content with being in the shadows.

Where do you prefer to be as a change-maker for justice? Can you serve in the shadows? Or, do you need to always be up front?

PRAYER:
O God, You Who represent the Light of the World, yet seem to always lurk in the shadows, we bless Your name. Hope us, I pray, to be content with being conduits rather than grasping to be power sources. AMEN.

HOPE US, LORD!

1 Samuel 2:1-10

"A New Song"

Songs have played significant roles within prophetic activity and social transformation. Songs have been known to bring poetic voice and rhythm to the hopes and dreams of oppressed people. Often what people could not say with words, would be voiced in song. The Bible provides a huge library of songs that give communal voice to their understanding of God acting in the midst of God's people.

The Song of Hannah has historically been tamed and domesticated by Western intoxication with individual salvation. When viewed through the lens of individual salvation, the Song of Hannah represents Hannah's response to God reversing the pain of her personal plight – the plight of a once barren woman. However, the themes of the song are clearly larger than an individual. The bows of the wicked being broken, the well-fed being hired out, the reversal of the rich and poor, and the needy being lifted up are issues of communal injustices. Although Hannah's personal plight was opportunity for rejoicing, the larger issue of Israel's plight being reversed from the oppression of the Philistines gave reason for communal praise. In essence, this is a song sung by a community, who see in the Hannah story their own story.

Again, song has long provided voice to the hopes and dreams of oppressed people. The protesting Africans of apartheid South Africa, the marching women of the suffrage, and the "We Shall Overcome" cadence of the civil rights movement are witnesses to the power of song. Song galvanized community and gave the oppressed rhythmic energy to forge forward. Even now, the restlessness of urban youth has been given voice in their songs, a voice that has been either shamelessly commercialized, or foolishly ignored. The hip-hop generation represents a prophetic voice giving expression to the pain and promise of an oppressed people.

What are your favorite songs? Are they songs of drunken individualism, or songs of the people? I challenge those who engage in the prophetic to put your hopes and dreams to song.

PRAYER:
O God, Who created us with singing capacity, keep us attached to our songs. Hope us, I pray, to embrace the songs of struggle and of victory. May our songs be songs of reason, rage, and reversal. AMEN.

1 Samuel 2:27-36

"Priestly Problems"

The regular and perfunctory duties of the priestly ministry are fraught with challenges. There is just something about doing the same thing over and over again that makes us extremely vulnerable to moral and careless lapses. Those who engage in priestly functions must be aware that the tedium of sacred duty calls for responsible and critical interventions. Perhaps the interplay between the prophetic and the priestly could energize us from the malaise of priestly doldrums.

We are not long into the Samuel story before we are informed that the priestly ministry of Eli had deteriorated. He had become disengaged and his sons had become notably immoral and inexcusably exploitative. They had lost touch with the need for sacred practices and rituals within the redemptive community. As a result, they used their sacred positions as opportunities for greed, graft, and sexual licentiousness. In incredible brevity, the narrator described their behavior as extremely corrupt.

An unnamed prophet intervened and informed Eli of God's intention. Noteworthy is that the prophet prefaced his announcements with a reference to the Exodus experience. The priestly office was grounded in the defining narrative of Israel, but Eli's disengagement and his sons' immoral exploitations had desecrated the Exodus perspective. Eli had allowed the priestly office to become a sanctified expression of Egypt, which was oppression wrapped in religion.

The prophetic ministry has a responsibility to critique religious practices. There is always the danger of priestly functions becoming too cozy with the culture. As I write these lines, among the news headlines is a story of another pastor resigning because of moral lapses. Somehow we must keep in tension the critique of the prophetic with the cultic of the priestly. The priestly should not be left to its own devices, nor should the prophetic ignore the priestly. What we do as priests should be scrutinized by what we expect as prophets. Unfortunately, it's become much too common to separate the two functions, to the peril of both. We cannot have priestly sanctity without prophetic urgency, nor can we engage prophetic urgency without priestly sanctity.

What are the dominant pitfalls of those within Christian ministry? How does your church deal with clergy misconduct? Your denomination? Is there a healthy connection between the priestly and the prophetic?

PRAYER:
O God, we need for our prayer life to be consistent with our prophetic intentions. What You do for us in redemption is not to be trivialized in our consecration. Hope us, I pray, to not neglect our worship practices as being nonessential to our prophetic practices. AMEN.

1 Samuel 3

"Confirmed as a Prophet"

Prophetic passion has to be nurtured. Unfortunately, the prophetic is often nurtured within unseemly contexts. There are no easy contexts for the nurturing of the prophetic. The prophetic has to live with that which it must contend with, and that is no easy or enviable place or space.

The narrative around the prophet Samuel begins in pain. His mother Hannah suffered the indignation of barrenness before he was birthed into the world. Both priest and husband misunderstood her as she suffered and believed, against her lived-out odds and agony. Nothing is more ironic than her giving her long awaited son to Eli, who represented everything that was wrong with the state of the priestly ministry.

Eli, however, served as a serious mentor of the young man. In spite of all the egregious behavior of Eli's sons, Hophni and Phinehas, the Bible notes that the child, Samuel, grew under the spiritual tutelage of Eli. When God called Samuel, it was Eli who conditioned him to hear what God was saying to him. God's message to Samuel was a fierce rebuke and rejection of Eli's household, a message so painful that Samuel was hesitant to share it. Eli insisted that he share the message, and when Samuel did, the narrator informs us that Samuel kept growing and was confirmed as a prophet.

Who we love and what we live with are our primary tutors of the world's realities. It is within the context of our lived experiences that we come face-to-face with our prophetic responsibilities. Martin Luther King, Jr. lived the segregation that he opposed. Mandela lived the injustice that he opposed. Sojourner Truth and Harriet Tubman lived the slavery they sought to escape. In all of those experiences, there were people who were loved and respected who had to be rebuked and rejected.

Who are the people who have nurtured you in the very systems that you assail? Can you name the people who helped you hear God's call, even if God's call was a rebuke of the evil they tolerated? How did you handle rebuking people you honor and respect?

PRAYER:
O God, You Who call us within less than ideal contexts, we are in awe of Your courageous ingenuity. May we be responsive to Your call, even if it finds us opposing those we love and respect. Hope us, I pray, to bless our nurturing agents with truth, even if it hurts. AMEN.

1 Samuel 7

"The Circuit Prophet"

Yesterday we mentioned that the prophet is nurtured within unenviable contexts. The places where prophetic urgency is nurtured and cultivated often become both the subject and the object of one's prophetic challenge. I want to add to that observation by stating that where we are nurtured is critical to our prophetic perspective. How we see God at work is largely determined by where we work.

Samuel's prophetic ministry took place during a critical time within the development of Israel. He served as the last judge of Israel. His ministry was primarily concerned with restoring theological integrity to Israel while dealing with the hostile and oppressive Philistines. Israel had a fierce enemy in the Philistines, but their biggest enemy was themselves. Their capitulation to the Baals and the Ashtoreths compromised their theological integrity. Theological confusion often found them mimicking the oppressive behavior of the Philistines.

Samuel distinguished his ministry by being a circuit judge. He went throughout the Israelite communities providing justice wherever injustice was being perpetuated among the people. His ministry was a mobile ministry that gave him access to a broad range of injustices that the people were inflicting upon themselves. The defeat of the Philistines was actually a defeat of the internalized oppression that caused them to perpetuate injustices toward one another. The people's recommitment of loyalty to God created a moment where God's help was so decisive that Samuel provided a memorable to signal that the "Lord has helped."

We do well to monitor the loyalties of our people. Too often the oppression being perpetuated among our people is self-inflicted, the inevitable result of the lack of theological integrity. We will never make real the liberating love of God with divided loyalties. The people we serve have much to do with the focus of our ministry, and we cannot limit where we serve them. To get an accurate picture of what we are up against, we will have to frequent the many places of their unjust practices and behavior. There needs to be a circuit dimension to our ministry. We need to see the injustices of the people from many different perspectives.

What has shaped your prophetic perspective? How have you interacted with people in ways that broaden how your minister? Cite a recent injustice you sought to mediate.

PRAYER:
O God, we know You to be a God of justice. Hope us, I pray, to develop a broad perspective. Create moments where we can experience the myriad expressions of injustice in order to better serve You. AMEN. AMEN.

HOPE US, LORD!

1 Samuel 8

"The King's Behavior"

We continue pondering over the context of prophetic engagement. The places where we are nurtured are rarely enviable, and where we are, critically impacts the shape of our ministry. Likewise, the work that we are called to do causes us to say things that are difficult to say, especially when they must be said to people for whom we wish the best.

Samuel labored long and hard among the children of Israel. He seemingly had a sterling record of making justice an honorable reality. However, his sons were not as prudent in their dispensation of justice. Like Eli, his predecessor, he suffered the indignation of wayward sons. His sons used the offices of judgeship to exploit and oppress. As Samuel aged and his sons strayed, the people lost hope in the office of judgeship and demanded a king. God's response was to allow Samuel to concede to their demands, but he was obligated to tell them what they were getting into.

Samuel's words to the people were to tell them what would happen to them once they accepted a king. In other words, their choice had consequences. The king's behavior, as spoken by Samuel, would be oppressive, exploitative, and detrimental to the quality of the people's lives. While the behavior of Samuel's sons was as shameful as Eli's sons, the acceptance of a king would normalize and give royal credence to shameful and exploitative behavior, essentially giving it political legitimacy. The request for a king would, in essence, begin the process of Israel sleeping with the enemy.

One of the most dangerous places for prophetic activity is to be cozy with the empire. I've witnessed people and leaders believe they could negotiate the conflicting values of the empire, only to learn they were wrong. When we make up our minds to be the prophetic voice for our people, we cannot do so from the platform of governmental privileges. To speak against the perversions of the empire we need to be free of the exploitative tentacles of the empire.

In what ways are your community's preacher-prophets aligned with the empire? How does your community deal with clergy compromises?

PRAYER:
O God, Who allows us the freedom to choose government, we pray for just expressions of government. Hope us, I pray, to be free enough to be prophetically responsible. AMEN.

1 Samuel 9

"Dinner with Saul"

The prophetic ministry places us in a lot of interesting situations. The ministry of the prophetic can be so publically known that it finds us at the intersections of varied community concerns. We can never allow ourselves to become aloof from normal, or extraordinary community events. It is those places where community interacts where we encounter the currents of prophetic concern.

The selection of Saul to be King of Israel was set within the context of very common community interactions. Saul was on the humble assignment of locating his father's lost donkeys and Samuel was in preparation for community worship. We are not told how Saul deduced that the prophet would be helpful in locating lost donkeys, but his inquiry resulted in the recovery of the donkeys and Saul being invited to share dinner with the prophet. Of interest in this pericope is what is said in the last verse of chapter 9: "But you stand still now, because I want you to hear what God has said."

What has become lost among our interactions with people of power and influence is our willingness to share what God has said. We have become so content at listening to politicians and people of power tell us what's on their mind, we neglect to inform them about what God has said. I've been in situations where I witnessed preachers so content with eating a politically sponsored luncheon that there was no desire to tell the politician what God has said. To make matters worse, the politician did not give us the respect of even sitting and eating with us. Worse yet, was the fact that I was made to feel uncomfortable because I raised an objection. We have to be able to tell people of power and influence to "Sit down because I want to tell you what God has said."

How have you fared when interacting with people of power and influence? Has what God said been an easy conversation to broach? If not, why not?

PRAYER:
O God, we appreciate the humble arrangements by which prophetic engagement transpires. Hope us, I pray, to remain humble enough to traffic within the normal affairs of community. Yet, keep us diligent of our responsibility to remind people of power and influence what You have said. AMEN.

1 Samuel 10

"Dancing with the Prophets"

A challenge of prophetic ministry is keeping the people in a position where God can be acknowledged. This sometimes calls us to do some creative things to keep God in the mix. We may have to work with some people who are not as serious about God as we are. We might also have to concede some battles in order to for God to win the victory.

The calling of Saul to be King of Israel was a challenge to prophetic ministry. It was a challenge because the office of king was a new experience within the community of the faithful. It was a shift from a theocracy, being God-led, to a monarchy, human-led. Because of the novelty of it all, Samuel had to keep his hands on Saul in order to maneuver him into kingly responsibility. Although Israel was slipping into a monarchy, a large part of Israel recognized Samuel, the prophet's role, as critical to the process. Therefore, Samuel mentored Saul into the role and responsibility of kingship, even though Saul showed early signs of being woefully ill-equipped.

One of the ways in which Saul mentored Samuel was by telling him to dance with the prophets. The dance with the prophets dramatized the continued relationship between the king and God. It was a way of understanding the rhythmic steps necessary for prophets to comingle with politicians and remain distinct. Since the prophets were known as people of God, Saul, hopefully, would become known as being in a relationship with God. The dance with the prophets would hopefully transform Saul into another person, a person God could use. However, it is noteworthy that some of the people questioned the authenticity of the relationship and his transformation. Some of the people did not see how a person of one tribe could be transformed with the prophetic gifts of this unique group. There was a crowd suspicious of Saul's transformative experience.

The intrigue of this pericope is that it seeks to provide a God-perspective to a human-initiated endeavor. As grand as our ideas may be, it is important for us to seek ways to provide a God-perspective to our endless efforts to shape community in our own image. The truth is: God really wants to be included! God can transform our grand schemes into divine opportunities. The dance with the prophets was Samuel's attempt to infuse the kingly aspirations of the people with a sense of what matters to God. God may allow us to do things, but we should do our very best to infuse them with godly purpose.

I have witnessed so many human-initiated endeavors flounder because of a lack of godly purpose. What grand project are you attempting that needs to be infused with godly purpose? Is there a sense of justice or "just us"?

PRAYER:
O God, You are a God of justice, love, mercy, and righteousness. Hope us, I pray, to be ever mindful that the clever plans we initiate, and the people we engage, always find a moment where we can be transformed by a dance with the prophets. AMEN.

HOPE US, LORD!

1Samuel 12

"Prophetic Integrity"

Our behavior matters! What we do before people matters. How we conduct ourselves in the day-to-day interactions of community life speaks volumes. It has been aptly said that our actions will speak louder than our words. Moreover, our actions will give weight and worth to our words.

Chapter 12 allows us to hear and witness the value of prophetic integrity. Samuel stood before the people and engaged in a personal assessment of his ministry. He noted the longevity of his years and service. He called upon the people to bear witness to his life among them. He opened himself up to be seen as a person who never used his prophetic office to exploit, oppress, or defraud anyone. He called upon the people to judge him in this matter, and none could provide an instance where he used his prophetic office to exploit, oppress, or defraud anyone. There was no incongruity between the way he viewed himself and the way the people viewed him. His integrity provided him the platform by which to speak with authority.

Using the platform of his integrity, Samuel placed the people's current plight in the context of their Exodus experience. He sought to provide a perspective by which the people could see where they were in light of where they had been. The goal of Samuel's words was to call attention to the faithfulness of God, in light of the faithlessness of the people. He wanted them to be clear that their desire for a king was an affront to the faithfulness of God, but God allowed it as long as God would be honored and obeyed. The God of the Exodus, and the Deliverer from enemies, would reluctantly become God of a king-smitten people.

The need for prophetic integrity is critical. We need men and women whose lives have not been marred and scarred with disingenuous behavior. We need people whose voice and view are morally congruent. We need leaders whose humble nobility is known, acknowledged and respected. For our words to have weight and worth, we cannot be guilty of exploiting, oppressing, and defrauding God's people.

Let's be clear! We serve a people who are constantly smitten by something. The unending bombardment of consumerism and the mad quests for materialistic comfort, accompanied by insatiable sensuality, has made prophetic integrity extremely challenging. We have lost our Exodus perspective when a "reality show-smitten" world seduces the clergy into dramatizing the depths of their moral depravity.

How can we speak a word worthy of being heard when we have no prophetic integrity? What view does the community hold of you? Does the view the community holds match up with your own?

PRAYER:
O God of grace and mercy, shadow us afresh with a sense of holiness. May the One we serve be seen by us as the One we depend upon. Hope us, I pray, to strive for a greater sense of prophetic integrity. AMEN.

1 Samuel 13

"The Illusions of Good Intentions"

What people do says a lot about who they are. People are rarely anything more than their behavior. Maya Angelou, the poet laureate, has wisely stated that if people show you who they are, we should believe it and not try to make them someone they are not. We should never operate with the illusion of good intentions.

The ill-conceived desire of the people to have a king was troublesome from the start. Saul, personally, never got off to a good start as king. During a crisis, he took it upon himself to offer the priestly sacrifice. He was losing the battle of political leadership and sought to secure his leadership by assuming a priestly role. Samuel was dumbfounded by his actions and confronted him. Saul's answer indicated that personal fear had prompted him. Samuel decried Saul's act as a foolish one and that his "kingdom shall not continue." Samuel did not neglect his prophetic responsibility just because Saul betrayed his responsibility as a leader. He was not swayed by the illusion of Saul's noble intention.

What is deeply troubling about this narrative is that Saul really saw no wrong in his action. Could it be that the prophetic office can become so close to the political that either could lose perspective? In this instance, the political assumed the responsibility of the priestly-prophetic. We have to be careful that we don't allow politicians license to engage in the work of the priestly-prophetic. It is foolish to believe that just because the people elect a person to an office that he or she has license to engage in God-anointed functions. I cringe whenever I see politicians assuming priestly-prophetic roles and responsibilities. The President of the United States risks losing "the kingdom" when intruding upon the priestly-prophetic.

What are limits of a political office? Do we see any danger in a politician, an ambassador of the empire, engaging in priestly-prophetic responsibilities? We are not to be swayed by the illusion of good intentions, because such intentions are rarely good.

PRAYER:
O God, forgive us for prophetic naiveté. Hope us, I pray, to be responsible stewards of the sacred, even when we seek to support the secular. May what is done for You never become trivialized by selfish ambition. AMEN.

1 Samuel 15

"Grieving Prophet"

The work of the prophetic is human work. We are called to engage in the most intimate and sacred spaces of humanity, often broken humanity, struggling to negotiate a broken world. We experience pain when the grand vision for the things of God is sabotaged by the frailty of human weakness. There is a grievous quality about the prophetic.

Saul had been allowed to proceed in the office of king. He experienced a measure of success and was victorious in battle over established systems of oppression. However, he compromised the intent of God by holding for himself prized possessions of the oppressive system. He sought to justify his behavior by asserting self-determined assessments about what was good and what was not. He essentially disobeyed God, and the pain it caused God was felt in the heart of Samuel. In other words, what hurt God was experienced by the prophet. As a result, "It grieved Samuel; and he cried unto the Lord all night."

I find grievous the decisions made by politicians and policy makers that inflict pain upon people who they vowed to serve and protect. The ongoing battle for justice and inequality is often undermined by self-determined assessments of what is good and what is not. We painfully witness decisions being made that deprive the needy and enrich the greedy, often done in the name of what's good for the country. It is becoming much too common for those elected from among the oppressed to use their office for egregious acts of greed. Such are the moments when those who work passionately for justice and equality are caused to grieve over the disparity of what God expects and the sordid behavior of those expected to bring it to pass.

Have there been moments in your ministry where you grieved? What does it take for you to feel the pain of God as an appropriate response for egregious human behavior?

PRAYER:
O God, Who feels the pain of oppression, and repents our foolish blunders, extend to us Your unfailing love. We admit disappointing You with willful acts of egregious behavior. Hope us, I pray, to be sensitive to how our disobedience brings pain to You. AMEN.

1 Samuel 16

"What the Lord Sees"

We are stuck with people. People will be the vehicles of transformation and the instruments God will use to initiate justice and equality into our broken communities. The challenge of prophetic ministry is in how people are assessed. We cannot allow the standards set by the populace to determine our assessment of who God will use. God perceives a person from their heart and such a perspective should assist us in determining allies for justice.

As previously stated, Samuel grieved deeply over the failures of Saul. Saul's repeated failures not only served as a painful disappointment to Samuel, but also disrupted the possibility of collaborative community building between throne and altar. God's concession to a king was contingent upon God remaining central to the people's lives and the prophetic-priestly function being honored and respected. Saul's failures were so subversive to the expectations of God that God initiated the process of replacing Saul. Samuel was directed to go to Bethlehem and anoint the king God provided.

Samuel's journey to Bethlehem represented a shift. There would be a shift in the selection process, as well as the assessment process. Who God had provided would be selected from a number of prospects, and would not be determined by external impressiveness. God's choice would not be limited to the narrow determinations of human perspective, but from a perspective that only God can perceive: the perspective of the heart. Samuel's role was that of prayerfully seeking divine discernment.

We are quick to say that a person has a good heart. It's as if we have been able to look into the inner workings of individuals. The reality is that we don't know what's truly in a person's heart. We can only see who a person is by what he or she does. The risks of our presumptuous assessments are legion. We risk having too lofty of an assessment of a good heart, or too low of an assessment of a good heart, or somewhere in between. What we really don't want to do is set a person up too high, or assess them too low. Heart issues are really God issues.

The involvement of Samuel clearly suggests that the heart of people in leadership is critical to a just community. How have the issues of heart in leadership been determined in our communities? Are we content with leaders who tell us what's in their hearts? Or, will we prayerfully seek divine discernment over human opinions?

PRAYER:
O God, the Seer of hearts and the Knower of secret things, we are humbled by Your perceptions. Hope us, I pray, to be diligent as we prayerfully discern who might more justly serve Your people. AMEN.

1 Samuel 16:11-13

"Stand Up until He Comes"

The sedentary life is seductive, particularly for people who have major responsibilities. We have been seduced into believing that the most important things in life are accomplished from a sitting position. Moses sat while the people came to him to be judged. Executives of power and influence sit behind great desks. I witnessed President Obama signing executive orders always from a sitting position. Yet, there are some things that demand that we stand.

Samuel busied himself discerning who God had prepared for the role of king. Jesse's sons were brought before him one by one, name by name. He knew he was at the right house, and he also knew that he had not seen the right person. He knew he was at the place of God's designation, but he had not discerned the person who God had prepared for king. He declared, "The Lord has not chosen these."

Samuel inquired about the presence of any other young men, and Jesse informed him of the youngest one, David, who was keeping sheep. Samuel demanded that he be brought to him and that he would not sit until he arrived. There was dogged persistence in Samuel that would not allow him to sit until he saw the one God had prepared.

I probably could not write this meditation from a standing position. There are things that must be done by sitting, but when God is trying to put in place people He wants to use for the building of a just community, we do well to stand. By standing, we send a message that what we are doing is not only personally important, but it is symbolic of what God is about to do. God wants us to stand. We have to stand up for justice. We have to stand up for righteousness. We have to stand up for peace. We have to stand up for the least, the lost, the locked out, left behind, and looked-over.

The late Harry Emerson Fosdick once said, "If a man doesn't stand for something, he will fall for anything." What are you standing for? Is there any cause in your life worthy of your taking a stand? When was the last time you stood for something?

PRAYER:
O God, Who created us as perpendicular creatures, we stand in awe of Your creative intentionality. Hope us, O God, to be emboldened and steadfast enough to stand for what You stand for: justice, freedom, equality, and peace. AMEN.

1 Samuel 17

"Is There Not a Cause?"

Life is best lived when attached to some noble cause. God gets more out of us. The world gets more out of us, and we get more out of ourselves when we link our lives to something greater than us. There awaits all of us some noble cause that will never be fulfilled without our faithful engagement.

David's introduction into the narrative of Israel's redemption is most dramatic. He was given a humble assignment to bring bread to his brother and cheese to the captains. Although David was yet considered a child, he was given chores that would bring him close to the conflict between Israel and the Philistines. The champion of the Philistines had struck fear into the hearts of Israel's army. Goliath had challenged Israel to send out their best, and upon David's arrival at the camp, no Israelite solider had responded. David is portrayed as inquiring about why the men were so reluctant to engage, and his brother, Eliab, became upset with his inquiry. David's response was to ask, "What have I done? Is there not a cause?" David would eventually accept Goliath's challenge and defeat the champion of the Philistines. His biblical notoriety began with him as a young man doing a child's chores, who undertook an adult's assignment. David slew Goliath, who symbolized the taunting antics of an oppressive power.

Admittedly, I leant toward the New King James Version for this text. I find in it a passionate expression for responsible prophetic engagement. I find it intriguing because it raises the pivotal question for all who would locate some noteworthy issue in which to invest one's life. The New King James Version may have issues with interpretation, but it does not fail to note what is crucial to prophetic engagement. David put his life on the line against a powerful, intimidating, and taunting power. Moreover, he used what he had to bring down the symbol of his people's oppression.

What cause dominates your life? Are you willing to put it all on the line for that cause? If not, why not?

PRAYER:
O God, Who positions us to make a difference, we give You praise and adoration. Hope us, I pray, to be diligent in discerning causes worthy of our life investment. May we be willing to put it all on the line for the causes of justice and equality. AMEN.

1Samuel 22

"Justice from a Cave"

The work of prophetic engagement is done wherever justice is being pursued. Personal comfort is a common sacrifice when fighting for injustice. The work is not always done in ideal settings, or in ideal conditions. In a very real sense, justice is awkward because it speaks to the awkward imbalances of society that have been maintained and sustained by powerful allegiances.

David's arrival upon the scene was received enthusiastically by the people, but was unwelcomed by Saul. Saul responded by trying to kill David, and became obsessed with removing David from the scene. In response to one of Saul's attempt at killing David, David takes refuge in a cave. The cave was called Adullam. Adullam means "justice for the people," or "equity for the people." Of note in the text is that the people who gathered around David were people who were distressed, in debt, and those who were discontent.

Although David was not identified as a prophet, his role has prophetic implications. For one, he was victimized. He was subjected to life-disrupting injustices just because of who he was. He did not choose his place in life, but was treated as a criminal and lived a significant part of his life as a fugitive. Secondly, the people who rallied to his side were people who shared similar injustices. Thirdly, the close relationship between the kingly and the prophetic provided him a prophetic perspective. Moreover, his penchant for fairness earned him the love and respect of people. In a cave, as a fugitive fleeing for his life, David became a powerful symbol for justice.

The work of prophetic engagement forces us into the tight spaces of personal preservation and the pressing needs of others. The tenuous space of our own wellbeing must be shared with the glaring injustices of others. Although we instinctively do what needs to be done to preserve ourselves, we do not isolate ourselves from the collective claims of community injustice. I suspect that the loss of prophetic urgency has been compromised by an obsession with self-preservation. Many who could and should share in the burden of prophetic engagement have become overly preoccupied with concern for the self.

Have you been able to share the space of your injustice with others? How have your own needs been negotiated while meeting the needs of others?

PRAYER:
O God, You created space and place for all Your creation. Hope us, I pray, to eliminate our tendencies to isolate. May we share our concerns for justice and equality with all who know the pain of injustice and inequality. AMEN.

1 Samuel 24

"When the Enemy is in Your Hand"

My dear friend, Reverend E. L. Branch, of Detroit, would probably ask us, "What do you do when God places your fiercest enemy in your hand?" It would be a query intended to examine our common responses. Yet, it would also be a set-up to challenge our most likely response. All of us have some preferred response when we gain advantage over our enemy, but is that response the right one?

Previously noted, a significant part of David's life was spent as a fugitive. Before he ever sat in the office of king, he lived on the run from the deadly schemes of Saul. In the text for today, David had come to rest in the stronghold of Ein Gedi. This was a place where David was safe and his forces strengthened. Saul, in pursuit of David, happened upon this place. Saul goes into the place to relieve himself, unbeknownst of David's presence. While Saul was in a vulnerable state, David's men encouraged David to kill him. David declined. Instead, he took his knife and cut a piece of Saul's garment.

David could have killed Saul and ended his fugitive lifestyle. He believed so strongly in God's justice that he did not see executing Saul as his assignment. Furthermore, he believed in his own sense of righteousness that he chose not to mar his sense of judgment by killing his enemy. David's actions moved Saul to remorse, and he conceded the righteousness of David's claim to be king.

America has long put forth the propaganda of being just and righteous. However, America's history with her perceived enemies contradicts such claims. We are not a nation given to kindness toward our perceived enemies. In fact, we are the only country to have dropped a nuclear weapon upon a highly populated area. We are not gracious toward our enemies. As a result, we have created a culture of violent vindictiveness.

When Jesus forgives his enemies, the shadow of David hovers over Calvary. The reality of enemies is real. We do have enemies to justice and righteousness. Oppressed people are unjustly isolated and made to live lives of quiet desperation, much of which is designed by people in positions of power and influence. What will our actions be when the enemies of justice are at our disposal? Will we pursue the common responses? Or, will we do that which most identifies us with Jesus? Killing all of our enemies will not make us any safer.

PRAYER:
Merciful God, who extends Your mercy even to Your enemies, extend to us a listening ear. Hope us, I pray, to be conduits of mercy rather than agents of vengeance. May Your justice serve as the measure of all justice. AMEN.

1 Samuel 25

"Abigail's Wisdom"

I borrow again from the wisdom of my dear friend, Edward L. Branch, of Detroit. E. L. Branch recently sermonically reflected upon this text and spoke of the "Voice of Reason." The voice of reason represents the presence of wisdom so decisive that it prevents calamitous possibilities. The potential for calamitous missteps looms large for those who engage in prophetic engagement. In our quest for a more just society, we can slip into behaviors that are shaped by self-righteousness. In the name of all that is good and just, we can easily become "accidental Pharisees."

This chapter opens with the voice of the prophet Samuel being silenced by death. His death is mourned and lamented by the masses. The text moves quickly from the gravesite of the prophet into a Davidic episode of perceived injustice. The presence of David had apparently discouraged acts of injustice and exploitation from being carried out in the region of Carmel. An obviously rich man had benefitted from David's presence, but refused to extend hospitality to David and his men. David's request for assistance was denied, and his person was severely disrespected. As a response to the harsh and insensitive rebuke, David prepared to inflict his own sense of judgment upon the person and property of Nabal. David chose a violent response.

As David rode into Carmel to dispatch his own brand of justice, Nabal's wife, Abigail, intervened and saved David from embarrassing himself. Abigail became the voice of reason, or the prophetic voice, that stemmed the tide of David's wrath. The voice of reason came from an unlikely source, a woman, who was also the wife of a perceived enemy. When the prophet died, God's prophetic intent for justice was articulated in a woman.

Issues of injustice are not always the product of clever design. Some acts of injustice are ignorantly dispatched. There are people of possessions and power who ignorantly act unjustly and perpetuate self-defeating realities. We need to be careful that we don't waste valuable social capital fighting battles with foes we do better to leave to their own devices. Moreover, we should be vigilant in giving ear to unlikely allies who potentially can be for us "voices of reason." We do well to reconsider who we might listen to, or we might find ourselves inflicting ourselves with unnecessary wounds.

How have you responded to social and political slights? Has anyone unexpectedly provided you with words of wisdom? What was your response?

PRAYER:
O God, You Who created a world primed for justice and prepped for equality for all, we honor You. Yet, we know that our efforts to advocate for justice can be blinded by self-driven motives and concerns. Hope us, I pray, to be sensitive to whomever You might send as the voice of reason for those moments when our better judgment is adrift. AMEN.

1 Samuel 26

"Valuing Life"

The driving force behind any and every act of social justice is the value of life. When life is held in high regard, justice is inevitable. There is a strong correlation between our estimate of life and our capacity to be a just community. Conversely, where there is a low estimate of life, injustice prevails and dehumanization becomes normative.

The love-hate relationship between Saul and David shapes the pages of 1 Samuel. There is a near comedic cycle of Saul pursuing David and David having opportunity to kill Saul, but he relents and spares Saul's life. David, again, seizes some symbol of his advantage and uses it to illustrate to Saul how easily he could have killed him if that was his intent.

In chapter 26, again, one of David's men sought permission to kill Saul and David would not allow it. David secured Saul's spear and water jug as evidence of Saul's vulnerability. David claimed that he would not kill Saul because he perceived value in Saul's life, and blamed Saul's guard, Abner, for failing to adequately protect him. His appeal to Saul was that Saul would value his life as he valued Saul's. Saul cried out in remorse and the narrator states in chapter 27 that "He sought him no more."

An obvious symptom of societal injustice is the loss of respect for human life. The senseless killing in urban streets represents a daily reminder of America's continued loss of respect for black life. It's easy for us to blame the young individuals who perpetuate the violence, but what about the systems that set the stage for violent reactions? Perhaps some Abner-like forces are in play that are leaving young men vulnerable to the forces of senseless violence. Any strategy to stem the tide of violence within our communities must include a heightened value for life.

How do you relate justice to the value for life? What are the primary examples of a lack of value for life within your community? What ministry response has developed as a result of it?

PRAYER:
O God, Who anoints all life with sacred value, we give You thanks. Hope us, I pray, to value all life, especially the lives of people cheapened by unjust social arrangements. May we view in others the value we want others to see in us. AMEN.

1 Samuel 28

"No Prophets, No Strength"

The political tendency to push the prophetic to the sidelines is eerily common. America's longstanding belief in the separation of church and state has done much to mute the voice of prophetic intent. It has become a unique challenge in America to honestly serve God, prophetically critique society, and remain in compliance with governmental regulations. Yet no social construct should ever mute those whose voices speak for justice.

Samuel 28 provides a sad commentary on a nation that mutes its prophets. Saul's incessant actions to maintain authority in a kingdom he no longer possessed heightened the anxiety about the presence of the prophetic. It appears that Saul had set policy laws that banned the prophetic (verse 3). However, when his kingdom was severely threatened by the Philistines, he reconsidered his anti-prophet ban. His need for prophetic intervention caused him to become desperate. So he sought out assistance from a witch, or a prophetess. Of note is the fact that he specified prophetic inquiry from a woman (verse 7), who discerned his deceit and designs.

Religion in America has often been a tool to accommodate oppressive policies and practices. I have witnessed the presidents of my life call upon certain noted preachers whenever the country faced a serious crisis, or some major decision needed to be made. The preachers often summoned are those who will not challenge the presidential position, or offer an alternative approach. Popular preachers, who are connected to the oppressive political machinery, are sought to give religious sanction to oppressive decisions. Meanwhile, the few prophets who could provide compassionate perspective are avoided and ignored.

Do you have a prophetic person in your life? How do you deal with serious and challenging issues? Is it important to have someone to agree with your decisions, or challenge your decisions?

PRAYER:
O God, Who sends forth prophets as reminders of what is good and just, restore us to Your righteous way. Hope us, I pray, to be strengthened by truth-tellers and not placated by fortune-tellers. AMEN.

THE FOURTEEN STATIONS OF THE CROSS

The Fourteen Stations of the Cross represent the Christian equivalent of Judaism's 42 Stations of the Exodus. It should be noted that numerically, the number 14 multiplied by 3 equals 42, a clear numerical connection with the Exodus experience. As the drama of the Exodus defines the liberating epicenter of the Jewish faith pilgrimage, the drama of the Cross defines the liberating epicenter of the Christian faith.

The Baptist tradition, from which I was shaped and formed, does not acknowledge or celebrate the Fourteen Stations of the Cross. Interestingly, neither of the Protestant seminaries that I attended lifted them up for academic consideration. Yet, I find the drama of the Fourteen Stations intriguing fodder for prophetic consideration. Out of the fourteen traditional Stations of the Cross, only eight have clear scriptural foundation.

I adventure now into this traditionally foreign liturgical territory with an eye for prophetic and meditative relevance.

Mark 15:1-15, Matthew 27:23-31

THE FIRST STATION:
"Getting Away with Murder"

Oppression and oppressive constructs exists because people are able to get away with it. Somehow, the convoluted constructs of power provide outlets where evil people can be absolved of responsibility for wicked deeds. A serious challenge for those who engage in prophetic ministry is the reality of people getting away with murder.

After years of reading this text, I'm still bothered by its blatant injustice. The narrative is clear. We are told of an obviously innocent man being subjected to an unjust legal system. The charges are obviously trumped up. The text says, "The chief priests accused him of many things," while the magistrate, Pilate, could see he was guilty of nothing. The animosity toward Jesus was so great that the community leaders made the release of a known murderer more acceptable than the release of an innocent man. Barabbas gets away with murder. Pilate washes his hands of the blood of an innocent man. The chief priests hide behind an oppressive practice of Rome and use it to kill an innocent man. Jesus's only words in the entire proceeding are, "You have said so." The story provides a medley of injustices where everybody, including the riotous crowd, gets away with murder.

As I write these lines, a governor, a utility company, a mayor, and a complex array of supposedly responsible people are getting away with murder. The murder will not be immediate, or sudden, like police shootings of unarmed black men and women. The murder will be slower, more gradual, far more expensive, and more difficult to bear. I speak of the Flint, Michigan water crisis, where a whole city has been lead poisoned. A financially motivated decision was made to deprive poor and black people access to clean water in favor of lead-poisoned water. To date, the most serious response to this decision has been to demand the resignations of politicians. I hold that even if the governor does resign, he lives on having gotten away with murder.

What are the situations in your community where systemic evil provides people outlets to get away with murder? How are you reacting to the fact that people in your community get away with murder?

PRAYER:
O God, You Who give life and call us to be stewards of the resources of life, hope us, I pray, to not be complicit in murderous behavior. May we be courageous, to challenge those forces that make it possible for people to get away with murder. AMEN.

John 19:13-17, John 19:5

THE SECOND STATION:
"Cross Bearing"

There are some things we do, not because we want to. We do them because we have to. In fact, not many things would get done if everything were done based upon our personal preferences. In particular, there are some expressions of evil that would never be confronted if not imposed upon us. Cross bearing represents the inevitable assumption of that which is imposed upon us. We assume it because we have to.

There is something deeply disturbing about the text used for the Second Station of the Cross. Pilate presents a whipped and humiliated Jesus, bloodied and clothed in garments of jest, as a man (verse 5). In verse 14, he shifts and presents him as "King of the Jews." The chief priests, as representative of the Jews declare, "We have no king but Caesar!" This was such painful irony for an oppressed people to hate one who loved them most, while claiming to reverence one who openly loathed them. The Cross Jesus carried was the burdensome and painful realization that what he was doing was not appreciated by who he was doing it for. His people would rather claim loyalty to their oppressor than embrace the one who sought to free them.

I am not sure that we who claim the Christian faith understand cross bearing. I believe the Cross has been reduced from the painful assumption of oppressive impositions to the pious denial of personal privileges. Cross bearing has lost its meaning to changing the way we live in the world, even at the risk of death, to accepting some frivolous personal flaw that we must live with. To know that we must love and serve people who insist on voting against their best interest is a burdensome load.

What does bearing the Cross mean to you? How are you bearing a cross? And what difference is it making?

PRAYER:
O God, You Who call us to service in pain-filled contexts, hope us, I pray, to obediently assume the painful realities that are brutally imposed upon us. May our faith in You hold us up in a world designed to crush us down. AMEN.

Isaiah 53:4-7; Matthew 11:28-30

THE THIRD STATION:
"The Weight of It All"

While cross bearing represents the inevitable assumption of that which is imposed upon us, it is no less burdensome. The overwhelming weightiness of cross bearing comes freighted with grief and pain. There is a painful weightiness that comes with prophetic engagement.

Isaiah's depiction of the suffering servant has long been used to scripturally color redemptive suffering. It reads like a communal testimony that details a Messiah-like figure who endures great suffering on the community's behalf. The redeemed community liturgically embraces the fact that for them to be where they are, someone endured great suffering.

Matthew puts on the lips of Jesus an invitation to all who are being grievously overburdened to embrace his yoke. It appears that the everyday transactions of life, compounded with Roman oppression, have made life unbearable. Jesus's invitation opens up a redemptive approach to countering life's grievous burden. He not only shares the grievous burden but provides considerable relief from the burdensome exigencies.

Today I observed a brother whose physical appearance was astoundingly burdensome. His frame was stooped and the painful toll of life showed up in his face. The loss of an eye accentuated the painful and grievous journey that had marred his life. Life, for him, had been burdensome. His resultant appearance provided evidence that his responses gave in to the weight of it all. He represented a significant part of the African American community who has given in to the weight of it all. Zora Neale Hurston once described a broken procession and beaten African Americans as being "ugly with ignorance and broken by poverty."

What does burdensome oppression look like to you? Are there signs of any who join in with those who are being crushed by the weight of it all? How do you respond to burdensome oppression?

PRAYER:
O God, You Who join with us in the burdensome experiences of life, hope us, I pray, to locate opportunities to participate in suffering that redeem us from the weight of it all. AMEN.

John 19:25-27

THE FOURTH STATION:
"Ministry in a Disaster Zone"

A common response to an experience with death and dying is a view of one's life flashing before one's eyes. Prophetic intrigue functions within life and death situations. It is within life and death situations where the prophetic engages in ministry. Prophetic ministry seeks to create life where death ought to be.

The Fourth Station of the Cross is one where Jesus is actually on the Cross. Within the experience of crucifixion, John provided the witness to Jesus seeing his mother and a beloved disciple. Jesus's response was to divert their attention from him and direct his mother's attention to the disciple and the disciple's attention to his mother. In essence, he diverted their attention from death and directed their attention to life.

Jesus's mother symbolized the womb of communal nurture, and the beloved disciple represented a creative future. In the midst of death, Jesus directed his followers to engage in creative ministry. The Bible says, "And from that very hour that disciple took her to his own home."

An imperative within our communities is to shift our gaze from the gory scenes of death and despair to the possibilities of a creative future. As long as we are fixated on the tragic consequences of oppression, we miss out on the possibilities of new life. New life is the creative result of responsible nurture and hopeful anticipation. Prophetic engagement bears the responsibility of creating hopeful opportunities of ministry within the disaster zones of oppression.

What expressions of death rivet the attention of your community? What opportunities for life and a future are present? How are you responding to ministry in the midst of a disaster zone?

PRAYER:
O God, You Who call us to love beyond the tragic consequences of sinful oppression, hope us, I pray, to direct our view away from death toward the creative possibilities of new life. AMEN.

Mark 15:21

THE FIFTH STATION:
"Compelled to Bear a Cross"

We all need help with something. There are some things in life that we cannot achieve with just our own strength. This is never more true than when it refers to the prophetic burden. Cross bearing represents the primary symbol of the prophetic burden. During our most challenging moments, painful burdens can be eased by those who are compelled to bear a cross.

The Markan account of the Passion of Jesus includes a powerful scene of a Cyrenian, a black man, being compelled to carry the Cross of Jesus. He is noted as a father, a named person, an accomplished and stable man, but he, too, was subject to the arbitrary whims of the Roman oppressor. As Simon made his way from the rural setting of his household, he was brutally forced to participate in the popular and defining punishment of those who threatened the realm of Roman rule. With no regard for his intended business in Jerusalem, the soldiers made him an unwilling accessory to state-sanctioned murder.

As scene after scene of police brutality is being recorded by the phones of ordinary citizens, we have become witnesses of men and women participating in state-sanctioned brutality and murder. Every time an officer is not charged for obvious acts of brutality, we share in the cross bearing of those victimized by violence. Just as Mark included the story of Simon, we have become innocent bystanders compelled to participate in the popular and defining punishment of those who threaten the realm. Prophetic engagement joins the procession of those who are compelled to bear a cross.

What are your feelings about Simon being compelled to bear a cross? Are there painful experiences within your community which people are being compelled to participate in? Name a few. What are your thoughts on the continuing drama of unarmed black men killed by police?

PRAYER:
O God, You Who don't stay safe on the sidelines of injustice, hope us, I pray, to live life, not avoiding painful realities. May we be available witnesses to the many painful injustices within our community and world. AMEN.

John 14:9, Matthew 25:40

THE SIXTH STATION:
"Done Unto"

My late homiletics teacher and doctoral mentor, Dr. Samuel Dewitt Proctor, used to assert that there were two kinds of people in the world: those who do and those who are done unto. In spite of my unshakeable admiration and respect for Dr. Proctor, I thought it a kind of narrow and limited perspective at best, and crude and cruel at worst. I know that he was seeking to encourage us to do all we could to make the best out of life, or we risk being victims to those who selfishly exploit all they can out of life. Yet, while the limitations of Proctor's assertion struck me as somewhat extreme, our faith testifies that Jesus, like so many who live among the exploited and oppressed, was done unto.

The Johannine text refers to a moment when Jesus was dismayed that not even those closest to him fully knew him. All that he had done had not been sufficient to reveal to them his relatedness to God. The Matthean text, however, speaks to Jesus's relatedness to the least of these. The good, or the lack of good, that the disciples did toward the hungry, thirsty, naked, sick, and imprisoned, were deeds done unto him, or not done unto him. Jesus identified with God the Father, but also identified with those who lived at risk of being ignored or forgotten. Faithful and discerning discipleship was a combination of seeing God in the lives of the least, last, lost, and left behind. This Station of the Cross reminds us that the One who did was also done unto.

I am not always sure that I adequately make the connection between discerning an awesome God in the awful positions of marginalized people. Admittedly, I struggle to interface my discernment with God's majesty and my deeds, or lack of deeds, with ministry to God's son. Yet, as I write these lines, I sense that my predilections toward helping the least, last, lost, and left behind comes from identifying them as people God loves. When we love people God loves, we love them where God loves them, and where God loves them is not always in desirable situations. Sometimes we are called to do unto those who are done unto.

What are your thoughts on those who do and those who are done unto? How do you normally respond to those who have clearly been done unto?

PRAYER:
O God, You Who do all You can to demonstrate Your love and concern, hope us, I pray, to be diligent in doing what we can to increase Your love and concern to those who are done unto. AMEN.

Hebrews 4:15, Isaiah 63:9

THE SEVENTH STATION:
"The Second Fall"

The Doctrine of the Fall has been a pillar in evangelical thought. I cut my theological teeth on the belief that we were created on one plateau of God-human relatedness, but through the sins of one man we descended to a lower plateau of God-human relatedness. Likewise, the near bestial tendencies exhibited in human behavior have been viewed through the theological lens of "the Fall."

The Seventh Station of the Cross depicts Jesus falling for the second time. The Second Fall underscores the intensity by which Jesus identified with us. Hebrews captures him as a high priest who "sympathized with our weakness," but he did not participate with us in our weakness. He stumbled with us, but did not stumble like us. Likewise, Isaiah is referred to as a means of connecting the redeeming work of God to the plight of fallen people. God used Jesus as an example of God's willingness to experience a second fall in order to lift us up.

I want to make a confession. I confess that I am not always comfortable with Jesus having to suffer so that we might recover our God-connecting sense. The Jesus-suffering-for-us theology gets us too cleanly off the hook. I embrace grace, but there has to be a way in which we assume some responsibility for our own behavior. Do people who do evil against other people get off the hook so cleanly? Does the redeeming work of Jesus relieve the oppressor of all responsibility? And what responsibility does the oppressed have for the experience of oppression? Perhaps our descent is so great that redemption demands a second fall.

What are your thoughts on the Fall? Do you believe the redeeming work of Jesus absolves the sinner of all responsibility?

PRAYER:
O God, Your redeeming work is not always crystal clear. There are questions that we have about the efficacy of the "proclaimed" work of Jesus. Hope us, I pray, to seek clarity in our thoughts about all that You did, and even what You did not do, to effect our redemption. AMEN.

Luke 23:27-31

THE EIGHTH STATION:
"Redirected Grief"

Largely missed in most acts of violence is the trauma inflicted upon the host community, particularly among the historically marginalized. People who are victims of violence are part of a community that is emotionally connected in joy and in suffering. However, when violence comes as response to prophetic engagement, our tendency is to focus our lament exclusively upon the stated victims. The greater loss that should be lamented is the community that suffers not only the loss of lives, but the loss of justice and equality. Prophetic engagement must redirect the grief of a traumatized community.

The Eighth Station of the Cross directs the drama to the anguished suffering of the witnessing crowd. The women who witnessed the gory and horrific scene of Jesus's painful walk through the streets of Jerusalem broke out in communal lament. The text suggests that they were weeping for Jesus. Their collective pain was for the one who was suffering the humiliating agony of another Roman crucifixion. However, Jesus's response was for the women to redirect their grief to the losses their children would suffer as a result of the apparent injustice being manifested in his crucifixion. As long as the Jews were subjected to the painful injustices of Roman oppression, the wellbeing of the children was at risk.

Nothing brings me such anguish as the painful looks of children who have to look upon the draped bodies of homicide victims, or attend funerals where the drama of grief is conspicuously displayed. All of our heroic efforts to stop the senseless killings among young black men mean nothing when children have to internalize repetitive experiences of trauma drama. While the community weeps for the deceased, I believe that our grief should be directed toward the children. Redirecting our grief could potentially mobilize us toward more creative responses to the root causes of our trauma. Directing our lament to those who are most vulnerable provides us a different lens through which to respond to our collective pain.

What brings your community the most grief? How does your community respond? What consideration is given to the children of the traumatized community?

PRAYER:
O God, You Who created us with capacity to feel deeply the pain of apparent injustices, hope us, I pray, to consider redirecting our grief toward the most vulnerable in our community – our children. AMEN.

Luke 22:28-32

THE NINTH STATION:
"Propping Up Your Faith"

Our estimation of ourselves, or our own strength and dedication, must never be presumed. We are all susceptible to over assessing ourselves, and such over assessments can lead to spiritual and emotional letdowns. The formidable and unpredictable proponents of oppression can prove challenging to the best of us. Prophetic engagement demands that our faith is propped up with the assurance of a caring and competent resource.

The Ninth Station is identified as Jesus Falling for the Third Time. While the text does not depict Jesus as falling, it does point out the potential for falling in those who follow him. While the heated dispute over who would be the greatest (verses 24-27) cooled down, Jesus used the aftermath of the experience to commend and encourage. He commended the disciples for sharing with him in his trials, and encouraged them to continue to do so. However, the prayerful concern for the one who followed him the closest was passionately interjected. Jesus informed Peter that he was praying for his inevitable fall and failure. Yet, Peter's fall and failure would be used to prop up the faith of the other disciples.

Perhaps the church's identification of the Ninth Station as Jesus Falling is creatively instructive. As followers of Jesus, we seek to represent him in all that we do and say. Yet, when we fall, Jesus takes a hit. Our falls and failures represent opportunities for Jesus to intervene in ways that empower us to strengthen our brothers and sisters. We must guard against becoming so self-obsessed that we miss out on using the experiences of falls and failures as spiritual props for the faith of others. What we go through as followers of Jesus prophetically aligns us to be conduits of strength.

In what ways have you experienced failure when in the act of faithfully following Jesus? How have you used your falls and failures to help others who are trying to follow Jesus?

PRAYER:
O God, You Who call us into the perilous journey of following Jesus, hope us, I pray, to not presume, or overestimate ourselves. May we consider You as an ever present resource of strength. Thank You for a Savior who intercedes on our behalf. AMEN.

John 19:23-24

THE TENTH STATION:
"Gambling on Seamless Garments"

There are some things that are of no use being ripped apart. The usefulness such realities potentially possess depends upon them remaining intact. For instance, the concept of justice is not good ripped apart. The concept of justice is only viable when pledged as "one nation, under God, indivisible, and justice for all." However, the constant and contentious wrangling on what it means to be America essentially represents partisan efforts to gamble on what is best when remaining intact. Prophetic engagement challenges the divisive gambles on justice and equality for some, but not for all.

The Tenth Station of the Cross represents the brutal act of Jesus's crucifixion. Interestingly, there is more scriptural detail given for the activities surrounding the crucifixion than the crucifixion itself, particularly the humiliating activities of being stripped naked and publically humiliated. The soldiers, the brute representatives of Roman oppressions, execute the crucifixion and parlay the spoils of his four-part garment. However, the tunic is noted as being seamless. Therefore, they "cast lots for it." We are not given the conclusion of the gamble, nor the name of the soldier who won. We are provided with a commentary that Scripture might be fulfilled.

A dangerous game played by oppressors is gambling with the seamless. History reveals that America has a painful legacy of gambling with the seamless concept of liberty and justice for all. While the primary proponents of oppression may lurk behind the scenes, their brute representatives boldly and callously execute their diabolical plans. The injustices historically inflicted upon African Americans have too often left us emotionally naked and psychologically humiliated. It is the responsibility of the prophetic to be attentive to the seamless garment of democracy so that all people will be beneficiaries of the American contract of freedom. Without prophetic engagement, we risk a nation being ripped apart by its own foolhardy gambling with seamless garments.

Can you name other democratic realities that are being ripped apart? What is your response to the senseless gambles upon the seamless fabric of our democracy?

PRAYER:
O God, You Who created us of one blood and one nation, we honor You as the God of one humanity. Hope us, I pray, to be attentive to the violent and brutal ripping of the seamless fabric of our democracy and humanity. May we be more sensitive to all that makes us one blood and one nation. AMEN.

Luke 23:39-43

THE ELEVENTH STATION:
"Not A Minute Too Soon"

Urgency pushes decisiveness. We do not have the luxury to procrastinate or obfuscate when immersed in matters of urgent concern. Unfortunately, we do not consider matters urgent until our economic wellbeing is being threatened, or life is at risk. The normal pace of life rarely pushes us to be decisive. Prophetic engagement sensitizes us to the urgent and calls us to action not a minute too soon.

The Eleventh Station of the Cross is a scene of urgency that provoked different responses. As three alleged criminals are being executed for crimes detrimental to national security, one of the executed turns upon one of his assumed fellows-in-crime. His conversation indicates that he knew "something" about Jesus's allegations and used them to callously deride him. He basically challenged him to use the power of what he'd been accused of to save himself. His words provoked a response from one of the other criminals rebuking him for such callous and insensitive utterances. After rebuking his partner in crime, this man turned to Jesus and asked to be included in the world-altering reality that Jesus had promoted. Jesus's response was to assure him that he would be included in the experience of the Kingdom, and it would commence at that moment. "Today you will be with me in Paradise."

I am always intrigued with the varied responses provoked by obvious experiences of oppression. Inevitably, significant numbers of people are desensitized when the painful realities of oppression are placed before them. Large swaths of oppressed people lack the capacity to empathize, even in shared experiences of obvious oppression. Also, there are those who do empathize, but misinterpret what's going on. Prophetic engagement calls us to use what the late Dr. Martin Luther King, Jr. called the "urgency of now." Now is the time when oppressive constructs are to be dismantled and liberating realities constructed. Now is the time to use the current moment to shape what we need, using what we have, to move us toward where we need to go.

What has been your default response to high-pressured experiences? Has urgency pushed you to do what is right, or do what is easy? How so?

PRAYER:
O God, You Who accompany us in the torrid haste of urgency, focus our minds and hearts on the creative urgency of now. Hope us, I pray, to not waste this day in callous and insensitive utterances. May the words we speak prod us to use this day constructing paradise out of painful circumstances and new beginnings from deadly situations. AMEN.

John 19:28-37, Matthew 27:50

THE TWELFTH STATION:
Purposeful Pain

None of us enjoy pain. Yet, pain occupies significant space on the landscape of our lives and unfortunately defines much of who we are. None of us are privileged to live pain-free lives. Among the oppressed, we know that oppression is painful. Racism is painful. Sexism is painful. As I walk into the senior years of life, I am daily made aware that growing old is painful, thus, ageism is painful. The challenge of the prophetic is to discover purpose in our pain. How does pain usher us into meaningful living?

The Twelfth Station of the Cross serves as a kind of redemptive climax to the painful drama of Jesus's crucifixion. It is not the end, but it registers the completion of the agonizing experience. Three words are used to capture one. The Greek word used for "It is finished" is "telos," which denotes purpose. In the midst of excruciating pain, Jesus closed this episode by declaring purpose. His pain had purpose and so did his death. Most Christians believe that he fulfilled his life purpose by using the Cross as a means of redemption. What was designed to humiliate and intimidate has become the focal point of what we celebrate. Paul would later write, "For the message of the cross is foolishness to those who are perishing, but to us who are being saved it is the power of God."

In 1969, a prison escape plan was devised for the late African nationalist, Nelson Mandela. The plan was abandoned because it was discovered to be a plot that would have had Mandela shot during the escape. Mandela would serve 27 years for crimes of government sedition, but would be released and become the President of South Africa, a once brutal regime of apartheid. The painful and dehumanizing prison experience has become the defining experience in the life and legacy of not only Mandela, but of the redemption of South Africa. All persons who aspire to freedom from oppressive regimes and realities look to Nelson Mandela for hope and inspiration.

Who do you look to for inspiration during painful experiences? Have you been able to find purpose in the painful experiences of your life?

PRAYER:
O God, You Who use painful experiences to work out Your purposes of justice and equality for all, hope us, I pray, to not shrink from painful experiences, but to use them as resources for redemptive purposes. AMEN.

John 19:38-40

THIRTEENTH STATION:
"Undercover Discipleship"

People are not always forthright in what they believe, or open in who they support. Too many have found it easier to function through clandestine operations. While such allies might render invaluable support, we are not always sure how much they can be trusted, or how genuine their support. How we include, or recognize, covert supporters remains a challenge to all who are on the frontlines of prophetic activity.

The Thirteenth Station of the Cross invites us to consider one of the Bible's most intriguing episodes. Two prominent men within the Jewish society make covert arrangements to secure and prepare for the burial of the body of Jesus. While the names of both are provided, both men are identified as persons who connected to Jesus in covert ways. One, Joseph of Arimathea, a "secret disciple," used governmental influence to secure Jesus's body. The other, Nicodemus, "came to Jesus by night" and made resources available to prepare his body for burial. It seems they collaborated to obtain a "new tomb" in which to lay his body. Of interest is the fact that their ministry efforts are death-focused and not life supportive.

I think it important to note that there is nothing necessarily nefarious about using influence and resources to support Christian ministry. What weakens such engagement, however, is one's unwillingness to be public in ministry efforts that call for public engagement. While we need Christians who can navigate governmental apparatus, as well as those who have resources, what is most needed are people who publically take risks to advance ministry that affects life and living. Undercover discipleship risks being on the prophetic edge when it shows up only to accommodate funeral proceedings.

There are people in my city who make themselves known only when death has violently impacted the community. They challenge city hall and contribute to the funeral needs of victims of violence, but where are they during the normal intercourses of life? Prophetic engagement must guard against allowing undercover discipleship to become normative.

When are you most useful to ministry? Who are the undercover disciples within your community? What might be done to pull them into more public engagement?

PRAYER:
O God, You Who make Yourself known in the world, hope us, I pray, to be more forthright in how we represent You in the world. May what we do for You do more to encourage life and not just accommodate death. AMEN.

Mark 15:46-47

FOURTEENTH STATION:
"Borrowing Tombs"

As observed in yesterday's reflection: people are not always forthright in what they believe and in who they support. Many wait until things have been settled before stepping up and registering their support. Unfortunately, when issues have been settled, it is too late to make a measurable difference. When controversial issues are assumed to have been settled, the best we can do is dress things up and lay them in borrowed tombs. Progressive prophetic engagement never functions post-mortem. Prophetic engagement pursues an agenda of life, and not one of death.

The Fourteenth, and final Station of the Cross continues the covert activity of burying Jesus. In Mark's story, only Joseph of Arimathea was involved. He recovered the confirmed dead body of Jesus and proceeded to prepare it meticulously and expensively. He wrapped Jesus's body in recently purchased expensive "fine linen." Once the wrapping process was completed, he then "laid him in a tomb," which is assumed to be the property of Joseph. The narrator makes a life-hinting observation that the entire proceedings were carefully observed by two women who had been faithful followers of Jesus. The presence of the women indicated that the tomb would not be final, for it was borrowed.

Nothing frustrates a movement more than post-mortem support. The glowing admiration that the nation now has for the late Dr. Martin Luther King, Jr., highlighted in the erection of a national monument in Washington, D.C., clearly amounts to a borrowed tomb. Where was all this support when Dr. King lived and fought for human rights, as well as for economic justice? Who in the nation's capitol dared to encourage King's denouncement of the Vietnam War, which the Vietnamese correctly label as the American War to resist colonization? The King Monument is a political Joseph of Arimathean construct that meticulously and expensively enshrouds the ministry of Martin Luther, King, Jr. in a borrowed tomb. I wonder if there are present any faithful proponents of justice who visit the monument and see hope beyond King's entombment?

What are your thoughts about the King Monument? Are there other moments and prophetic personalities who have been enshrouded in borrowed tombs? How do we move faith beyond tombs?

PRAYER:
O God, You Who call us to choose life over death, hope us, I pray, to be vigilant in the long struggle for justice. May we not be distracted by the meticulous and expensive entombments of those who come late to the struggle. AMEN.

1 King 1

"A Game of Thrones"

I have been intrigued by the HBO series, "A Game of Thrones." The intrigue of the series is the endless and maddening display of power, scheme, and subterfuge for power. I am weekly surprised by the vicious outbursts of those who will do anything to hold on to their version of power and control of a vast and largely unmanageable kingdom. The presence of magic, dragons, old gods and new gods, along with the prodding presence of the walking dead, make mockery of any divinely inspired sense of justice. In the Game of Thrones, the just and unjust are eternally imperiled.

1 Kings opens up with the drama of a game of thrones. David has become old and nonresponsive to governmental responsibilities. One of his sons, Adonijah, acts compulsively to assume the throne for himself and provokes a governmental crisis. The priest and prophet are not consulted, and the prophet intervenes. The prophet's intervention constitutes a plan to establish Solomon as king. David authorizes the establishment of Solomon as king, consequently, dethroning Adonijah. Thus we are introduced to the opening stages of the biblical version of a game of thrones, where the lives of all aspirants are imperiled.

Two things stand out in this biblical drama of the game of thrones: one, that Adonijah was able to assume kingly authority without the king's knowledge. The text notes, "David, our Lord, does not know it." David was so out of touch with the goings and comings of the kingdom that he not only did not know of Adonijah's intrusion upon the throne, but David had never done anything to discipline his son's compulsive tendencies. The other thing that stands out, which I believe the most egregious, is that there is no mention of Moses, Egypt, Exodus, or the Lord who brought them out of bondage. Lost in the game of thrones is the defining narrative for Israel's existence.

How can we expect justice when those responsible for dispatching justice are out of touch? Is there a correlation between undisciplined citizenry and compulsive leadership? The maddening realities of our world are clearly the result of a game of thrones, in which the prophetic narrative of justice and equality has been long forgotten. If there is no defining narrative of justice, we doom ourselves to the maddening drama of a game of thrones, where the plight of the most vulnerable is perpetually at risk.

What side of the game of thrones in American political drama are you? How does American leadership reveal how out of touch they are with American life? Whose lives are the most imperiled?

> **PRAYER:**
> *O God, You Who, in the words of our spiritual ancestors, "sit high on a throne and lifted up," hope us, I pray, to recover the narrative for justice, liberation, and equality. May we be empowered to use that narrative as prophetic critique of a world immersed in a game of thrones. AMEN.*

HOPE US, LORD!

1 Kings 3

"A Closer Look"

Not everything happening in the world fits into easy packages of religious suitability. There is much in the world that could easily offend our most treasured religious sensibilities. Yet, what offends our religious sensibilities does not exempt us from our prophetic responsibility. Our prophetic responsibility demands that we pay attention to the happenings of the world, without feeling the need to impose our religious assumptions, or promote our religious sensibilities.

1 Kings 3 opens up with a surprising move. The narrative of the Solomon kingship began with him forming alliances with Pharaoh. This is clearly not something we would expect from a people whose identity was shaped by deliverance from Pharaoh. Yet, it is biblically clear that the politics of Solomon included forming alliances with oppressive regimes. The narrative continues with two other interesting observations: Solomon prays for wisdom to execute justice, and then was made famous by a so-called act of justice experienced among the marginalized and exploited. The wisdom of Solomon is noted as becoming legend because he spared the life of a child he was set to cut in half.

Although Solomon's wisdom has been celebrated, a closer look at who is the recipient of his wisdom and how it was executed raises questions. How is it that two harlots, exploited women, are privileged to come before a king? What is truly just about using your power to cut in half a disposable child? The wisdom of Solomon should be viewed within its political and sociological context. There are many questions that could be raised about Solomon's wisdom before bestowing upon him sacred honor.

Although there are no prophetic engagements evident in the text, the text should prepare us for an obvious departure from the defining narrative of Hebrew faith. I consider chapter 3 because it provides us a prophetic lens by which to view what will follow. The world of Solomon began with radical departures from the justice-seeking community of Moses. Solomon's form of justice takes violent liberties with a community that has historically been exploited.

What are your views of the dynamics of this text? Is allying with our enemies a path to a just society? How can we be just to those who are historically exploited?

PRAYER:
O God of justice and righteousness, grant us eyes to see what we need to see rather than what we want to see. Hope us, I pray, to view with prophetic scrutiny even those we have been led to love and admire. AMEN.

1 Kings 4

"The Cost of Excess"

We look again at an expression of obvious injustice. Wherever anyone is living in excess, someone is being deprived. The opulence of one is usually because of the deficiency of many. There is no economic formula or theory that allows one to have excess, while at the same time no one is being deprived.

The ascendency to the throne by Solomon is marked with noted difference from that of David, his father. David's throne was marked with ruggedness, while Solomon's was marked with opulence. David fought. Solomon negotiated. David had enemies. Solomon had allies. David was loyal worshipper of Yaweh, alone. Solomon worshipped Yahweh, and other gods for political convenience. David was known as a warrior. Solomon was known as wise.

What really sets Solomon apart from David was his excess. 1 Kings 4, verses 20-23, notes that Solomon's daily rations were excessive. It is noted that his household consumed on a daily basis supplies adequate enough for an average size city. It is further noted that his excessive consumption was made possible by an elaborate taxing system (verses 27-28), clearly the result of a well-armed military (verse 26). Solomon's technology, military, and political savvy privileged him with a lifestyle of excess.

A recent candidate for the presidency of the United States, Mitt Romney, has a home with an elevator for his car. Very few homes in the United States have an elevator for anything. Anyone who can afford an elevator for his or her automobile lives in excess. The current president lives in a New York tower with gold plated toilets. If Solomon's excess was the result of oppressive exploitation, is it likely that anyone can live such a life as America's current president without oppressive exploitation?

What kind of leadership can we expect from someone who is living a life based upon the spoils of economic inequity? How do you think some live in such opulence while others linger in destitution?

PRAYER:
O God, Who created a world with more than enough, we offer You praise and thanksgiving. Our prayer, O God, is for just appetites that are not given to excess. Hope us, I pray, to understand the connection between our excesses and another's deprivation. AMEN.

I King 5 - 7

"The Religion of Excess"

An irony of life is that the assumed and promoted greatness of God historically has been used to camouflage greed and excess. When God is believed to be majestic and mighty, those attributes can give opportunity for egotistical narcissism and uninhibited consumption. What we think of God can be expressed in excess if we have the means and the manner of pulling it off. Yet, excess of any kind is the result of inequity every time. Someone always suffers when we bring our excesses to expression.

The excesses of Solomon's personal life segue into the excesses of his religious life. The excesses described in the building of his personal house are mirrored in the excesses described in building the temple. He includes the exploits of political allies and thousands of servants to complete the task. It is noted that he parlayed imported laborers through political pacts (5:10-12) and used forced labor (5:13-15). The use of slave and cheap labor intensified the excesses of personal consumption. He maintained his insatiable diets while overseeing a massive construction project that was sustained by oppressive labor practices. In the name of God, a magnificent structure was erected that served to give religious sanction to political oppression.

Throughout our nation are towering structures built in the name of God. Many of these structures have come at the cost of oppressive and exploitative means. I do not suggest that God is not worthy of our best. I believe we should give God our best. I am questioning whether the God who liberates us from oppressive social arrangements is honored through oppressive religious arrangements. Slavery by another name is still slavery. Exploitation to build a church or a ministry is still exploitation. The God who supplies daily bread is not honored by the deprivation of bread.

Is it possible that we can use God to project our insatiable appetites and compulsions? How so? Do our penchants for excess deprive those who God wants to bless?

PRAYER:
O God, how excellent is Your name. We proclaim that the earth is Yours and the fullness thereof, and Your concern for all who dwell therein. Hope us, I pray, to see Your concern for justice even in our places of worship. May we not use You as a tool for our excesses. AMEN.

1 Kings 9-10

"The Psychology of Excess"

The objectification of life opens the pathway to serious sociological and psychological distortions. When who we are is determined by what we accomplish and accumulate, we lose a significant part of who we really are. Jesus called a man on such a journey a fool, because accomplishments and accumulations summed up his total self-understanding.

When I read the accomplishments of Solomon, I am both impressed and troubled. I am impressed by how much he was able to accomplish and the psychological impact it must have had on Israel. His ability to establish peace allowed him to expand the influence of Israel, as he allied himself with the most powerful and influential leaders of his time. His commitment to build the Lord a house, as well as the kingly palace, placed him in an enviable position. The chapters unfold in rapid succession, each one highlighting more and more of Solomon's wealth, technology, military, academia, and economic policy. It's almost as if the narrator subconsciously connects the maddening pace of having and doing too much too fast. Solomon was a man on a mission to do more than anyone of his day. In fact, in chapter 10, verse 23, it is stated in Trumpian delusion, "So King Solomon surpassed all the kings of the earth in riches and wisdom."

However, I am troubled by Solomon's seemingly insatiable appetite for more and more because it drives him further and further away from the religion of Moses. Moses led a liberation campaign away from Egypt; Solomon negotiates an economic relationship with Egypt. Moses is profiled as a desert warrior, whereas Solomon is lost in the gluttony of wealth. It just seems that the psyche of excess has detached Solomon from the original vision of a covenant people, identified by justice and equity. Brueggemann even cites that "Solomon had a social vision contradictory to that of Moses." There can be no equity when the leadership is driven by excess.

When is enough enough? What more do you need when you have more than enough? The psychology of excess shapes a mental construct that distorts reality. What does it mean for a person to be noted as having "surpassed all the kings of the earth in riches and wisdom?"

PRAYER:
O God, You have been noted as the Owner of earth's silver and gold. We are humbled that You consider us as Your stewards, yet we confuse stewardship with ownership. Hope us, I pray, to protect ourselves from being distorted by the psychology of excess. May what we hold in stewardship be used to Your glory. AMEN.

1 King 11

"A Heart Turned Away"

It is commonly purported that where our mind goes, there goes our soul. The Bible, however, views life as being determined from the heart. "As a man thinks in his heart, so is he." "Out of the heart come the issues of life." We have been known to do well by changing our minds, but not so when our hearts are turned.

As swiftly as Solomon accomplished and accumulated, he just as quickly neutralized the impact of his success, what Elton Trueblood called "a holy conjunction" imposed itself into the narrative. "But King Solomon loved many foreign wives" served as an announcement that all was not well within the kingdom. In the midst of mind-boggling accomplishments and accumulations, there was a steady erosion of that which really mattered, a passionate sense of loyalty to Mosaic or Davidic faith. The narrator wants to blame Solomon's wives, but Solomon's wives would not be held responsible, because "his heart was not loyal to the Lord his God, as was the heart of his father David."

Solomon's behavior triggered the anger of the Lord and his lavish kingdom/empire construct was terminated. A broad contingency of enemies rose up and set their sights upon Israel. Ironically, the most exacting toll on the kingdom of Solomon came from within. Solomon's Secretary of Labor, Jeroboam, led a God-inspired rebellion against Solomon, consequently ripping apart the kingdom/empire from within. A prophet by the name of Ahijah framed Jeroboam's revolt as God's response to idolatrous behavior. Could it be that idolatrous behavior serves to shape exploitative labor practices, where human beings are objectified for the idols of excess? Noteworthy is that Jeroboam was given over 80% of the kingdom. This is an interesting analogy of our day when over 80% of the wealth is being controlled by less than 20% of the population.

The kingdoms/empires of excess are inherently susceptible to "holy conjunctions." It does not matter how mighty the military, extravagant the palace, or vast the surplus of the National Treasury, the idols of excess do not prevail. The rebellion of exploited labor can always terminate kingdoms/empires of excess. The anti-labor policies of our world are futile attempts to maintain the fleeting constructs of a kingdom of excess. Perhaps the missing ingredient in our fight for economic equality is prophetic framing. We need a voice to frame America's demise as God's response to idolatrous behavior.

What are some of the obvious signs of excess in our country? How are such signs being addressed? Where are the labor exploitations within your community? Who is enriched by them?

PRAYER:
O God, Who is ever aware of the constructs of our humanity, hear our prayer. Indeed, we are guilty of being silent as the machinery of excess runs amok. Hope us, I pray, to recover our prophetic voice that we might frame a redemptive reaction to the kingdoms of excess. AMEN.

1 Kings 12

"Bloody Scourges or Golden Calves"

We are the sum total of the choices we have made in life. It could be said that the choices we make end up making us. A closer look, however, reveals that there are some givens in our lives. Simply stated, there are some things that were given to us, of which we had no choice. For instance, my race, my skin color, my gender, my family, and my birthplace are givens. I had no choice in those matters. Yet, outside of my race, skin color, gender, and family a strong argument can be made that I am living out the fulfillment of my choices.

The 12th chapter of First Kings is a troubling read. It is troubling because it highlights how the choices of people in power can adversely affect healthy community life. Solomon's death led to Rehoboam, his son, becoming king. Rehoboam failed to listen to the people's concern about relieving the burden of oppression imposed by his father. Instead of listening to the wise counsel of the elders, Rehoboam chose to listen to the gratifying folly of his peers. He chose not to relieve the oppression, but to intensify it with scourges.

Jeroboam, who had the potential to do good, slipped into self-serving idolatry. He built idolatrous shrines of golden calves and induced the people to worship them. Those led by Rehoboam were grievously oppressed and those led by Jeroboam were offensively idolatrous. When the choices made by people in power were all bad, it imposed a culture of hopeless corruption. The only saving moment was Rehoboam receiving prophetic intervention from Shemaiah, who brought a word from the Lord.

Perhaps what we are witnessing in our world is the drama of a culture of bad choices. No sane American can claim that Donald Trump was a good choice as a president. Likewise there are those being oppressed by the collective choices of their own making, and others are bowing down to offensive idolatry. The choices between self-absorption and idolatrous prostrations are all bad. What do people do when all choices are bad choices? Is there a Shemaiah-presence who will call for a retreat from the idols of bad choices?

PRAYER:
O God, Who created us with the wondrous capacity to make choices, we offer You praise. However, we confess that we have not always made good of the gift of choice. Hope us, I pray, to hear the prophetic voice when the choices imposed upon us are all bad. Grant us an opportunity to retreat from the idols of our bad choice and make the one choice that matters, which is to serve You. AMEN.

HOPE US, LORD!

1 Kings 13

"Lions and Donkeys"

Inasmuch as we live out the fulfillment of our choices, we also live and die by what bears us and what tears us. On the one hand, God has provided us incredible resources to bear us and assist us in the fulfillment of our prophetic responsibilities. We have people in our lives who assist us in doing the tough things in ministry and life. On the other hand, there are forces and realities whose purpose and design is to tear us apart. Ironically, the forces that bear and tear are not always adversarial toward one another.

The leadership of Jeroboam was rife with idolatrous claims. He misled the people and justified it with religious pageantry. However, God sent an unnamed prophet to critique and condemn Jeroboam's idolatrous constructs. With keen prophetic incision, the prophet dismantled the offensive altars that symbolized Jeroboam's idolatrous claims. Jeroboam's response to arrest the prophet resulted in the shriveling of his hand, which the prophet compassionately consented to restore. When invited to Jeroboam's home, the prophet refused to eat at the king's table, and initially refused to eat at the table of a lying prophet. Interestingly when the prophet rode off on donkey, he was met by a lion, who mauled him to death. The narrator noted what was unusual, which was that at the site where the prophet lay dead stood both the donkey and the lion. All who passed by witnessed the body of the prophet and the unusual sight of the lion and donkey standing by.

My predecessor, Dr. Abraham Henry Newman, held to the prophetic stance that he would "rather eat bread and drink muddy water than eat sumptuously at the table of those who would oppress him." He held that position throughout his life and his 40-plus year tenure at the Bethlehem Missionary Baptist Church, Richmond, CA. Something needs to be said to those of us who rush to accommodate those who oppress us. It needs to be brought to our attention that there are forces in this world that will bear us and tear us. The prayers of the faithful will bear us, but the favors of the enemy will tear us. The witness of those who have gone before us will bear us, but the guile of the enemy will tear us. The God of our ancestors will bear us, but the idols of materialistic consumerism will tear us.

What position in prophetic ministry have you assumed? Are you willing to be humbly borne? Or, are you positioned to be regally torn?

PRAYER:
O God, You Who seek to use us to Your glory and honor, may Your truth be established. Hope us, I pray, to accept our humble task of declaring Your liberating truths. Deliver us from the forces that will tear us from our assignments and leave us as spectacles of public derision. AMEN.

1 Kings 15-16

"From Bad to Worse"

There are some choices we make that have generational consequences. When we decide that life is best lived a certain way, we set a precedent for future generations. The people who follow us will usually find a way to continue what we started, even if they don't fully understand why we did it the way we did it. Without a clear understanding of why an action was taken, the succeeding generations can turn a good activity into something bad, and a bad activity into something worse.

When Israel decided they wanted a king like the other countries, they set the course for succeeding generations. The biblical narrator is clear about framing the choice of a monarchy over a theocracy as a bad choice. As much as God is portrayed as being amenable to the choice, God's expectations were always set in tension with Israel's actions.

Chapters 15 and 16 move through the reign and rank of Israel's kings. From the southern kingdom to the northern kingdom, Israel and Judah, the practices of the kings are pictured as deteriorating from bad to worse. All the kings fail to rule according to the covenantal plans of God. Their rule and rank was considered "evil in the sight of the Lord." By the time we get to the King Ahab, the last king mentioned in chapter 16, we are told that he was more "evil than all who came before him." The idolatrous and exploitative practices of the choice to have a king moved from bad to worse.

I am not sure America has fully examined the legacy of its founding fathers. Both Washington and Jefferson were unrepentant slave owners, who set the course for the nation's continuing dilemma all the way to Donald Trump. While we elected and re-elected our first African American president, we have not divested ourselves from the continuing legacy of racially charged politics and policies. One need not know the history of our country to note the racial drama being daily played out in the script of white supremacy, sanctioned by religion and codified in political policies. The idolatry of racism has in so many ways gone from bad to worse.

What are our children being taught about the legacy of racial exploitation? Will America ever divest itself of the idols of white supremacy? What conversations exist within your community around America's original sin?

PRAYER:
O God, You Who have created us in Your image and likeness, with a will to shape our destiny, hope us, I pray, to truthfully examine the idolatrous legacies of our past choices. May we become faithful in divesting ourselves from any and every idolatrous choice and perception. AMEN.

1 Kings 17

"Prophetic Alternatives"

The work of the prophetic is always about alternatives. When social and political realities are seriously at odds with the wellbeing of all people, and only concerned with a select few, a prophetic shift is required. Alternatives to the stagnant realities of an oppressive status quo constitute the critical work of prophetic engagement. What we do in word and deed dramatizes alternative options to existing structures and policies, particularly those that demean and dehumanize the vulnerable masses.

Elijah's presence represents an abrupt intrusion into the protracted drama of royalty gone awry. In the first fifteen chapters of Kings 1, the drama of royalty is narrated, with all regimes being marked as provoking God to anger. It is assumed that the lavish lifestyle set by Solomon accompanied the drama of empire and evokes the prophetic announcement of drought. Elijah intrudes upon the lavish story of empire with drought realities. He personally survives, not from the purse of the empire, but by the surprising provisions of God. He is further sustained from the meager resources of the most vulnerable of the community, a widow and an orphan. The widow's son becomes gravely ill and Elijah intervenes and restores him to life.

All of what Elijah does is according to "the word of the Lord," and not from the mandates of the empire. In fact, empire lacks power to stop the economic crippling realities of drought. The life of Elijah, through a widow and an orphan, is sustained by alternative sources to empire.

This story speaks so powerfully to America's current economic realities. Contrary to any boasts of economic health, the truth is that many have not recovered from the economic downturn of '08, which was preceded by lavish living in the empire. Strangely, we are precariously situated to repeat the economic drought of that time because of a lack of a progressive economic alternative. The vulnerable in society remain at risk, even with the establishment of the beleaguered Affordable Health Care Act. We stand in need of a prophetic alternative.

What vision are we casting of economic parity? Can we remain silent while the lavishly rich keep getting lavishly richer, while the poor among us deteriorate into economic desperation?

PRAYER:
O God, Who created enough for all, speak to us of Your eternal concern for economic parity. Hope us, I pray, to disrupt the drama of empire with an alternative word from You. AMEN.

1 Kings 18:1-15

"Undercover Prophet"

God has an unusual way of positioning people for prophetic work. There are a lot of surprises in prophetic engagement, none more amazing than who God positions and where God positions them. We must never close our minds to who God will use as allies for prophetic engagement.

Chapter 18 represents the primary and pivotal text of the Elijah narratives. It brings Elijah into direct confrontation with Ahab. It is one of the Bible's most tense confrontations of the prophetic with the empire. Of note in this confrontation is the presence of a prophet, Obadiah, who doubled as the Chief of Staff to an established, evil, and exploitative king, Ahab. Obadiah is noted as a fierce believer in Yahweh, and had demonstrated his belief by using Ahab's vast resources to save the lives of 100 prophets. Although he worked in the empire, he subverted the power of the empire with prophetic ingenuity.

When Obadiah met Elijah, he bowed in humble respect. Obadiah knew the potential risks of allying with Elijah, yet he chose to assume the assignment of announcing to Ahab that, "Elijah is here." The announcement of Elijah's presence in the empire represented a serious disruption to empire. Elijah's presence was an open protest against the oppressive and exploitative policies and practices of empire. Obadiah took the risk and announced to Ahab, "Elijah is here."

The long night of oppression and exploitation creates heightened suspicion among the oppressed. A person of suspected alliances among African Americans has historically been referred to as an Uncle Tom. Clarence Thomas, the only African American Supreme Court Justice, is an example of someone who is largely detested among African Americans. His positions have consistently been adversarial to the quests of African Americans, and all others who yearn for equal rights. However, the traditional Uncle Toms have used their places of privileges as opportunities to subvert empire. While strangely mute and invisible, there remains a need for some proverbial "spooks" to sit by the doors of empire and ally with the oppressed.

Where do your serve within the echelons of power and privilege? How are you using your positions of privilege to self-enrich, or to subvert?

PRAYER:
O God, we thank You for positioning allies for justice. Hope us, I pray, to be open to allies of subversion, no matter how awkward their position. AMEN.

I Kings 18:16-18

"Prophetic Troubler"

The ironic work of prophetic engagement necessitates social troubling. The oppressive systems and practices of empire remain unless they are troubled. A major obstacle of prophetic engagement, however, is defining trouble. If the definitions of "trouble" and "troubler" are shaped and controlled by the oppressor, it leaves the prophet vulnerable to stigmatization. We must provide our own definition of trouble so that we can be effective troublers.

The confrontation of Elijah and Ahab sees Ahab using his enormous resources and position of privilege to label Elijah. He announced Elijah as "the troubler of Israel," as if Elijah was responsible for the economic drought that placed widows and orphans in danger of starving and as intractable victims of inadequate healthcare. Ahab sought to deflect Israel's economic woes away from himself and empire. From his perspective, Elijah was the cause of the trouble.

However, Elijah refused to allow Ahab to shape and control the perspective. From Elijah's perspective, which obviously had been disseminated, Ahab was the troubler. Ahab's policies and practices, as shaped by his idolatrous belief system, were indeed the source of Israel's trouble. Elijah dared to confront Ahab and his troubling empire.

Martin Luther King, Jr. and the advocates for civil rights, were labeled as troublemakers. Their bold but nonviolent confrontations disrupted longstanding assumptions of American racial policies. The continuing policies and practices of America that oppress and exploit will remain until significant "trouble" is created. Unfortunately, we face a powerful media that operates 24/7 shaping and controlling the public narrative. We have bigoted ideologues pumping billions of dollars into the media in an attempt to control and shape the public narrative.

How are you being perceived within the community where you serve? Have you ever been labeled a troubler? If you are not a troubler, you are probably an enabler.

PRAYER:
O God, Who calls us to trouble all that conflicts with Your will and way, hope us, I pray, to be diligent in our call to bring prophetic trouble. May the work we do trouble the perpetrators of oppression and injustice. AMEN.

1 Kings 18:19-40

"The Problem of Two Opinions"

Life is a commitment. How we live is determined by the commitments we make. For life to be fully lived, we must make specific commitments. We miss life's depth when we fail to make clearly defined commitments. More specifically, ministry without social specifics usually supports oppressive realities.

The most memorable story of Elijah is the conflict on Mount Carmel. Out of nowhere, Elijah challenges the defining deities of Israel's most wicked king. The exaggerated numbers, 450 prophets of Baal and 400 prophets of the Ashtoreth, all on royal payroll, magnify the drama and Elijah's confidence. Elijah challenges Ahab, but the real challenge was for the people. Putting Ahab's prophetic entourage in a contest actually put the people's faith to test. Disproving Ahab disproved the conflicting loyalties of a capitulated people.

Everything Elijah did was because the people were "limping between two opinions." The political sway Ahab held over the people had diminished their capacity to live life as Yahweh intended. The oppressive and exploitative practices of empire had dulled their sense of community. The boisterous claims pronounced by the prophets of the empire had to be rendered useless for faith in Yahweh to be restored.

Without a doubt, the boisterous claims of American individualism have dulled the senses of American Christianity. Our belief that we somehow control the outcome based upon personal initiative has become a prominent feature of our faith expressions. Trusting in God and having authentic compassion for one another has been displaced with self-enriching materialism. We have failed to make the connection between our greed and our oppression. We are a people "limping between two opinions."

What are you committed to? How is that commitment expressed? How has Americanism distorted and/or compromised your faith?

PRAYER:
O God, Who calls us to faithful living and healthy community, hear our prayer. Hope us, I pray, to silence the voices of those who would cause us to limp. May we be found loyal to You and resistant to any faith claim that promotes and embodies oppression. AMEN.

1 Kings 18:41-46

"The Sound of Heavy Rain"

Much of what plagues our attempts to build authentic community are the issues of power and control. These issues distort harmonious community arrangements in all forms, from basic family relationships to the complexity of nation-states. Wherever and whenever we can bring clarity on issues of power and control, we move closer to becoming communities of grace and truth. Community moves toward authenticity when we realize that there are some things we have no power over and some things we will never control.

1 Kings 18 ends with Elijah giving orders. He orders King Ahab to get up, eat and drink. He orders his servant to go look. The orders issued forth by Elijah were based upon the "word of the Lord" received by Elijah. The word of the Lord serves as the catalyst for all orders issued and the word of the Lord is not under the control of empire. A drought caused extreme economic challenges for the empire, and the end of the drought brought much-needed economic relief. Israel moved from a time of no rain to the sound of heavy rain, and neither drought nor rain are instruments of empire control.

Elijah's orders are instructive to those of us who engage in prophetic ministry. We stand as arbiters of the uncontrollable and the idols of power and control. We must keep before the empire that there are some realities beyond its control. Likewise, there are some essentials to economic health that are outside of the influences of those who seek to exploit and oppress. Prophetic engagement understands the symbolism of the sound of heavy rain.

As I write, hundreds of firefighting personnel are risking their lives fighting thousands of acres of bushfire. The hot weather combined with human carelessness and/or wickedness has created a deadly inferno, threatening the neighborhoods of the wealthy and privileged. The need is great for the weather to change and for rain to come, but no one in government can make that happen. What is our word to people who run from trouble, but trouble finds them? Are we prophetically sensitive to the sound of heavy rain?

PRAYER:
O God, Who calls us into ministry with no regard for who thinks he or she is in control, hope us, I pray, to be bold in our assertions of You being able to bring the hopeful reality of heavy rain. AMEN.

1 Kings 19:1-8

"Living with a Target at Your Back"

Any engagement that disrupts the status quo of an oppressive and exploitative system becomes a target. Oppressive powers never relinquish power without some form of violent defensive reaction. A common defensive reaction is to target those with death who disrupt oppressive systems and assumptions.

As could have been expected, Elijah's incredible assault upon the oppressive regime of Ahab was not received well. Ahab, the king who is noted as most oppressive, consulted his equally oppressive wife and cohort, Jezebel. Jezebel responded by putting a death warrant on Elijah, one that appeared so ominous that he fled in fear for his life.

With a death warrant on his head, Elijah removed himself from the territory of one threat only to arrive in the territory of another threat. Jezebel's threat was replaced by the threat of personal despair and starvation. Under a broom tree, he sunk into deep despair, but was surprisingly nurtured and sustained by an angel of the Lord. In the midst of his tenuous reality, Elijah responded to the support provided by the angel of the Lord and was able to go forth.

The work of prophetic ministry is an enemy-making undertaking. Those who benefit from oppressive arrangements think nothing of eliminating those who are a serious threat to the status quo. The burden of living with a target on your back can be depressive, and in those times, we need to be receptive to surprising systems of support. I am recovering from being hopelessly self-reliant. This condition has had me insensitive to surprising systems of support. I am given to being suspicious and apprehensive of those who sought to support me. I am now learning how to be open to God's surprising support systems, especially when there is a target on my back.

How are you when there is a target at your back? What systems of support are in place when you are fearful and despairing? What are your feelings about receiving surprising sources of support?

PRAYER:
O God, we do not always know what to do when the enemy paints a target on our back. We instinctively become fearful and anxious for life. Hope us, I pray, to be receptive to Your angelic interventions. We thank You for never leaving us without surprising sources and systems of support. AMEN.

1 Kings 19:9-14

"The Silent Voice of God"

The idea of God has historically been attached to the dramatic. Unfortunately, the Bible often frames God's interventions in dramatic ways. From the call of Moses at a burning bush, the three Hebrew boys in a fiery furnace, the Resurrection of Jesus – God's interventions are dramatically portrayed. Yet, such an exclusive portrayal of God limits our experiences of Him.

Elijah's desperate and despairing flight from Jezebel placed him in an unusual place. He ended up in a cave. He moved from being surprisingly sustained under a broom tree to being painfully isolated in a cave. The cave is noted as Horeb, Moses's mountain of God. I am not sure if the cave mentioned is literal or metaphorical. Perhaps the cave symbolized the despairing state of the prophet. Twice he noted that his zealousness for God had not changed anything. In fact, his zealousness had resulted in the death of prophets, and his own life had been threatened.

From the cave, be it literal or metaphorical, Elijah was summoned. The dramatic expressions of an earthquake, wind, and fire brought no solace from the voice and presence of God. The voice and presence of God was experienced in a "still small voice," translated "heard in silence."

Interestingly, a voice heard in silence! Could it be that the prophet heard what he was supposed to be: a voice for people who have no voice? Prophetic engagement brings loneliness with it because we speak for people who have no voice.

How has God been prominently expressed in your life and/or ministry? What confirms God's presence for you? What voiceless community do you speak for?

PRAYER:
O God, forgive us for limiting You to the dramatic. Hope us, I pray, to not be overcome by the loneliness of our assignments. May we find solace and substance in knowing that Your voice is spoken through our voice for those who have no voice. AMEN.

1 Kings 19:15-21

"Go Your Way"

Oppression and exploitation represent a malignancy of human community. The presence of an oppressive power seems to eternally malign our greatest efforts toward justice and equality. There seems to be no relief, and victories are short-lived. Rare is the prophet who does not hit a wall of despondency.

Elijah's slump into isolation and despair was not consoled. He was ordered to resume the work, with specific orders to do three things. He was ordered to anoint two kings and a student-prophet. Whereas Elijah believed his work futile, God wanted his work to continue. In fact, Elijah's work was so vital to the transformation of Israel that he would begin the work of prophetic succession. And by the way, Yahweh asserted, there existed a 7,000-member cohort of prophets who had not succumbed to the idolatry of Baalism or Ashtoreth.

The loneliness of prophetic ministry can create serious neuroses. I have yet to talk with a person seriously engaged in prophetic work who did not feel alone, unsupported, frustrated, and largely ineffective. The enormity of evil and the persistence of oppression often appear unfazed. As a product of the '60's when civil rights were fervently pursued, I believed that the big battles were over. As I currently witness the felonization of black men, and the huge success of the prison industrial complex, I often despair at the loss of so much social capital. How will we ever maximize our human potential when black men are being Jim Crowed out of community?

The lesson of Elijah is to stay in the fight, continue the struggle, and equip other would-be prophets. We can be encouraged that, unbeknownst to us, there are always people engaged in prophetic activity.

Name some time when you hit a wall of despondency. What was God's word to you in that moment? What keeps you going when ministry appears futile?

PRAYER:
O God, I confess that I have had moments of deep despair and experienced painful moments of isolation. Yet, I know that Your work is greater than my despair and You are eternally committed to justice and equality. Hope us, I pray, to stay engaged, to continue the struggle, and to have faith to equip others for prophetic activity. AMEN.

1 Kings 20

"Drunken and Resentful"

The great German philosopher, Friedrich Nietzsche, once stated, "Power corrupts and absolute power corrupts absolutely." I wonder what he would have said about people who have delusions of absolute power? I suppose a deluded sense of absolute power would give a deluded sense of absolute corruption. Scary!

Interestingly, 1 Kings 20 introduces a character with an apparent deluded sense of power. Benhadad, the King of Syria, believed he had absolute power over the fate of Israel. After defeating Samaria, he assumed that Israel would be easy prey. In fact, he demanded that Ahab surrender and give him all the gold, silver, beautiful women and children. Obviously, Benhadad represented another expression of oppression and exploitation. Note: he wanted gold, silver, and the most vulnerable as plunder. Benhadad sought to destroy what was crucial to a society: the economy and the family.

Ahab, apparently, convinced of Benhadad's might, agreed. However, the king's cabinet did not consent. As Benhadad prepared to carry out his boisterous assault, a prophet suddenly appeared. The prophet, a representative of Yahweh, declared victory for Israel, with Ahab as the Commander in Chief. Israel defeated Benhadad and Syria, as well as the Syrian allies, thus, preserving the essentials of its society.

Three unnamed prophets appeared in this chapter, none of whom are controlled by empire of any expression, and declared what thus says the Lord. Benhadad was defeated in his drunken delusion, not once but twice. Ahab became resentful of a prophet's bold declarations, and went home sullen and displeased.

Prophetic engagement calls for bold intervention. There are moments when the prophet will stand with the people of God, even when their lives are outside of the will of God. The essentials of community must never be sacrificed to make a theological point. Likewise, a stance with the people of God does not relieve us of prophetic denouncements against the people of God. What is crucial to a society are issues of justice and equality for all families. In the language of the young, "Don't get it twisted!"

How has delusional power been expressed in America? In your community? What role did you play when delusional power plays were made in your community?

PRAYER:
O God, You have clearly made choice of a people who are called by Your name. However, the claim You make of us is not always faithfully represented in our world. Hope us, I pray, to be diligent in the Word You speak, both for our liberty and against our apostasy. AMEN.

1 Kings 21:1-16

"Scoundrels at a Banquet"

We continue to consider the corruption of power, and also add the corruption of privilege. Those who are positioned in power are always vulnerable to corrosive ethical influences. The moral imperatives of a just society are at risk when leaders are not insulated with prophetic perspectives. Prophetic engagement has a responsibility to check those who are delusional.

After the defeat of Benhadad, and the sullen response of Ahab to prophetic proclamations, the corrosive character of power and privilege reemerged. Ahab coveted a tract of land owned by a Jezreelite, named Naboth. Apparently, it was an attractive tract of land; even the text states that it "was next to the palace of Ahab." Ahab offered to purchase the tract of land, or even give Naboth another tract in trade. Ahab apparently wanted to expand his holdings. He wanted to enlarge his territory.

Naboth refused, as was his prerogative, and Ahab took issue with being refused. He sunk into depression, and his wife, Jezebel, intervened and responded by concocting a devious plan to deprive Naboth of his land. Jezebel organized a banquet and hired some known scoundrels to deceitfully discredit Naboth, to criminalize him, and have him put to death. The scoundrels were to do their dirty deeds at a banquet, in a context of gaiety and celebration, where all the movers and shakers of the community would be witnesses. Consequently, Naboth was discredited, criminalized, and put to death, after attending an event of gaiety and celebration.

As I read this story, it echoes with the strategies of American expansionism. Our oil companies would be one example of scoundrels at a banquet. American oil companies have been known to expand their oil excavations by discrediting local leaders of foreign countries, and are even suspected of causing untimely deaths. They provide banquets of assumed opportunity with the intent to beguile and deceive. There is no limit to what corporate giants will do to expand their holdings and enrich their coffers.

What is the history of the corporations in your town? Do you care that they might have used scoundrels to discredit, criminalize, and murder innocent people? How would you respond to such a strategy?

PRAYER:
O God, You created a world big enough and adequate enough for all to have enough. However, we have scoundralized the banquet of Your bounty with greed and covetousness. Hope us, I pray, to call to responsibility any and every act of covetous expansion. AMEN.

1 Kings 21:17-29

"Blood Licking Dogs"

There is an inevitable "come uppance" about life. In other words, what you do will come back upon you. The Bible states it thusly: "You reap what you sow." Jesus said, "Whatever is done in the dark will come to light." The facts of power and privilege provide no exemption from the moral arc of the universe. Prophetic engagement is often a reminder of judgment inevitabilities.

Naboth's prerogative to not sell his land was rudely and violently responded to. Jezebel's scheme to deprive a humble peasant of that which identified him and his family evoked a prophetic rebuttal. Although Ahab did not concoct the scheme, nor did he carry it out, he is held responsible. He was the king. His policies allowed for devious encroachments and unjust seizures. Moreover, he profited from Jezebel's scheme and he had to give an account.

Elijah's pronouncement of "dogs licking blood" could be symbolic of what happened to Naboth. Jezebel and Ahab used their positions of power and privilege to carnivorously lick the life out of a proud peasant. Elijah's pronouncement implied that what they did to Naboth would also be done to them. They would reap what they sowed. Dogs would, indeed, lick their blood.

I am not convinced that the current possessors of power and privilege are concerned with moral imperatives and judgment inevitabilities. The behavior of those currently in power strongly suggests a kind of obliviousness to moral responsibility. The continued deprivation of fair wages to hardworking employees is likened unto dogs licking blood. The greedy encroachments of corporate giants upon the humble holdings of powerless countries are likened unto dogs licking blood. What is needed is a disruptive reminder that what one does unto others will come back upon one.

Where is the Elijah voice for our day? Who will tell modern day Ahabs and Jezebels that dogs still lick blood?

PRAYER:
O God of justice and moral responsibility, may we remain mindful of Your presence and power. Hope us, I pray, to be diligent in our responsibility to promote justice and fairness. May we be the voice for those who lose theirs to political thievery and injustice. AMEN.

1 Kings 22

"Prophetic Minority"

The force of public opinion rarely equals the force of the politically popular. When a government makes up its mind, the will of the people is often lost. It is during these times when the need for a prophetic word becomes urgent. Empire listening to empire voices can only be disrupted by the voice of a prophetic minority.

The popularity of Ahab's kingship was enhanced by an extended period of peace and assumed prosperity. Apparently, the policies of Ahab seemed to have solidified national support and attracted the attention of Jehoshaphat, the king of Judah. They both agreed that a common enemy, Syria, possessed a strategic tract of land. Once again, the issue of land became the obsession of Ahab. However, this time Ahab, along with Jehoshaphat, wanted to use a military option. The military option would be considered only if they could receive prophetic sanction.

A significant number of prophets, 400, sanctioned the military operation. However, one prophet, who was known to be critical of Ahab, was sought. Micaiah initially supported the military option, but when chided by Ahab, he provided a scathing and critical pronouncement. Ahab went to war in disguise and was killed by an unknown soldier, who didn't even know he had shot him. As prophesied by Elijah, the dogs licked the blood of Ahab.

I recall when America sought to sway public opinion to invade Iraq. While there was significant public opinion against the war, the political fervor was so intense for the war, that America, along with a cadre of allies, invaded Iraq under false pretenses. I lived in New York at the time and I wrote a scathing objection to the war, utilizing Augustine's basis of a just war. I was among the minority voices lost in the tide of overwhelming political popularity, even lost among the voices of consenting religious leaders. A popular presidential candidate, Hillary Rodham Clinton, would lose the presidential nomination to the lone vote against the war cast by Barak Hussein Obama. She largely lost because of a vote to fight a politically popular war that soon became politically unpopular.

Are there moments in your professional or religious life when you represented the minority voice? Or, are you one who generally goes along with popular opinions?

PRAYER:
O God, Who has identified in One-ness, we stand ever in reverent awe of You. Hope us, I pray, to embrace Your call to stand for truth, even if we have to stand alone. May we forever see in You the power of engaging in prophetic minority. AMEN.

2 Kings 1

"Messengers of the King"

Positions and power delude. Those who occupy seats of power and are in a position to influence lives are often deluded into believing their own hype. The dominant hype of the deluded is that they can manipulate life to their favor. Unfortunately, they often do so at the cost of personal and national shame.

Ahaziah, the son of Ahab, had a short-lived term on the throne. His reign was marked by the same evil as his father, and he had to deal with the same prophetic nemesis as his father. His reign was ironically shortened by an accident. He fell and was gravely injured. The severity of his injury prompted him to begin a quest of manipulating the gods to act in his favor. His quest to inquire of Baal was interrupted by Elijah, who expressed God's contempt of an Israeli king seeking assistance from a foreign god. Ahaziah responded to Elijah's proclamation by sending a military contingency to influence Elijah. His failed manipulations resulted in the deaths of 100 soldiers, who represented messengers of the king.

The rabid and tenacious attempts of the powerful to shape the dominant narratives are the expressions of the deluded. The slick use of the media and political intimidation has caused many a charlatan to believe their own hype. Such manipulations are not the exclusive exploits of politicians. It has even been employed by those in clergy garb. Who Ahaziah employed as messengers of the king, Carlyle Marney identified as "beggars in velvet." A religion that manipulates always necessitates a counter word from the Lord.

Prophetic engagement must always counter the manipulative maneuvers of those in position and power. Messengers of the king are always powerless before messengers of the Lord. What has been your response to the manipulative maneuvers of the powerful? Can you identify manipulative maneuvers currently in the making?

PRAYER:
O God, You Who determine the outcome of our lives, deliver us from manipulative maneuvers. Hope us, I pray, to trust Your word to face down the manipulative maneuvers of the king's messengers. AMEN.

2 Kings 2:1-11

"When Prophets Cross Over"

No one stays on the scene forever. Just as there is an expiration date stamped on perishable goods, there is an expiration date stamped on the mortality of every human being. As eternal as our work might be, we, the workers, are not eternal. We pass on and prayerfully leave a prophetic inheritance.

As abruptly as Elijah appeared, the announcement of his departure is abruptly inserted into the narrative. After announcing a counter word to the manipulative maneuvering of Ahaziah, a descriptive announcement of his departure is made. For a prophet who was a known loner, Elisha, his prophetic protégé, appeared and was faithfully attached to Elijah's side. When asked what Elijah could do for him, Elisha requested a double portion of Elijah's spirit. Whatever it was that made Elijah who he was and do the things he did the way he did them, Elisha wanted it two times over.

Elijah's departure is prefaced with prophetic movement, as he is sent from one locale to another, and finally makes his way through the Jordan. As Moses crossed over the Red Sea, Elijah crossed the Jordan and Elisha went with him. It seemed to have been common knowledge that Elijah was going to cross over, but when it happened, it still surprised Elisha and the other prophets. It happened suddenly, and Elisha was separated from Elisha and the prophetic work.

The imminence of our departure seems a difficult one for us to embrace. Very few of us live with the Pauline sense of "the time of my departure is at hand." I have witnessed great ministries die because the prophet stayed too long. The lesson of Elijah is for us to not only prepare for our own departure, but also to prepare someone else for our departure. Prophetic work continues long after the prophet crosses over.

Do you ever give serious thought about your departure? What preparation have you made for your departure? Who have you shared it with?

PRAYER:
O God, You Who are from everlasting to everlasting, humble us to the fact of our mortality. Help us, I pray, to embrace our time as being in eternity, but not of eternity. AMEN.

HOPE US, LORD!

2 Kings 2:12-25

"Taking Up the Mantle"

Someone has noted that succession is a vital part of success. My observations in ministry, especially in prophetic ministry, are failures on our part to intentionally prepare successors. There exists an erroneous assumption that those matters are best left to God and chance. Perhaps we might want to consider that anything that was worth doing could best continue being done if we prepare someone to do it.

Just as Moses passed the mantle of prophetic responsibility to Joshua, Elijah passed it to Elisha. Elisha accompanied Elijah and they developed a relationship, one in which Elisha was grievously impacted upon Elijah's departure. Although Elijah's departure was unusual, it pained Elisha, nonetheless. As requested, Elisha took up the mantle of Elijah and assumed the prophetic walk by returning to the territory of prophetic challenge. He crossed back over the Jordan.

Of interest is that Elisha's prophetic position was challenged. Fellow prophets who were reluctant to believe that Elijah had been taken up challenged his position. They wanted to confirm Elijah's death, so they went looking for him. The second challenge was in making sure that the place where they lived could sustain life. It was noted as a nice place with bad water. A nice place with bad water is a place unable to sustain life. Elisha's first miracle was to heal the water. His third challenge was to not be taken seriously by a group of young men. He was derided and mocked. Elisha cursed the young men and they were eventually mauled by she-bears. The mauling does not indicate to death, but the young men clearly received a serious beating.

The lesson of Elisha is that mantle passing is a serious part of prophetic work. It takes time to nurture relationships and to prepare someone to continue the work of prophetic ministry. Even when we have done our best, those who we mentor and prepare may not be quickly embraced. It took years before Jesse Jackson and Al Sharpton were embraced as authentic successors to the civil rights struggle, as expressed by the late Dr. Martin Luther King, Jr. We should wonder about who they are preparing? Mantle assumption comes not without challenges, and will even suffer derision. Yet, the mantle of prophetic ministry must always be passed on.

Where are you in the process of succession? Are you a successor, or a successee? How do you feel about being responsible for continuing the work of prophetic challenge?

PRAYER:
O God, Who calls us unto a great work, we confess that we were not eager to embrace the work and we face struggles with letting the work go. Hope us, I pray, to accept our roles as mantle passers or as mantle receivers. AMEN.

2 Kings 3

"War, Water, and Words"

I believe life will present us with enough adversity without us concocting any. We will have enough to contend with without our seeking out additional venues of contention. Neither does the prophetic mantle serve us well when we are drawn into the petty, ill-planned skirmishes of others. Our words must count for something more than the endorsements of someone's petty scheme.

2 Kings, chapter 3 draws us back into the arena of empire. The prophetic mantle was settled in chapter 2 and the scene shifted back into the arena of prophetic engagement. The matters of the prophetic are to be played out on the stage of empire antics. The antics of the empire are introduced when tension breaks out over Mesha, who is identified as a sheep breeder, and Jehoran, who is identified as a slightly improved version of his father, Ahab. He was evil, but not as corrupt as his father. Mesha, king of Moab, ceased to pay a rather exorbitant tax to Jehoran, and Jehoran took issue. In fact the Bible cites Mesha's move as "rebellion against the king of Israel."

Jehoran responded by organizing for war, recruiting Jehoshaphat, who remained loyal to Yawheh. The king of Edom was also brought in as a willing ally to go against Mesha. However, their war effort was frustrated because the area where the armies were to assemble lacked water, an essential resource to sustain life. How could they wage a war when they could not even sustain the life of their war apparatus? It appears that their war was a poorly planned excursion, and Jehoshaphat suggested that they get a word from the Lord.

Elisha reluctantly speaks a word into this dire situation, and God provided water. Their ill-planned excursion was salvaged and Mesha was defeated. Mesha responded to the battle by sacrificing his first son!

I am not sure what the intent of the writer of this episode of empire and prophet was. I see no serious problem with the assertion of Mesha to be delivered from unfair taxation. Perhaps the lesson has to do with enemies so intent upon destroying God's people that prophetic expediency makes challenging exceptions. Perhaps this strange military stratagem underlines a fundamental truth of all war: the horrific sacrifice of sons (and daughters) on the battlefields of political and religious nonsense.

What do you see in this strange episode of political and religious alliance? How have you viewed our country's ill-planned military strategies, from the war in Vietnam to the latest excursions into Afghanistan and Iraq?

PRAYER:
O God, we are not always privy to Your long-term intentions. Hope us, I pray, to be discerning when a word from You is solicited by those who do not know or love You. May we speak a bold truth that saves lives rather than destroys life. AMEN.

2 Kings 4:1-7

"Prophetic Pastorate"

It has been noted that the political is personal. Whenever we consider our personal challenges, we come in touch with our political realities. This is also true for the concerns of the prophetic. Prophetic engagement always finds its root in the personal.

The Elisha ministry turns quickly from the strange alliances of empire-at-war to the local concern of widows and orphans. The widow mentioned was a part of the prophetic family. The death of her husband left her and two sons seriously at risk. They were candidates for debt-slavery, a cruel concept that would have reduced the dead prophet's family to a lifetime of poverty. Elisha's intervention allowed the woman to pay her debts and live comfortably for the rest of her life. Of note, is that her economic challenge was solved within the context of community. Everything she needed was provided within her immediate community.

We, who engage in prophetic ministry, must never overlook the pressing needs within our immediate communities. There are always present persons who are vulnerable to the vicious machinery of economic expediency. The prophetic is at its best in the role of the pastoral, because the pastoral puts us in touch with the pains of the local. Moreover, within the pastoral role, we empower communities to be free of the oppressive realities of an insensitive empire.

Are there personal and local concerns in your neighborhood that call for pastoral intervention? What is the connection of that pastoral concern with your prophetic perspective?

PRAYER:
O God, You Who are concerned with the least, the lost, the last, the left behind, and the left-off, sensitize us to Your heart. Hope us, I pray, to see in the pain of our local parishioners the wide vision of our prophetic call. AMEN.

2 Kings 4:8-17

"Kindness to the Man of God"

The ministry has, indeed, produced a fair share of charlatans. It is no question that clergymen, and clergywomen, have used clerical privileges for ignoble gain and purposes. In the main, however, the majority of men and women of God have been faithful to their calling as they have understood it. The ranks of clergy, particularly those who serve in oppressed communities, have sought to bring some sense of the hopefulness of God into the lives of people.

The goings and comings of Elisha caught the attention of a woman of means. Although her name is not mentioned, she apparently was a woman of substance and respect. For one, she could make decisions about how resources were used in her home. Moreover, unlike the prophet's widow, she had adequate resources. She had enough to make special provisions for the man of God. She even included her husband in her plan to show kindness to the prophet.

The kindness shown to Elisha prompted him to want to do something for her. Of note is his suggestion to speak to the king or the commander of the army on her behalf. Speaking to the king or the commander of the army implies seeking some form of relief from those who had the power to oppress. Her answer is telling: "I dwell among my own people." In other words, she was able to sustain her life from the resources created within her own community. She was industrial and independent. The one thing she lacked, however, was a son. She did not have anyone who could protect and provide for her future.

The blessing of being kind to a man or woman of God has far-reaching consequences. Those who boldly stand against oppressive powers can bring relief to the oppressed. Although the relationship between prophet and empire is often adversarial, it can also be advantageous. Prophets should be able to bring relief to oppressed people. In addition to relief from the oppressed, the prophet has the power to speak new life into barren situations. I have witnessed where the word of God birthed new possibilities into the lives of those who love, respect, honor, and support prophetic ministry.

Who among those you serve show unusual kindness? What word do you have for those who generously share and support prophetic ministry?

PRAYER:
O God, You always position someone to provide support and relief to those who serve You. Hope us, I pray, to not just receive, but to seek opportunities to speak new life into those who unselfishly support us. AMEN.

HOPE US, LORD!

2 Kings 4:18-37

"Pick Up Your Son"

The matter of a future is enormous. Endless are the possibilities when a people embrace a sense of a future. To know that tomorrow offers possibilities emboldens present-day living with creative imaginings. We are emboldened to dream when we believe life has a future.

The strange dynamics of the story of the unnamed woman from Shunen have but one end: the restoration of a future. The narrative has some strange and dramatic twists and turns. A child given in verse 17 is dead in verse 20. Her strange exchange with Elisha's servant, Gehazi, must be perceived as a statement of hope. Her son is dead and when asked, "Is it well with you?" Her answer was, "It is well." Elisha's dispatching of Gehazi with a staff to restore the boy was unsuccessful, and more startling was the woman's insistence on staying with Elisha. It took the unbearable pain of the woman to communicate to Elisha that he must personally engage before he returned to the house. The extravagant and quite physical ritual of restoration performed by Elisha added to the strangeness of this story. Yet, the end result was that the boy was restored, resurrected from the dead, and a future was established.

As a million African American young men languish in prisons, and countless others are at risk of premature death or crippling injuries at the hands of their peers, the future of a people is bleak. What chance stands a people when the repositories of their future are systematically being destroyed? The prophetic word for the African American community is to "pick up your son." If it takes strange maneuverings, inexplicable rituals and conversations, we must position ourselves to collectively pick up our sons. Our sons are God's gift to our future and we must not leave them to the random destruction of a racist and cruel society. We don't have to explain to anyone why we do whatever we do, let's just restore a sense of future to our people.

What risks are you taking to restore life-options to African American young men? How can you become more involved in positioning our community to pick up its sons?

PRAYER:
O God, Who gifts us with future possibilities in our sons, grant us a sense of the radical importance of a future. Hope us, I pray, to engage in the prophetic work of restoring life to our young men. AMEN.

2 Kings 4:38-41

"Healing Poison Stew"

What we ingest determines our success. If we are constantly partaking of that which is toxic and poisonous, we place our lives at risk. Unfortunately, when a community is forced to make do, the chances of toxic ingestion are increased. People, including people of faith, who have internalized lack and scarcity, are prone to take risks to survive.

The school of prophets was not exempt from the effects of famine. The lack of adequate food supplies brought a crisis upon the prophetic community. Elisha ordered that a pot of stew be prepared for the famished prophets. One of the prophets, who sought vegetables and herbs, secured an unknown gourd. The stew was prepared and consequently served. To the dismay of the hungry prophets, they discovered that the stew was poisoned. They cry out to Elisha, "There is death in the pot!"

Although Elisha did not prepare the stew, he was expected to do something about the inedible concoction. Elisha asked for flour that he added to the stew. The stew was then served as an edible substance. A known substance from the ground cured the stew of an unknown substance that was found.

When our children can learn the most complex and vulgar rap but not know the Bible, and speak more text talk than acceptable English, someone has placed an unknown substance in the pot. When being glued to couches playing video games has replaced muscle-building outside activities, someone has placed an unknown substance in the pot. The famine of healthy living has allowed the irresponsible to gather unknown substances, which have poisoned our communities.

Prophetic engagement must also consider ways of bringing healing to our respective communities. We must reassert the healthy good that we know as an antidote to the unhealthy unknowns that are poisoning our communities. Someone has to take responsibility for correcting what we are ingesting.

How has your community been poisoned? Where did the poison come from? What are you doing to correct the poison in the pot?

PRAYER:
O God, everything that You made is good, but it is not all good for ingestion. Hope us, I pray, to remedy the poisonous unknowns with healthy knowns. AMEN.

2 Kings 4:42-44

"Days of Plenty"

The scarcity syndrome has the capacity to rob us of days of plenty. When we are inundated with the scarcity narrative, we normalize scarcity. We never see ourselves as having enough. When abundance enters into our world, we can so easily negate it with the scarcity narrative.

Immediately following the episode where famine poisoned the pot, a visitor showed up with abundance. The man is noted as being from Baal Shalishah, a place of Baal worship. However, he comes with twenty loaves of fresh-baked bread and fresh fruit. He offers it to the prophets and Elisha commands that it be passed around. However, a student prophet can't see how twenty loaves and fresh fruit will be adequate for a hundred hungry prophets. Elisha insists that the bread be shared and the results are more than enough. There were even leftovers.

The scarcity narrative has so impacted the lives of some communities that many can't see beyond it. One of the strange manners in which scarcity has poisoned our communities is in the problem of obesity. Obesity, the gluttonous response to the scarcity narrative, is a disorder of uncontrolled consumption. Many are so afraid that there is not enough, they consume more than they can healthily ingest. As a result, many of us walk around with excess fat that adversely affects our total wellbeing. The ironic testimony of obesity is that there is more than enough.

Elisha's word to a servant, whose perspective is distorted, challenges us to consider prophetic intervention to disrupt the scarcity narrative. Overindulgence is as deadly as poisonous indulgence.

What words have you for the scarcity narrative? What response has your ministry to the obesity-scarcity dilemma? Can we see ourselves living out our days of plenty?

PRAYER:
O God, You created a world of abundance and declared that it was good. Hope us, I pray, to see beyond the distorted scarcity narrative and see where there is more than enough. AMEN.

2 Kings 5:1-19

"Barriers to Healing"

Does it really matter how God heals us? What's more important: the style of our healing or the fact of our healing? There seems to be a struggle with our willingness to be healed on God's terms. The apparatus of our hubris seems to have created some well-constructed barriers to our social, psychological, emotional, spiritual, and political healing. In a very real sense, we are in the way of our own healing.

In 2 Kings 5, we are introduced to Naaman. The greatness of Naaman was negated by one reality – he was a leper. He is noted as an important figure in politics, a genius in military strategy, a well-respected and decent person, but he was a leper. The Lord had favored him with significant victories, and he was a doting husband and family man, but he was a leper. His greatness was negated because he couldn't live a normal life. He couldn't maximize his potential as a social being, because his affliction isolated him. It kept him at arm's length from all people. He couldn't even normalize his relations with his wife, without causing her a similar affliction. Like the late Elvis Presley, Howard Hughes, and Michael Jackson, his greatness could not heal him from his isolation.

However, he inadvertently made a smart move. He placed in his household an unnamed slave girl, a prisoner of war. She was a believer of Yahwism and knew about the prophet Elisha. Naaman's healing had to cross several barriers. He first had to negotiate the political apparatus of the empire. The Kings of Syria and Israel had to agree that his healing was in their best interest. Secondly, he had to get over his own deluded theological expectations. He believed that the prophet needed to come to him and perform a grand healing ceremony. Thirdly, he had to get over himself and do as the prophet commanded. He was healed, but he had to overcome some significant barriers.

America is a sick a nation. America boasts of being the last superpower, but we Americans know that we are global lepers. We have isolated ourselves from a normal life. There's nothing normal about being an American anymore! We can't maximize our potential as free people without the fearsome apparatus of our national security. We can't even normalize our relations with one another without holding one another at arm's length, viewing one another as competitors rather than comrades of intimacy. We delude ourselves with national religion, believing ourselves favored over other nations. We need a healing!

What determines healing in your community? How do you believe Americans can be healed? Name some of the barriers to our nation's healing.

PRAYER:
O God, You want us to call You by Your name, but we are apprehensive, not humble, contrite, prayerful or repentant. Hope us, I pray, to remove whatever barriers keep us from being healed socially, emotionally, globally, psychologically, spiritually, and intimately. AMEN.

HOPE US, LORD!

2 Kings 5:20-27

"Profits of Healing"

Why does every good deed have to be rewarded? Why can't we just do what's right and that's enough? There is a scheming dimension in us that needs to be healed. We need to be healed of the need of always seeking a way to get something for ourselves. The scarcity narrative has left a wound within our soul that leaves us painfully susceptible to covetousness.

The healing of Naaman was a humbling experience. It was humbling for Syria to seek a healing collaboration with an enemy, Israel. It was humbling for Israel to consent to Syria's request that Naaman be allowed an audience with Elisha. It was humbling for Naaman to consider the words of a servant girl, listen to the advice of his servants, and to reluctantly obey the humbling prescription of a foreign prophet. It was humbling for Elisha to reject payment, and to hear Naaman seek alliance with Yahweh. Humility is always a necessary component in the process of healing.

However, in the midst of a humbling and healing experience, an opportunist emerged. Gehazi, a servant with a name, asserts himself into the process. He sees a way to enrich himself from the healing experience. He concocts a convincing lie and executes his plan for self-enrichment. Elisha is not fooled, and the very disease of which Naaman was healed became the family legacy of Gehazi.

While visiting England for the Baptist World Congress, a senior member of our party fell and cracked her knee. She was rushed to the hospital, cared for, given pills for the pain, and released. That happened over 10 years ago and she has never received a bill. Why? England had free healthcare! There are forces in America that are convinced that national healthcare is an enemy to the American way of life. With nearly 50 million known uninsured people, we have people with a Gehazi spirit who covet profits for healing. The insurance and pharmaceutical companies have elected and hired Gehazi to make sure that profits are made for healing. We need an Elisha movement that exposes the Gehazi-minded industries, even at the expense of isolating them with their own dis-ease.

What are your thoughts on national healthcare? Should profits determine the outcome? What are you doing about it?

PRAYER:
O God, Who created a world where healing can be found within the leaves of Your creation, for this, we give thanks. Hope us, I pray, to speak truth to the profit-powers of our nation. May we be emboldened to expose and condemn all who would scheme and skim exorbitant profits from healing. AMEN.

2 Kings 6:1-6

"Floating Axe Heads"

The intervention of the prophetic is never more necessary than when we become overly dependent upon technology. Our dependence upon technology has robbed us of our capacity to wonder. Without the capacity to wonder, we become tools to our own machinations, which is a serious form of idolatry.

2 Kings 6 opens with an episode within the life of a school of prophets. In chapter 4, the prophets were seen as being susceptible to the economic woes of the empire. When famine struck the empire (4:38-41), it adversely affected the community of the prophets. In chapter 6, things seemed to have changed. There has been an expansion within the community that caused obvious discomfort with their living arrangements. The request was made to expand and Elisha consented. The expansion program was pursued in earnest and was facilitated by the use of surplus technology. A prophet is noted as using a borrowed axe, the head of which he loses while busy chopping down a tree.

A crisis emerged as the result of the loss of the axe head, which called for prophetic intervention. Elisha asked only where was the place where the axe head was lost. Once the location of the lost axe head was given, Elisha took a stick, threw it in the water, and the axe head begun to float and was recovered.

Like lost axe heads, we have lost our capacity for awe and wonder. As a result, everything, including our worship, has become an elaborate display of technology. This tendency to control and manipulate life has obviously increased the range of our oppression. When life is viewed as being controlled and manipulated, the powers line up to control the levers of control and manipulation.

In a sense, the young prophet's words are helpful. The technological prowess of our age is borrowed. It is not germane to who we are. What is germane to who we are is the capacity to live life in endless awe and wonder.

When was the last time you engaged in wonder? What evoked it? What are your thoughts on our dependency upon technology?

PRAYER:
O God, "when I in awesome wonder, consider all the worlds thy hands have made, how great thou art." Hope us, I pray, to recover our sense of awe and wonder, so that we might be liberated from the false claims of our own machinations. AMEN.

HOPE US, LORD!

2 Kings 6:8-23

"Seeing Servants, Blind Armies"

A lot of unnecessary pain and grief comes as the result of blind fear and presumptuous power. Conflicts escalate and community life is disrupted when people panic over what they cannot see, while others assume power over what they think they see. How do we facilitate sight to those who need to see? And how do we divulge the blindness of those who think they see?

2 Kings 6 moves from the ambitious building program within the community of the prophetic to the ambitious plotting of a warmongering king of Syria. The military strategy of this unnamed king was repeatedly disrupted by insights provided to the king of Israel by the prophet Elisha. We are not told how Elisha became privy to military strategy. Yet, the information provided by Elisha disrupted the war plans and upset the warmongering king. Once it was discovered who was responsible for sharing the military plans, the king of Syria prepared a massive assault upon the humble habitat of the prophets.

Two things of note take place: The servant to the prophet panics when he sees the intimidating forces of the enemy that encircle the city. Elisha prays that the servant could see the forces supporting Elisha's cause. God opens the eyes of the servant and he sees the army of God that encircled the mountains. Secondly, Elisha prays that the intimidating forces of the enemy be struck blind and they were subsequently blinded. The blinded army was then led captive to the King of Israel. Instead of killing the blinded army, the king of Israel was ordered to feed them. Instead of a bloodbath, community was created and the war strategies ceased.

In an age of a cowering church and warmongering politicians, the role of prophetic ministry is to open fear-blinded eyes and demonstrate the blindness of presumptuous power. The empire's ready use of military force is often blinded by political ambition, and the church's fear of the empire's retaliation blinds us to our power. We need to see that "those who are with us are greater than those who are against us." May the end result be not more bloodshed, but an opportunity to build peaceful communities.

What fear blinds the people within your community? What power blinds others? How would you respond to having advantage over people who sought to kill you?

PRAYER:
O God, You Who created us to live in peaceful community, restore our vision of the ministry of reconciliation. Hope us, I pray, to be emboldened by our faith in You. Grant us creative impetus to turn instruments of war into tools of community building. AMEN.

2 Kings 6:24-7:20

"Troubles at the Gates"

A city can usually be assessed by what is seen at its city-line, its borders, or its gates. The gates provide invaluable perspective to the social and economic dynamics of a city. Thus, who is seen at the gates usually provides an adequate barometer of the social, economic and spiritual wellbeing of a city, a state, or even a nation.

The drama of today's text is dictated and determined by the activities at the city gates. Of interest, is the dynamics of trouble as manifested at the gates. The first gate encounter is deeply disturbing. As the king goes in and out of the city, a woman whose life has been reduced to cannibalism confronts him. She is complaining that an agreement had been made with another to share in the cannibalistic consumption of their respective sons. Her son had already been eaten and she wanted the king to force the other woman to share in the consumption of her son. The king is appalled and grieved at the severity of the famine, but is unable to provide any relief. His anger is provoked and he directs it with a threat to kill the prophet, Elisha. Elisha responds by declaring an end of the famine, about which an officer of the king did not believe him.

The second gate scene is just as desperate. A quartet of lepers is positioned at the gate and ponders their plight. They could either go into the Syrian camp where they might either be fed or killed. Or, they could stay at the gate and die. They took the chance of being killed or filled with food. Their desperate chance paid off because God had caused the Syrian army to flee the camp. The lepers not only ate well, but also began plundering the camp. Their consciences bothered them, so they went and told the king's household, and the king cautiously responded by sharing in the plunder.

The average American city has become a lesson in extremes. On the one hand, we see booming constructions and the obvious plunder of regentrification. On the other hand, we see homeless camps dotted on the city-lines. It is obvious that the vendors of construction and the plunderers of regentrification will stay on their self-enriching course. Yet, among the homeless encampments are voices prepping to disrupt that which "we do not well." The change that is needed in our cities must necessarily arise from troubled communities at the gates.

What do you see at the gates of your city? Who in your city is being eaten alive by the plunderers of regentrification? Is your ministry positioned to hear the voices of the troubled?

PRAYER:
O God, You Who desire that all people have access to the world's goods, open our hearts and minds to the people who are being denied. Hope us, I pray, to be conduits of Your bounty and not be trampled by the belief of scarcity. AMEN.

2 Kings 8:1-6

"Prophetic Residuals"

What we do now should have some impact later. The good we do ought to live beyond the moment. There ought to be some residual outcomes in the work we do.

The pastoral ministry of Elisha continued even as his prophetic ministry became legendary. He continued to assist the Shunammite woman on a personal level by directing her to leave the famine-afflicted land of her residency. The woman leaves for seven years, and during that time the government confiscated her land. Upon returning, she sought the audience of the king, so that she might reclaim her land. As she entered into the king's presence, the king was inquiring about the feats of Elisha. The text suggests that as she was approaching the king, the resurrection of her son was one of the feats in discussion. Gehazi, Elisha's disgraced servant, points her out. She verified the incredible feat of Elisha, and the king restored her land plus residual incomes.

We do well to embrace the witnessing aspect of our faith. There are things that the Lord has done through us that are worthy of repeated discussion. The living for the moment attitude of our culture undermines prophetic residuals. When we don't "legendize" our victories, the enemy can easily trivialize them. Who knows, what we do now might be the testimonial conduit of someone's restoration. Let us not minimize the significance of our work by moving on too quickly to the next thing.

What are some noted victories in your prophetic engagements? How can they be canonized in ways that build up legend? Who within your community has been victimized by the government?

PRAYER:
O God, how magnificent are Your works among us and through us. Hope us, I pray, to not minimize and trivialize what You have done. May what You have done through us have residual impact on the restoration of others. AMEN.

2 Kings 8:7-29

"We Three Kings"

The bane of community is often played out in the idolatry of nationhood. Ethnocentricity, the exclusive loyalty to one's group, often becomes the central stage upon which the drama of oppression is played out. The assumed protection of privilege has led many a nation into idolatrous encroachments, of which a prophetic word was neither heard nor heeded.

Although the kings of Israel, Judah, and Syria occupy much of the space in the narrative, it was Elisha who spoke the word that disrupted. Ben-Hadad was destined to die from an undisclosed illness, and his messenger Hazael would become the deadly oppressive successor. Jehoram, who reigned in Judah, continued the evil of his oppressive predecessors. Ahaziah, the king of Judah, advanced the evil policies of his predecessors. All three kings promoted their oppressive policies by use of military prowess and political intimidation.

Strange it is that our world remains a planet of conflict. We hear daily of the political encroachments of one nation upon another, as well as the continuous embroilment of civil unrest. The violent drama of the Middle East rotates on the stage with the unending of violence of the African nations and the tenuous turmoil of Eastern Europe and Asia. America, the so-called last superpower, finds a way to assert itself into most world conflicts. The so-called American interest has become the pretext for imposing our will upon other countries.

Where is the prophetic outcry? And, if the prophet would speak, would anyone listen? The call is for the prophet to speak the truth, even if no one seems to listen.

PRAYER:
O God, You Who are Sovereign over all, inspire Your truth to be uttered and proclaimed. Hope us, I pray, to be faithful to the truth of Your word, even if no one seems to listen. AMEN.

2 Kings 9

"Prophetic Instigation"

The sordid arrangements of oppression never surrender to good intentions. There is never a benevolent awakening of those who hold claim to entrenched powers of oppression. Something has to be said. Something has to be done. Something must serve to instigate the demise of oppressive powers.

2 Kings has provided a lengthy narrative of the conflict between the oppressive rule of the Omridian dynasty and the prophets of Yahweh. The Omridians ruled long and wrong, with Jezebel as the matriarchal symbol of its wickedness. Beginning with Elijah, the contest between Yahwism and the perverted policies of the Omridians have dominated the prophetic narratives. In 2 Kings 9, the Omridian dynasty comes to a violent end, all of which was pronounced by Elijah in 1Kings 21:19.

An unnamed prophet is commissioned by Elisha to instigate the demise of the Omridian dynasty. A revolution ensued in which empire loyalists switch sides, kings were assassinated, and those who were considered impotent, threw Jezebel from a window. As the dogs ate Jezebel's body, the prophecy of Elijah came to reality.

I have not lived a very long time, but I've lived long enough to see Omridian-like dynasties come to an end. The Jim Crow South, the Soviet Union, Marcos's Philippines, and South African apartheid are examples of Omridian-like dynasties coming to an end. Although blood was shed and lives were lost, moral pronouncements served as primary instigators of their demise. If the continued Omridian-like behavior of America is suggestive, it suggests that America has not taken note.

What do you see as evidence of a conflict between American practices and policies versus the will of God? Are you willing to become a prophetic instigator?

PRAYER:
O God, You Who speak of justice and righteousness, sensitize us to Your word. Hope us, I pray, to become bold instigators of Your justice and righteousness. May the reality of Your Kingdom demolish any and every proud kingdom of this world. AMEN.

2 Kings 10-11

"The Lord has Done What He Spoke"

It is true that to completely eliminate a tree, we have to pull up the roots. The same holds true for a culture. To change a culture, we must dig deep and uproot the relational systems that sustain the culture. Unfortunately, we have not learned how to change a culture without shedding blood and destroying lives.

2 Kings 10-11 present the gory drama and detail involved in dynasty change. The chapters are filled with blood and deceit, and military and political cunning. There is little effort to negotiate, or inject humane discourse into the political process. We witness the brutal and bloody destruction of family lineages, political allies, and religious adherents. The strategy is brutally simple: destroy the key families, murder allies, and kill all who believe in the god of the system. What validates the bloody drama is the belief "that nothing shall fall to the earth of the word of the Lord which the Lord spoke concerning the house of Ahab; for the Lord has done what He spoke by His servant Elijah."

I find this bloody and gory drama disturbing. I know it's in the Bible, but just because it's in the Bible does not mean we need to like it or not take issue with it. I do not agree with the "take no prisoner" approach of militarized religion. Our world has been ravaged by bloodshed of religious adherents. We have the uncanny capacity for justifying brutal and bloody behavior as an expression of religious belief. While Islamic fanatics are dramatized as bloodying the world with terroristic behavior, Christians have not been innocent of violent and gory drama. We have a horrid history of bloodying up the world with violent expressions of our belief.

What are your views of the bloody drama of religious beliefs? Do you think we can justify genocide with a "thus said the Lord?"

> **PRAYER:**
> *O God, You Who author life and death, give us a reverent respect for both. Hope us, I pray, to temper the fervor of our faith with respect for all life. As we seek to discern the truth of Your Word, may we also detect the trouble in the text. AMEN.*

2 Kings 13:14-21

"The Bones of the Prophet"

The power of the prophetic often gets buried in the symbolism of the sacred. We know God was doing something powerful in the prophetic, but we lack the foresight to integrate it into the fabric of community life. Therefore, we build monuments that serve as sacred symbols of something that happened once-upon-a-time. Such monuments do little to incorporate prophetic energy and insight into community life because their prophetic meaning has been buried.

The preceding chapters in 2 Kings move quickly through the quirky antics of kings and the so-called protectors of the realms. The tensions of empire upkeep are summarized, and the idolatry of kings is duly noted. The voice of Elisha seemed to no longer confront and agitate. Elisha reemerges as sick. It seems that the illness of Elisha happened suddenly and would be terminal. The word of his sickness evoked a cry of grief from the kings of Israel, and an enfeebled gesture to honor a last command from the stricken prophet. Elisha dies and another dead man is buried on top of him. Yet, when the dead man touches the prophet's bones, he is revived and lives again.

Gone are the voices of those who boldly confronted and agitated. The quirky antics of the empire dominate our attention with 24/7 reports and endless political commentaries. Once a year, there are enfeebled attempts to honor the legacies of Martin Luther King, Jr., Fannie Hamer, Sojourner Truth, Frederick Douglass, Malcolm X, and others who lived to confront and agitate. The best we do is "strike the ground three times," which provides only temporary relief from our ongoing oppression. What is needed, however, is for us to make contact with the bones of dead prophets. We need a communal experience where we descend into the abyss of our collective deaths, so that we might experience the resurrection of the spirit that confronts and agitates. The truly resurrected make contact with death.

Where lie the bones of your community's prophets? How serious are you about experiencing new life?

PRAYER:
O God, Who raised Jesus from the dead, forgive us for our enfeebled gestures of following Him. Hope us, I pray, to feel what Jesus felt, so that we might experience what He experienced – resurrection from the dead. AMEN.

2 Kings 17

"Carried Away"

A saying of my youth described behavior that had gone too far as being "carried away." For instance, a person who took things to dangerous extremes was described as having been "carried away." To be "carried away" is not limited to personal behavior, but communities and nations can also be carried away.

A defining experience in the life of Israel was the experience of exile. The experience of exile represented Israel being literally and forcefully displaced by the Assyrians. It is described in 2 Kings 17:6 as "Assyria took Samaria and carried Israel away to Assyria." The people were deported from their homes and familiar surroundings, and were placed in an alien and oppressive setting. The narrator of 2 Kings interpreted the experience theologically and viewed it as a result of Israel engaging in behavior "like the nations whom the Lord had carried away before them." Exile, the experience of being carried away, is the consequence of recreating oppressive systems, policies, and idolatrous prostrations. Simply put, people were carried away whose behavior had gotten carried away.

Currently, we are witnessing some of the most "carried away" beliefs and behaviors in American history. Not since the days of chattel slavery and Jim Crow have we heard espoused the extremism of American politics. The presidency of Barak Obama, followed by the hateful campaign and presidency of Donald Trump, has emboldened groups of people to give voice and expression to thoughts once believed dead and gone. Racial bigotry and misogynistic tones openly fuel the American political landscape. I witnessed in Texas blatant demagoguery as politicians campaigned by presenting demonic portrayals of President Obama. Texas politicians felt safe in giving expression to their extremist thoughts and positions.

Has American been ideologically and theologically displaced? What do you see as expressions of our people being "carried away?"

PRAYER:
O God, who knows us wherever we are, meet us in this alien space. We confess that we have been "carried away." Hope us, I pray, to regain our sense of You and Your will for our lives and community. AMEN.

2 Kings 19

"The Sword in Your Own Land"

History is replete with the failed plans of the arrogant. Arrogance has a reputation of blinding the proud into believing their own hype. The Bible identifies pride as a conduit for shame (Proverbs 13:10) and that "Pride goes before destruction and a haughty spirit before a fall (Proverbs 18:12)."

The drama of 2 Kings 19 revolves around three realities: a righteous king, a boasting nation, and a praying prophet. Hezekiah served as a righteous king, who sought to restore justice and righteousness within Jerusalem. Sennacherib served as the Assyrian king who believed himself invincible, and who mockingly threatened to destroy Jerusalem. He believed that he and his warmongering allies were more powerful than the God of Israel. Isaiah was the prophet who Hezekiah turned to as a spiritual mediator. Isaiah intercedes and assured Hezekiah of Jerusalem's safety against Sennacherib. The word to the mocking and intimidating King Sennacherib was that he would die by the sword in his own land. Sennacherib, indeed, dies by falling on his own sword.

What is your view of America? Is there something mocking about America's relationship with other countries? When I listen to our national leaders speak to, and of other countries, America is presented as extremely arrogant. When American athletes compete against other nations there is a mocking arrogance. Our athletes never see losing as an option. There is a mocking arrogance throughout America's discourse. My fear is that one day this will lead us to a Sennacherib moment. We are setting ourselves up for death by falling on our own sword.

How do you view America's self-understanding? Are there signs of America reneging on justice initiatives and embracing self-righteous isolation? What prophetic voice calls us to humility?

PRAYER:
O God, You detest the proud of heart and the haughty of spirit. Hope us, I pray, to find our place of humility. May we as a people, a nation, even a church, be convicted of our arrogant tendencies and seek a more humble station. AMEN.

2 Kings 21

"Extended Time"

Our world is always selling things with guarantees. Extended warranties have become the norm for most purchases. Yet, we are not given any guarantees or extended warranties on life. Life is fragile and can either end or be fundamentally altered in a moment. Prophetic engagement speaks to the fragility of life.

Hezekiah is noted as being a good king. As noted, he sought to restore justice and righteousness in Jerusalem. However, Hezekiah's goodness did not exempt him from sickness. He became sick and death was imminent. The prophet Isaiah commanded him to "set his house in order, for you shall die." However, Hezekiah prayed. Of note is the fact that he does not pray for extended time. He only prays to be remembered. God's response was to command the prophet to reverse his previous position and inform Hezekiah that he will be given extended time. Hezekiah received an additional fifteen years, only to become a conduit for the Babylon deportation – a good man, with extended time, used as a sign of bad times.

I truly believe President Barak Obama is a good man. I believe he wanted to see America become a more just and righteous nation. I voted for him twice and attended both inaugurations. However, I did not see his re-election as a good thing for America, neither would it have been with the election of Mitt Romney. America is at a bad place and risks the deportation of its greatest asset, which is the vision of a responsible democracy. The senseless bickering in Washington and the inability of elected officials to make sound and compassionate decisions is a sign of bad times. America cannot get past its racist obsessions and classist bigotries in order to do what is right for this country. Obama was given extended time, but he only exacerbated what is a sign of bad times: the election of Donald Trump.

PRAYER:
O God, You Who give life and provide opportunities for the enhancement of life, I offer You praise. Hope us, I pray, to be more diligent when You extend our time. May we view the gift of extended time as opportunities for goodness and not mere maintenance of the status quo. AMEN

HOPE US, LORD!

Isaiah 1:1

"Prophetic Vision"

What is seen has much to do with what is said. Seeing and saying go together. Prophetic engagement must utilize the dynamics of seeing clearly and speaking convincingly. Major contributors to oppressive constructs are the combination of social blindness and twisted truths. Jesus said, "Watch and pray." We have to see as well as say.

Isaiah opens up with one of the most powerful precursors for contextualizing prophetic ministry. The book begins with two words, "The vision." In academia, it is called a superscription. Isaiah's prophetic ministry was shaped by a vision. Note, however, that the vision was formed within the concrete realities of human existence. It was formed by what he saw, or what was seen in a particular place, at particular times, during particular activities, by particular people. There is nothing nebulous about Isaiah's vision. The words that shape his prophetic utterances are based upon what he saw "concerning Judah and Jerusalem in the days of Uzziah, Jotham, Ahaz, and Hezekiah, kings of Judah."

Our world will only be transformed through responsible vision. We cannot distort the world and speak in irresponsible ways. To engage in prophetic ministry is a call to be responsible visionaries. We must look through God's lens of justice and righteousness and gaze realistically upon the harsh realities of our time. Our vision cannot ignore human personalities, and the roles they play in shaping society. We must offer responsible critiques of the prominent players of our day and let the chips fall where they may. Transformative speech must be constructed out of the harsh realities of what we see.

What do you see as obstructive to the process of God's justice and righteousness? Who are the players of inequity and oppression? What will you say about what you see?

PRAYER:
O God, Whose first act of creation was to create the light of comprehension from the chaotic abyss of hopelessness, hope us, I pray, to see clearly our world so that we might responsibly speak words of the truth and the light. AMEN.

Isaiah 1

"Prophetic Reasoning"

Prophetic engagement is creatively logical. Although uttered in colorful metaphor, it reasons. Clearly inspired by a moral obligation, prophetic engagement, while anchored in reality, lays out a logical argument for social and spiritual transformation.

Isaiah opens this incredible book with the foci of a court lawyer. There is a case to be made, and the evidence is displayed in a people's moral disconnect from their redemptive legacy and responsibility. The refusal to adhere to the moral standards of God had deeply corrupted the people, and the evidence was compelling. There was nothing logical about the people's behavior, "The ox knows his master, the donkey his owner's crib, but Israel does not know, my people do not understand." Although the people had maintained religious rituals and ceremonies, they were of no avail. In fact, the onerous ceremonies and rituals had become burdensome to God.

The obvious results of the people's moral lapse were systems of injustice, oppression, and exploitation. Isaiah called for prophetic reasoning. Prophetic reasoning opened up the possibility for moral transformation: "Though your sins are like scarlet, they shall be white as snow; though they are red as crimson, they shall be like wool."

The prophet still has an obligation to make sense. He or she must present a case that is sensible, logical, and compelling. Unfortunately, much of what goes for the prophetic in today's church lacks sense, logic, and compulsion. We have reduced prophecy to personal and individualized concerns. There is a need for a strong case to be built that addresses the moral, social, and global affronts of our day. The evidence available and accessible must be used to present a strong case for prophetic reasoning.

What do you see in your world that is in the way of people living as God intends? How do you provide a case that is sensible, logical, and compelling about this situation?

PRAYER:
O God, You Who created a universe from emptiness and chaos, grant us a sense of Your creative essence. Hope us, I pray, to see our chaotic world in creative new ways. AMEN.

HOPE US, LORD!

Isaiah 2:2-5

"From Violent Enmity to Vibrant Economy"

Prophetic engagement thrives best when energized by a transformative vision. The capacity to see something different motivates us to do something different. A transformative vision, however, must be formed from a transcendent Source. It takes a word, or an insight, from "elsewhere" that invites us to live life in a new way.

Isaiah 2:2-5 is probably as loved as Psalm 23. It is one of those passages that invite us to see the world in a new way. The exaltation of the Lord's house, or the place of revelation, draws the various nations to learn a new way of living. The text indicates an eagerness on the part of the nations to learn how to live life in a new way (verse 3). The weariness of warmongering and the relentless narrative of scarcity seem to no longer work well in the world. The word from the Lord is decisive. It rebukes those who have upheld this destructive way of life. Yet, the word that most defines the moment is the vision of transforming weapons of war into tools of economic usefulness.

Although we have read this text, preached it, and offered up memorable songs in honor of it, have we really heard it? I speak of hearing it as did the first readers, who heard it in a way that changed them. God's word is not intended for mere spiritual exercise or pious aesthetics. God's word is an invitation for us to consider life in a new way.

I consider nothing as more wearisome to our world than the relentless antics of warmongers, both foreign and domestic, and the pervading narrative of scarcity. A world shaped by such a troublesome narrative needs to re-envisioned. On this day, a 21-year-old white man decided, after sitting in a bible study for an hour, to shoot and kill nine African Americans. He said, "I came to shoot black people."

What will it take for us to hear a transformative word that reimagines our world? Are we motivated enough to envision a world that takes the energy and intellect used for war and use it to provide a more humane world where every stomach is full, every naked body covered, and every person protected with justice?

PRAYER:
O God, Who loves mercy and justice, continue to speak to us, Your hard of hearing people. Hope us, I pray, to hear like we have never heard before, so that we might do what we've never tried before. AMEN.

Isaiah 2:6-22

"Bowing to the Works of Our Own Hands"

We are an amazing species. The genius of human beings never ceases to amaze me. Our potential to create and improvise has become the measurement of national strength, wealth, and military prowess. However, a continuing difficulty is our capacity to exalt our genius above measure. We are woefully inclined to the delusional and to giving homage to the idolatrous.

After the incredible transformative vision had been cast, Isaiah took an existential plunge into the abyss of human idolatry. The broad and diverse range of idolatrous activity was essentially reduced to one source: "They bow down to the works of their hands." The technological advances that have produced unprecedented wealth appear to have turned the people's heart. What they had created, compounded with alien influences, became for them the focus of their attention and adoration. The results of such idolatrous prostrations heightened the people's pride and increased oppressiveness.

Whenever a people's accomplishments become the object of their affection, the likelihood of national haughtiness creating venues of oppression is increased. The last Republican Presidential Convention highlighted speeches that distorted the American dream as a self-generated reality. We have yet to internalize what the late Martin Luther King, Jr. noted as the interdependence of human existence. No one does anything without some kind of support from someone else. Prophetic engagement exists to critique the oppressive constructs of delusionary thinking.

What are some of the idols that we have created and to which we now give homage? How are these idols oppressive? What are you going to say about them?

PRAYER:
O God, Who created us for relatedness, wired us for dependence, and called us into community, hope us, I pray, to humbly assess our place in the world. May we see clearly the health of being dependent on You and interdependent on one another. AMEN.

Isaiah 3:1-15

"Children Will Govern"

A favorite game of childhood has always been to "act adult." It seems that children find adult roles and behavior intriguing and a primary source of amusement. Interestingly, no one seems to find adults acting like children with the same level of intrigue and amusement. In fact, such behavior is discouraged and strongly rebuked.

Isaiah 3 rolls out a prophetic vision of a national crisis. The handwriting was on the wall. The economy was in a tank, military prowess had been drastically diminished, and family life had deteriorated, all while an elite few plundered the poor and oppressed the masses. A once proud country and its leading city had been reduced to a shameful state. The sad state of Judah and Jerusalem was solidly the responsibility, or irresponsibility, of local and national leadership. Isaiah viewed the leadership as being basically childish. "I will give children to their princes, and babes shall rule over them." In other words, the leadership will behave like children.

Again, no one finds childish behavior intriguing or amusing. We have witnessed our country held hostage by the childish antics of so-called leadership in Washington. Our current president consistently behaves with the compulsivity of childishness. We've witnessed America risk its national credit standing, diminish the capacity of the military, weaken a fragile economy, and inflict pain upon poor and vulnerable people. All of this was done in a silly attempt to defund the Affordable Healthcare Act. Childish politicians led the nation to the brink in an attempt to get their way.

When we fail to evolve into responsible adults, our childish antics inevitably produce an unhealthy nation, family, and church. Where are you seeing childishness undermine social health? What role are you playing in our nation's childish drama?

PRAYER:
O God, You Who created us to enjoy childhood and to evolve into adulthood, hope us, I pray, to consider our roles as leaders of our family, communities, and nation. May we be more like Jesus who "increased in wisdom and stature," and evolved into responsible adulthood. AMEN.

Isaiah 3:16-4:1

"Eating Our Own Food"

The complexity of oppression is often resolved when inquiry is made about who benefits from oppressive constructs. Unfortunately, who may seem to benefit openly may not be the ones who are benefitting actually. This is often the case with women of oppressive constructs. The women may seem to benefit openly, but are not actually the oppressors.

The drama of chapter 3 presents a comprehensive portrait of an oppressive society. Verses 1-15 present a stunning portrait of failed leadership. It encompassed leadership failures in key areas of community. The leadership failures are noted as all male and childish. Interestingly, verse 16 begins a colorful portrait of female leaders. The women of Jerusalem are portrayed as haughty and pretentious. They are a vain group who have benefitted from the oppressive arrangements set up by the male leadership, and they gaudily present themselves as sexual ornaments of oppression.

The prophetic word to this gaudy and haughty group of pretentious women is severe. The downfall of the city will literally strip the women of all that propped up their gaudy and haughty lifestyles. In a state of desperation, the women bargain for marriage by agreeing to provide for themselves for the privilege of having a man's family name. The devastation of Judah and Jerusalem essentially affects all social arrangements, inclusive of power structures based on class and gender.

Although I appreciate the social honesty of the text, I find it troubling. It is troubling because of the patriarchal portrait of women. Women are portrayed as being responsible for the sexual distortions of the culture. The shame attached to the community's sexual failures is attributed to the behavior of women. This perspective finds easy expression in our culture. We have not moved too far from using women as scapegoats for the sexual immoralities of our communities. The patriarchal delusion of our culture leads many to believe that women will "eat their own food" just to be in a relationship with a man.

Who ultimately benefits from oppressive constructs within your community? How are women portrayed? What roles, if any, have women played in perpetuating oppression?

PRAYER:
O God, You Who created us in equality, male and female, hope us, I pray, to restore a sacred sense of gender and human sexuality. May we be mindful of our portrayals of women and their contributions to the health of our community. AMEN.

Isaiah 4:2-6

"The Filth of the Daughters"

The continuing saga of oppression maintains certain characters. History seems to hold on to its victims and recycles evil and oppression. Some people never seem to get out of the loop of oppressive structures, and some people seem ever in the position of oppressors.

Isaiah 4 anticipates the transformation of Israel and the great city of Jerusalem. The return of the captives and the deliverance of those who remained buoy the hope of this testimony. However, the hope of this text is negatively charged by the demonization of women. The shame of the exile experience, according to this text, is blamed on "the daughters of Zion." If the city's failure rested on childish male leadership, then its moral lapse was the result of the haughty and gaudy pretentiousness of the women. According to this text, the renewal of the city will take place "when the filth of the daughters of Zion" has been purged.

The drama of this text reflects the potential patriarchal blind spot of prophetic engagement. While giving expression to a powerful and hopeful declaration, the issue of gender discolors the text. I have just had a conversation with an amazing clergywoman, who has singularly impacted a static denomination. In spite of all she has done, she was refused a well-deserved opportunity because she was a woman. An otherwise progressive young man declared, "That's too much responsibility for a woman."

Could it be that many are holding to the belief that our communities will never be fully healed until cleansed of "the filth of the daughters" of our people? What would it take for us to no longer feel the need to blame? How are women viewed within your faith community?

PRAYER:
O God, Who created us free of blame and shame, grant us a greater sense of You. Hope us, I pray, to live beyond our need to genderize our deliverance. AMEN.

Isaiah 5:1-7

"Looking for Justice"

It has been noted that "the most certain way to perpetuate injustice is to allow justice to remain in abstraction." A lot is said about justice, but what is meant is not always clear. Prophetic engagement bears the responsibility of making the issue of justice clear.

Isaiah 5 is brilliant in rhetorical composition. A major truth is proposed in a song that ends up not being a song. In metaphorical brilliance, the issue of injustice is viewed as the primary cause of Israel and Judah's demise. However, in this incredible text, the lack of clarity in its call for justice is ambiguous, in spite of the poetic genius for justice.

The New Interpreter's Bible provides four perspectives of justice that are noteworthy. First is distributive justice, which is the equitable distribution of resources. Secondly, there is retributive justice, the dispatching of punishment or retribution for offenses suffered. Third, there is procedural justice, the intentional ordering of rules and procedures necessary for a just society. Finally, there is substantive justice, which is the understanding of that all acts of human justice are a response to the conviction of a just God.

Justice is too critical to be left as ambiguous. What do you mean when you speak of justice? How is injustice being perpetuated in your context? Where has the lack of clarity been a contributor to injustice in America?

PRAYER:
O God, You Who we know to be a God of mercy and justice, hear our prayer. Hope us, I pray, to be clear on what You consider as just, so that we might be more clear in our calls for justice. AMEN.

Isaiah 5:8-24

"House to House, Field to Field"

We have noted the danger of not being clear on matters of justice. Again, we assist in perpetuating injustice when we leave justice in the abstract. When we are clear about the expression of injustice, we become clear about the justice focus needed in a particular situation. Not all injustices are the same, therefore, not all responses need be the same.

The issue of justice in Isaiah 5:7, becomes quite clear in verse 8 and the succeeding verses. The justice issue driving Isaiah seems to have been distributive justice. There was a lack of equitable distribution of resources, especially the resources of houses and land. An elitist construct had corrupted the process to the degree that the rich were getting richer and the poor were getting no better. Isaiah proclaims: "Woe to those who join house to house; they add field to field." It appeared that a spirit of excess had overcome the leadership at the neglect of the community.

Recently, America has been witnessing stock prices skyrocket. We had never had a 16,000 Dow Jones, and now we have a 25,000 one. If the market informs us of anything, it is informing us that stocks are being served and someone is getting wealthy as a result of it. As I gaze upon the continuing disparity between the wealthy, or super wealthy, and the working poor, I become fearful of another economic meltdown. What are we doing that is so radically different from the behavior that drove the last collapse of the economy? As more houses, both local and global, are being joined, who is benefitting? Who is being deprived?

PRAYER:
O God, Who created a world with adequate resources for all, incline us to Your economic perspective. Hope us, I pray, to cultivate a spirit of distributive justice. AMEN.

Isaiah 6:1-7

"Prophetic Dates"

Prophetic engagement is always contextual. The work we do is shaped by where we live, the times in which we live, and the events that shaped the times in which we live. We never operate out of a vacuum. We are invited to serve in a real world, among real people, in real time.

The testimony provided by Isaiah dates his ministry. His ministry was defined by a memorable experience – the death of Uzziah. Assyrian oppression had dominated so much of Judah's life that the death of Uzziah was definitive to his perspective of prophetic ministry. As defining as were the chain of events in the year of Uzziah's death, nothing, however, was more definitive for Isaiah than his experience with God. In the year of Uzziah's death, a temple vision of God defined for him his impetus for ministry. In essence, his sociological engagement was defined by his theological understanding.

The dizzying speed in which events are currently reported has the potential to minimize reality. We are exposed to so much so often that our capacity to reflectively process is impaired. We are at risk of blurring our way into prophetic incoherence. Like Isaiah, our challenge is to anchor our prophetic work into some memorable experience that heightens our sense of God in our midst.

What dates what you do? Are there any defining historical realities that impact your perspective on ministry? What theological perspective shapes your sociological engagement?

PRAYER:
O God, who manifests Yourself in the harsh realities of our lives, speak to us in our time. Hope us, I pray, to not be overwhelmed by the dizzying pace of current events. May we know You in some concrete way so that our service will be specific. AMEN.

Isaiah 6:1-7

"The Wings of the Call"

Prophetic engagement comes from a sense of a call. One does not authentically engage a life into transformative work without being overcome by a powerful sense of divine compulsion. Without such a powerful sense of divine compulsion, we risk trivializing social transformation.

Isaiah 6 is probably the most well known of all prophetic calls. The death of Uzziah positioned Isaiah to be more receptive to the dynamics of a divine call. Free of the obstruction of a dominating personality, he is overcome by a vision of God as a God that protects, deflects, and reflects. The angelic presences were identified as having six wings: two were used to cover their faces, two were used to cover their feet, and two were used to fly.

The two wings that covered their faces represented humble anonymity in the presence of the awesome holiness of God. The two wings used to cover their feet were symbolic of prophetic obedience, a proper response to the call of God. The third set of wings allowed them to fly, symbolic of the experience of sacred movement, or freedom to serve. The activity of the angelic beings resonated with the being of Isaiah. He could not stand before the holy and remain the same. The seraphim who touched his lips with the coal purged him of oppressive constraints. There was a shift in Isaiah that resulted in the acceptance of the call to prophetic ministry.

We, who engage in the prophetic, do so through compulsion. In other words, we have to. The old preachers of my community called being overcome with the "can't-help-it." The late C.A. W. Clark once noted in regards to preaching, "If you can keep from preaching, do so. If you cannot not preach, you will preach." Likewise, if you can avoid the prophetic ministry, do so. (You will probably be in the way anyhow.) However, if you cannot not do it, you will be prophetic.

Can you avoid ministry? How easy is it for you to quit? Or, what keeps you in the fight?

PRAYER:
O God, You Who summon us into prophetic ministry, make Your will known. Hope us, I pray, to be humble in our work, so that You might get the glory. AMEN.

Isaiah 6:1-7

"Touched By the Holy"

We look again at this incredible summons into prophetic ministry. The "call" as it is commonly referred to, could also be identified as divine compulsion. As stated, we are smitten with a case of "can't-help-its." We must go because of what we have experienced.

Isaiah did not enter into prophetic ministry casually, or without reservation. His overwhelming experience with God caused him pause. The God who revealed awaited a response. Isaiah's assessment of himself and the people disqualified them all. He understood himself as being a woeful person among woeful people, inadequate to speak to an inadequate people.

However, the capacity to speak was not left up to Isaiah. The capacity to speak for God was left up to God. Isaiah received a touch from one of the angelic beings he saw. The touch of the holy prepared him for prophetic engagement.

We do not do the work of God without being touched by God. Woeful are our works when we operate out of the energy of our own devices. The God who reveals is the One who compels. May we never move out of our own compulsion, but always by the compulsion of the holy.

What has been your experience with God? Have you had a compelling touch?

PRAYER:
O God, Who yet reveals and compels, we honor Your presence and power. Hope us, I pray, to be sure of Your touch as we serve Your people in Your world for Your glory. AMEN.

Isaiah 6:8-13

"Divine Intersections"

The magnitude of God's work calls for willing service. Whereas the call of God can be compelling, faithful service must be done willingly. According to Isaiah 6, prophetic engagement is best fulfilled when there is an intersection of the compulsion of God's presence with the willingness of our hearts.

Isaiah witnessed the prophetic call on three levels. He saw the Lord, as best as we can see the Lord, through the intermediaries of angelic beings. He was touched by the holy, and experienced God's mercy and forgiveness. He finally heard from the Lord. What he heard was a call for willing service. "Whom shall I send, and who will go for Us?" Isaiah's response was to volunteer himself. He said, "Here am I! Send me."

Perhaps the lack of substantive callings has reduced the number of compelling personalities in prophetic engagement. I was asked about who currently holds the prophetic mantle and I was hard-pressed to provide a noteworthy list. Prophetic engagement must move on the strength of a sensory experience of the Divine. God must be seen at work. The prophet must be touched by the power of God, and the distinct voice of God must be heard. It is this type of call that makes authentic the willingness of a person to say, "Here I am! Send me."

How was God experienced in your call? Have you seen, been touched, and heard? What was your response?

PRAYER:
O God who reveals, touches, and speaks, manifest Yourself among Your people. Hope us, I pray, to be sensitive to how You are revealing Yourself in our midst. AMEN.

Isaiah 7:1-9

"Politics and Prophets"

When does the politician engage the prophet? The question of politics and religion has been historically confusing. We have not been able to have politics make friends with religion. We see no connection, therefore, we work hard to keep them separate, or we hardly work to make them collaborate.

Isaiah 7 provides an experience when the politicians needed prophetic assistance. Notice, the safety of the community was being threatened and the king was powerless. The prophet, who was not under the power of the empire, was called by God to intervene. The ministry of Isaiah and the administration of Ahaz were summoned into a collaborative. Although Ahaz' oppressive views and practices were antithetical to God, Isaiah spoke a comforting word to the king on the crisis, informing him that the danger to the community would not come to pass.

There has been a demise of the legacy of prophetic collaboration with politics in the African American community. On the one hand, politicians have been deluded into believing that they longer need the input of the African American preacher beyond the day votes are cast. On the other hand, most African American preachers have decided to limit their work to maintaining a self-serving religious institution. As a consequence, we have irresponsible politicians and disconnected preachers.

What are your thoughts on religion and politics? Are you free to speak for God about the issues of politics? If not, why not?

PRAYER:
O God, Who made one world and made us of one blood, deliver us, I pray, from bifurcated visions of faith. Hope us, I pray, to realize the connection between what we believe and how we live in the world. AMEN.

HOPE US, LORD!

Isaiah 7:10-17

"A Virgin and a Son"

Power and the expressions thereof are wrapped in symbols. Symbols are the carriers of meaning and the detached arbiters of a community's sense of justice. We are influenced by the symbol of a matter long before we act on the matter.

Ahaz was offered an opportunity to secure a sign of God's presence and power. Being influenced by the economic and militaristic symbols of his own sense of power, he refused. Isaiah provided a prophetic announcement of a virgin conceiving and birthing a son. The virgin represented a symbol of the potential for new life, whereas the birth of a son symbolized the endless potential of a future. Both of the symbols represented expressions of power that are beyond human capacity. Life and future are exclusive activities of God.

The facts and practice of oppression are upheld by symbols. Those symbols are in the possession and control of the oppressor. For instance, military might and law enforcement are powerful symbols of those in power and in control. Whoever controls the levers of military and law are usually the arbiters of power.

Isaiah's pronouncement of new life and a powerful future provide a necessary strategy for those who would overcome oppressive powers. The creation of new symbols is a necessity for prophetic engagement. In order to envision a new life and a future filled with endless possibilities, new symbols are best constructed from a Power beyond that of the oppressor.

What symbols are used for new life within your community? What symbols for a powerful future are utilized? If you have no symbols, what's in the way of you creating some?

PRAYER:
O God, You Who transcend our most powerful symbols and expressions of power, hope us, I pray, to maintain a sense of You and Your presence as we seek new life and a future of endless potential. AMEN.

Isaiah 7:18-25

"Briars and Thorns"

Prophetic engagement involves radical transformation of societal systems and practices. Unfortunately, the rigid forces of oppression often force a negative transformation before there can be a positive one. Things often have to get worse before they get better.

The dogged rigidity of Ahaz's idolatrous practices and oppressive policies resulted in a negative transformation before there ever was a positive one. Isaiah's words to Ahaz portrayed a dismal outcome for the Israel of Ahaz's day. In classic prophetic prose, Isaiah proclaims, "It shall come to pass in that day." In the day of God's judgment, the systems and policies that once supported oppressive behavior and practices would experience negative transformation. The economic barometers that fueled the systems would revert into useless commodities. The change would be so humiliating that places of abundance would be transformed into useless venues of briars and thorns. Briars and thorns symbolized the intensity of surplus uselessness.

We are daily exposed to experiences that support longstanding rigid and idolatrous practices. Like Ahaz, who would cut deals with those who would betray him, we have accepted many inhumane practices as normative. What is becoming clear is what one generation experiences as normal, another generation considers abhorrent. The rising generation, the progeny of my generation, views much of what we valued as briars and thorns. Could it be that what we are holding on to is nothing more than surplus uselessness?

Can you identify spaces and places in your life that are no longer worthy of continued cultivation? What are the responses to surplus uselessness within your community?

PRAYER:
O God, You Who speak to us in the times of our arrogant resistance, hope us, I pray, to be mindful of Your negative transformations so that we might experience Your positive transformations. AMEN.

Isaiah 8:1-18

"Making Love to the Prophetess"

Prophetic engagement is life-encompassing. There are no places or spaces that are out-of-bounds for prophetic insights and inferences. We, who are called to this work, avail all aspects of our lives to being conduits of prophetic activity.

In chapter 8, we are privileged to see where Isaiah's family life became a symbol of prophetic activity. The intimate interactions between him and his wife, who is identified as a prophetess, are noted as significant channels of prophetic expression. Her being noted as a prophetess strongly suggests her engagement and involvement in the ministry of Isaiah, and most likely her personal engagement in prophetic ministry. The public pronouncement of Maher-Shalal-Hash-Baz, "quick to plunder, swift to spoil," manifested the personal naming of their son. The son who was conceived became a symbol of God's judgment on Syrian and Ephraim.

Again we consider the schizophrenic nature of America's idea of separation of church and state. The psycho-socio-sexual-spiritual tension inherent in life makes this American idea incredulous. We cannot honestly bifurcate our humanity to accommodate a social ideal. Who we are as social, sexual, and spiritual beings shows up in all our human interactions. Who we make love to and the consequences thereof are highly reflective of the dynamics of our social consciousness. We are either socially connected and engaged, or disconnected and exploited.

What has your love life said about social justice? Do you separate your love life from your socio-spiritual life? Why? Are you mutually engaged or disparately exploitative?

PRAYER:
O God, Who created us in Your image and likeness to bear fruit befitting of You, hope us, I pray, to envision a just society being expressed through our most intimate expressions of love and community. AMEN.